# CAVEMAN's GUIDE TO BABY's FIRST YEAR

## EARLY FATHERHOOD FOR THE MODERN HUNTER-GATHERER

DAVID PORT, JOHN RALSTON, AND
BRIAN M. RALSTON, M.D., F.A.A.F.P.

WITH ILLUSTRATIONS BY GIDEON KENDALL

STERLING

New York / London
www.sterlingpublishing.com

*For the enlightened troglodytes who shepherded us to cavemanhood*
*and showed us how to stand tall in the modern world:*
*our fathers and fathers-in-law, Paul Port, Wally Knack, David Ralston*
*and Bruce Falls; and our grandfathers, Clyde Port, Bob Stringer,*
*Herbert Ralston, and Michael Ryan.*

PUBLISHED BY STERLING PUBLISHING CO., INC.
387 PARK AVENUE SOUTH, NEW YORK, NY 10016

PREPARED BY
SCOTT & NIX, INC.
150 WEST 28TH STREET, SUITE 1103
NEW YORK, NY 10001-6103
WWW.SCOTTANDNIX.COM

TEXT © 2008 BY KNUCKLEDRAGGERS, LLC AND SCOTT & NIX, INC.

ILLUSTRATIONS © 2008 GIDEON KENDALL

DISTRIBUTED IN CANADA BY STERLING PUBLISHING
C/O CANADIAN MANDA GROUP, 165 DUFFERIN STREET
TORONTO, ONTARIO, CANADA M6K 3H6

DISTRIBUTED IN THE UNITED KINGDOM
BY GMC DISTRIBUTION SERVICES
CASTLE PLACE, 166 HIGH STREET, LEWES
EAST SUSSEX, ENGLAND BN7 1XU

DISTRIBUTED IN AUSTRALIA
BY CAPRICORN LINK (AUSTRALIA) PTY. LTD.
P.O. BOX 704, WINDSOR, NSW 2756, AUSTRALIA

ISBN-13: 978-1-4351-0139-5

ISBN-10: 1-4351-0139-1

PRINTED AND BOUND IN THE UNITED STATES OF AMERICA

10 9 8 7 6 5 4 3 2 1

FOR INFORMATION ABOUT CUSTOM EDITIONS, SPECIAL SALES, PREMIUM
AND CORPORATE PURCHASES, PLEASE CONTACT STERLING SPECIAL SALES
DEPARTMENT AT 800-805-5489 OR SPECIALSALES@STERLINGPUB.COM.

# CONTENTS

# CHAPTER 1

# YOU'RE A DAD NOW, UNIBROW

AND YOU THOUGHT LABOR ENDED WHEN
THE PLACENTA LEFT THE BUILDING....

YOU ARE NOT ALONE. SINCE THE DAYS WHEN THE PAINT on the walls of Lascaux was still fresh, newly minted fathers have been prone to making that assumption. Now, having just witnessed the miracle of childbirth and an act of true heroism by your woman, you are awash in pride and comforted by the knowledge that you have weathered the worst the stork could throw at you. Here at labor's supposed conclusion, you have never felt so fulfilled as a man, a father, and a partner.

Congratulations, caveman, for you not only have persevered through the mind-altering (and for her, body-altering) experience that is pregnancy, you also have committed your first parental misstep in assuming delivery of the placenta marks an end to labor. In fact labor has only just begun. But that never dawned on you as your baby's due date approached, nor during delivery, when, *Homo erectus*-like, you stood tall in your supporting role, whether the wee one arrived via the birthing canal or surgical airlift.

Referring frequently to the pictograph birthing plan you had earlier scrawled on a cocktail napkin, you were a rock throughout the birthing experience, even during the most visceral moments. You stayed close by your woman's side from beginning to end, fulfilling her every request and offering comfort and reassurance as she morphed into Wonder Woman in a hospital gown (minus the gold tiara, matching bulletproof bracelets, and magic lasso). If the process involved a cesarean section, you were afforded the chance to view a sight that has buckled the knees of many an imperturbable lad: that of a loved one's working organs on display through a

neat little window in the abdomen. For those whose baby was delivered by more conventional means (for you clinical types, the term is *vaginal delivery*) there was the unfolding drama of labor. The textbooks told you it would occur in three stages, from the first stage's early tremors to the crescendoing contractions that foreshadow the sanguine sight of your partner pushing the little human you helped create through and out of the birthing canal, then to delivery of the afterbirth.

Only minutes ago, with a look of steely determination, you had grasped the surgical scissors offered by the doctor and unflinchingly snipped the umbilical cord connecting baby to Mom. You had gotten a little misty but never wavered as your woman, then you, held your matted, mucusy, and mottled offspring for the first time. Then, hardened by middle school insect dissections and repeated Tarantino film viewings later in life, you had fixed your gaze down below as the placenta passed into an awaiting receptacle, this being labor's third stage, supposedly the concluding (and somewhat anticlimactic) act of the three-part labor drama. Now your baby, having conquered the Apgar test (we'll explain that in a moment), is safely in the arms of Mom. Exhausted but elated, she's bathing in the afterglow of this immensely strenuous and immeasurably rewarding experience. Why, then, is your wide-eyed, new-daddy naïveté fading fast?

Because the just-described drama, you sense, isn't exactly over. Somewhere in the recesses of your cavernous cranium stir stories you've heard about early paternity, anecdotes and experiences that fellow knuckledraggers have related to you in hushed tones in locker rooms, casinos, bowling alleys, hunting blinds, watering holes, and other places where men of your ilk tend to congregate. Why, you wonder, did these stories always conjure expressions of such consternation and bewilderment on the faces of the men telling them?

As the question crosses your mind, rivulets of perspiration begin to flow from the gaping pores of your forehead into the bristly caterpillar above your eyes. Your quickening pulse resonates between your temples like a tribal drum. All the voices and computerized blips in the room blend into a single unintelligible hum. Sweat clings to the coarse fur of your palms like morning dew on a mountain meadow. Your mind struggles to piece together a coherent thought. The attending nurse, who scolded you during labor for repeatedly pressing the anesthesiologist for "a little taste" to relax you, now eyes you with concern.

These telltale signs can mean only one thing: You are entering the fabled—and in some quarters, feared—fourth stage of labor, the one primitives across the centuries have spoken of only in whispers, and only in exclusively male company, as if it were some mythic beast that from the shadows strikes fear in the stoutest, stoniest of men. You're not apt to hear about the fourth stage of labor in parenting books or birthing classes, but we are here to tell you it is no fabrication. It is as real as the Sasquatch.

New parents know labor's fourth stage to be at once wholly fulfilling and incredibly draining, at times mentally and physically taxing for the prehistoric pop and his fairer partner alike. Unlike labor's first three stages, where for obvious biological reasons your woman was the focal point and you the supporting partner, this stage is as much about the new dad as it is about the new mom. It is about parenthood, and in that a new dad can and should be an equal partner, even if he has no experience in such a role.

It is a role you likely will play for an extended period, for the fourth stage lasts a looooong time—like, indefinitely, or at least until you send the caveling out into the world, hopefully sometime before the age of 30. But fear not labor's fourth stage, caveman. With careful planning, steadfast commitment, and an ability to adapt to highly changeable and sometimes stressful conditions, the work you put in as a parent and a partner in the days, weeks, and months ahead will in retrospect turn out to be a labor of love—and oftentimes not a labor at all.

This book is here to help the 21st-century troglodyte dad come to grips with and navigate the initial phase of fourth-stage labor, representing baby's first year, as well as the first year of fatherhood. There's no underestimating the importance and enduring impact of these 12 months, for this is when your words, actions, mindset, and attitude can set a lasting tone for your lives together going forward and set the mold for a healthy, happy family dynamic.

*That's right, big daddy, it's time to shed the hair suit in favor of a well-fitting but spacious paternity suit, one with plenty of room to grow.*

By sporting a game attitude and drawing from the same reserve of resiliency that allowed many generations of pelt-clad *Hominidae* to survive the harshest of Pleistocene winters, what seems like one of the toughest stretches you'll ever experience very well could turn out to be one of the most memorable and rewarding.

## Apgar Awaits

As if the trip out of the womb wasn't traumatic enough, most newborns must submit to testing within 60 seconds of entering the world. Developed in the early 1950s by anesthesiologist Virginia Apgar, the Apgar test is administered by medical staff right after birth, first at one minute and then again at five, to see how the young unibrow is adjusting to the postpartum environment. Babies are rated from zero to two in each of five categories: appearance, pulse, responsiveness, muscle activity, and breathing (there's no balance beam or uneven bars in most birthing facilities). Based on those assessments, the youngster then is assigned an Apgar score from zero to 10, which will dictate the sort of care he or she receives from that point. A score of less than 10 is quite common, particularly for the first test at one minute. Receiving a less-than-perfect score should not preclude him or her from later matriculating at a top-flight nursery school, however.

Indeed, scores in the seven to 10 range usually indicate a newborn is destined for routine post-delivery care, with no need for special medical attention. And while a score in the four to six range usually means the baby needs some measure of extra medical attention, it's generally no cause for alarm, though no one can blame new parents for wigging out about it in the emotionally charged moments after delivery. A score of three or less (rare) means there's a serious condition warranting immediate intervention, such as to address difficulty breathing. But even in those cases, a baby who needs some form of urgent medical attention at the one-minute mark can rebound quickly to tally a stronger score when the second test is administered at five minutes.

As expectant fathers, many a caveman throughout the epochs has demonstrated that the fetal position isn't just for babies. Now comes an even more formidable test of the new dad's wherewithal: fatherhood. The concept of having a child with your mate was hugely appealing. In rare moments of abstract thought while your woman was with child, you fantasized about having a product of your union, an offspring to carry on your bloodline, someone to mold into a resourceful hunter-gatherer and an upstanding, contributing member of society. In a purely theoretical sense, the idea of you and your woman bringing a child into the world seemed eminently enticing and manageable.

Now, your reproductive fantasies fulfilled and your offspring safely delivered, reality has hit home with more force than a stone hurled by a rival tribesman. Confronted with the realities of fourth-stage labor, your first urge could be to flee. But for the new dad, there is nowhere to run—and really no good reason to run. You emerged from your partner's pregnancy a better man, a better person. Now it is time to reap one of life's most profound perks: parenthood. You will need survival skills, intrepid new father, as well as an aptitude for diapering bottoms, handling household duties, assembling equipment, juggling tasks, managing stress, and, of course, doing what's right for a small, somewhat fragile human who bears your genetic stamp (or at least shares your surname).

Are you up to the challenge? The next section could provide a solid indication.

## YOUR F.A.T. SCORE

Before we move along, sharpen up your No. 2 pencil and steel yourself for a "pop" quiz: The Father Aptitude Test on the facing page. Compare your answers with those provided at the bottom of the test (no cheating!), and compute your F.A.T. score:

**0-3 correct answers:** The Menace—Even your pet fish fears for its life; unsupervised contact with baby is prohibited until you demonstrate basic babycare competencies.

**4-6 correct answers:** The Apprentice—The foundation to be a good father is there, but significantly more seasoning is required to achieve full competence.

**7-9 correct answers:** The Sensitive "Guy" (French pronunciation)— You are equipped to handle fatherhood in a studly fashion, though

# F.A.T. Father Aptitude Test

Activities involving females, fire, clubs, motors, and meat come easily to the typical Stone-Ager, for they are pursuits that let a guy dwell comfortably in his own densely follicled skin. Few things can jar a man out of his comfort zone like the birth of a child. Even men who throughout pregnancy were confident in their competence to handle anything a baby might throw at them are susceptible to ambush by the new parent experience.

Like many dudes, you're probably curious how you measure up (insert locker room joke here) versus other new dads as you begin your journey through baby's first year. To gain a sense of your parental aptitude and your absorption of trivial postpartum facts, grab a piece of char from the fire (or other suitable writing utensil) and see how you stack up. Even guys who've been through the fatherhood thing before may be surprised with their scores.

**1. The practice of male circumcision began how long ago?**
a: around 10,000 BC, within Aboriginal tribes in Australia
b. around 2,300 BC, in Ancient Egypt
c. around 600 BC, within the Hebrew faith
d. in the mid-1800s, in Great Britain

**2. Typically how long after a complication-free vaginal birth can a woman safely resume sexual intercourse?**
a. 1,000 full rotations of the Earth on its axis
b. one full orbit of the Earth around the Sun
c. one full orbit of the moon around the Earth
d. 1,440 minutes

**3. How many bowel movements does the average newborn produce per day?**
a. 1-2   b. 4-5   c. 6-8   d. 12-14

**4. You can expect to pay the most for:**
a. a top-shelf bottle of 15-year-old single-malt Scotch
b. a top-end electric breast pump
c. a top-end pair of golf shoes
d. a topless table dance

**5. On average, how many times per day does a newborn breastfeed during the first month of life?**
a. 3   b. 6   c. 10   d. 16

**6. The average age for a baby to sleep through the night without waking to feed is:**
a. 3 weeks   b. 3 months   c. 6 months   d. 1 year

**7. The average number of doctor visits for baby during the first year is:**
a. 4   b. 8   c. 12   d. 15

**8. What is a baby's Babinski Reflex?**
a. baby's toes fan out when the sole of the foot is stroked firmly
b. baby's fingers close in a grasp when the palm of the hand is stroked
c. the sound of a siren or other wailing noise causes baby to howl
d. light stroking of the abdomen causes repeated kicking of baby's leg

**9. The average newborn sleeps how many hours per day?**
a. 12   b. 14   c. 16   d. 18

**10. What is colic?**
a. a skin condition common to newborns
b. a sleep state unique to a baby's first weeks of life
c. a baby's chronic, inexplicable, and inconsolable crying
d. hair formations that manifest on the scalp of some newborns

**11. It's considered normal for the average newborn to cry for *this long* over the course of a day:**
a. 20-30 minutes   b. 40-50 minutes   c. 1-2 hours   d. 3-4 hours

**12. At what age does a baby typically sample its first solid food?**
a. immediately after the first successful hunt
b. 3-4 weeks   c. 2-3 months   d. 4-6 months

1. Ⓐ Ⓑ Ⓒ Ⓓ    2. Ⓐ Ⓑ Ⓒ Ⓓ    3. Ⓐ Ⓑ Ⓒ Ⓓ    4. Ⓐ Ⓑ Ⓒ Ⓓ    5. Ⓐ Ⓑ Ⓒ Ⓓ    6. Ⓐ Ⓑ Ⓒ Ⓓ

7. Ⓐ Ⓑ Ⓒ Ⓓ    8. Ⓐ Ⓑ Ⓒ Ⓓ    9. Ⓐ Ⓑ Ⓒ Ⓓ    10. Ⓐ Ⓑ Ⓒ Ⓓ    11. Ⓐ Ⓑ Ⓒ Ⓓ    12. Ⓐ Ⓑ Ⓒ Ⓓ

Correct Answers: 1.a  2.c  3.b  4.b  5.c  6.b  7.b  8.a  9.c  10.c  11.c  12.d

there's still room for growth; eventually your rearing skills may even elicit praise from your mother-in-law.

**10–12 correct answers:** The Manny—Not only are you eminently equipped to raise your own child, you have a solid fallback career as a male nanny.

## PERKS FOR NEW POPS

On that fateful evening of conception close to a year ago, you stashed some 150 *million* gametes in your woman's safe deposit box. And boy has the value of that deposit appreciated, as you and your partner now have a tiny tyke to call your own. For proactive papas who invest fully in parenting their new child, the blessings don't end there. The effort you make to shape yourself into a caring, sharing, and responsible pop and partner should pay immeasurable dividends for years into the future, in forms both tangible and intangible.

Some of the perks you may enjoy so much you'll soon feel compelled to make another deposit and watch it grow, too. But let's not get too far ahead of ourselves. Better to savor the moment and save your energy, for you will need it to focus on reaping what you've just sown. What sort of fringe benefits might the can-do cavedad expect to enjoy for his efforts? Here are some of the biggies:

**THE CHANCE TO ADOPT A HEALTHIER LIFESTYLE.**
A major life event such as the birth of a child also tends to be a good time to size oneself up, reassess one's priorities, and scrap bad habits in favor of those that offer a better chance for longevity. Smoking or using chewing tobacco, relying too heavily on brachiation for locomotion, eating too much junk food, driving a motorcycle at high speeds sans helmet—these are the kinds of activities that become dispensable when, as a new parent, you become indispensable.

**AN EXCUSE TO BECOME A MORE RESPONSIBLE ADULT.**
Now is the time to get your proverbial house in order and pay heed to things you've neglected or put off, since baby-related responsibilities likely will consume much of the free time you had prior to the birth. Balance the checkbook. Complete household projects. Get your back waxed. Tying up these kinds of loose ends can provide a much-needed sense of stability and accomplishment as you venture into the yawning unknown of fatherhood.

**A MEANS TO HONE YOUR HOUSEHOLD SKILLS.**
There may be appliances and processes in your home with which you have zero familiarity. Now it is time to forge working relationships with the stove, the washer and dryer, the iron, the broom and vacuum cleaner, the mop, and common cleaning solutions, even the cat's litterbox. Becoming a full partner in the parenthood venture means developing proficiency with these and other contemporary household tools.

**THE OPPORTUNITY TO FURTHER EXPLORE AND EXPAND YOUR EMOTING SKILLS.**
Babies tend to do a lot of crying, which in extreme circumstances can drive their parents to weeping as well. But the emoting we're talking about here refers primarily to a guy expressing himself in new ways to his woman, his offspring, and others with whom he interacts. Having a baby opens new vistas of sensitivity to you. Openly cooing to a caveling now is not only acceptable but expected. Opening up to loved ones about how your baby and fatherhood make you feel is hunky dory, the mark of a more advanced male. Spearheading a family picnic instead of your normal Saturday golf outing is cool. Melting at the sight of your child's toothless, round-mouthed grin is certainly no cause for embarrassment. Just know where to draw the line. If you suddenly become engrossed in the Hugh Grant film pantheon or find yourself shedding tears after particularly poignant scenes of the "One Tree Hill" television program, you are in danger of crossing over to the dark side.

**THE OPPORTUNITY TO TAKE THE RELATIONSHIP WITH YOUR WOMAN TO A HIGHER PLANE.** Of all the things you share and have in common with your lady, few things strengthen the bond between you quite like a baby. It can be as simple as the moments spent together marveling at your baby's every motion and mannerism, where no words need pass between you.

**THE CHANCE TO MEET NEW PEOPLE AND MAKE NEW FRIENDS VIA THE KID CONNECTION.** One thing about new parents: they just can't keep themselves from thinking and talking about their kids. So when you meet other new parents, you immediately have conversation fodder. And you can usually carry on those conversations without fear of alienating your counterpart with too much kid talk. Eventually, such dialogue may provide the gateway to more adult-level repartee, where you find you have things in common other than offspring. That's how friendships are born.

**THE MEANS TO TAP ONE'S PATERNAL INSTINCTS.** Somewhere in the genetic make-up of the modern caveman there resides a chemical that drives him to do dad-like things—to rest the naked caveling on one's bare chest for a cuddle, to feed the youngster spoonfuls of gruel, then coax him or her to a roaring belch, to comfort the crying baby in moments of distress, and eventually to pass on some of one's wisdom and know-how, such as how to fashion a lunar calendar from an antelope bone. When the urge to do daddy things seizes you, go with it!

**THE OPPORTUNITY TO SHAPE ANOTHER HUMAN LIFE.** There was a time in the caveman's adult life when he may not have been able to adequately care for himself, never mind another. But those days are long gone. Here is the chance to mold and positively influence another human being virtually from the moment he or she exits the womb. Whether you believe in nature, nurture, or a blend of both, the opportunity to shape the future course of your youngster's life is within grasp.

**THE CHANCE TO CULTIVATE A LIFELONG BOND.** Relationships come and go over the course of a lifetime, but the one you have with the fruit of your loins, while it surely will ebb and flow, could outlast many of them. Investing time and effort now to connect with your child lays the groundwork for an enduring bond. The youngster won't remember a thing about the experiences you share in the first year, but rest assured, you will be making a lifelong impression somewhere deep in the subconscious. With such a strong connection in place, your offspring should be more apt to seek you out for a hug, for advice, and for money.

**THE CHANCE TO EVOLVE FROM A CAVEMAN TO A FAMILY MAN.** You've always wondered what it would be like to wear the boar-tooth necklace that, under clan tradition, is handed by tribe elders to new fathers upon the emergence of their first-born. Now you can wear the necklace with pride, for it represents your entry into an exclusive club of cavemen who've shown the courage to take a momentous step in their lives and in their relationships. But beware: the necklace is subject to repossession if certain devolutionary actions by the cavedweller so warrant.

**THE RIGHT TO BE CALLED CITIZEN CAVEMAN.** As a childless person, you had bigger things to worry about than the neighborhood watch, school bond issues, the speed of cars driving down your street, and the neighbor who fetches his paper each morning in nothing but a nightcap. But as a parent, such issues suddenly become relevant. Here is your chance to become more engaged in civic activities and other goings-on that affect not only you but your child and your family unit. So while there may be too many skeletons in your closet to feasibly seek public office without subjecting yourself and your family to supreme embarrassment, a run for neighborhood block captain is right up your alley.

**ATTENTION FROM BABY-OGLERS.** Remember the deodorant commercials where a whiff of the whistling sailor's fragrance prompted beautiful women to stop, turn, and wantonly leer at the source of the olfactory bouquet? Maybe not, but a guy with a baby in tow has the ability to stop women in their tracks. Of course, their stopping has nothing to do with you sporting a snug-fitting sailor's suit and cap or a spicy underarm scent— and everything to do with that little morsel you're pushing in the stroller. But who are you to turn away the attention?

We saved perhaps the best fringe benefit of proactive paternity for last. And this one is a clincher, a deal-closer, especially for "show me the money" types in the crowd who demand documentation to substantiate any daddyhood-related claims.

Scientific studies of our close genetic relatives in the primate order indicate that males who take on extra parenting responsibilities may actually live longer as a result. One such study hypothesizes that "the sex that bears the greater burden in the care of offspring will tend to survive longer" and that "in the species where the father does a greater amount of care than the mother, males tend to live longer."

As evidence, study co-authors offer males in the owl monkey and titi monkey species. Fathers from those two species of monkey typically carry their offspring from shortly after birth, relinquishing them only for short periods to let them nurse or to catch rides on older siblings. It may be no coincidence, they say, that males in both species tend to live longer than their female counterparts. They go so far as to suggest that the strength of the bond between father and offspring produces neurochemical and hormonal responses in the father that might enhance his survival. (Reference: "Parenting and survival in anthropoid primates: Caretakers live longer," Allman, John and Rosin, Aaron and Kumar, Roshan and Hasenstaub, Andrea (1998). Proceedings of the National Academy of Sciences of the United States of America, 95 (12). pp. 6866–6869).

This is compelling information, whether you are a purely rational numbers guy or an emotionally charged monkey man. Alchemists, shamans, and scientists through the centuries have vainly searched for the secret to longevity, and now, as a new father, you might just hold the key to unlocking that secret. Who knew the caveman could wield such power merely by standing erect as a father?

While they may not be privy to the latest research, male members of certain pygmy tribes in Central Africa clearly are doing their best to extend their lifespans. A study of one such tribe, the Aka net hunters, found that fathers among these so-called forest foragers do more infant caregiving than dads in any other known culture. (Reference: "Cultural Diversity Among African Pygmies," Barry S. Hewlett, http://www.vancouver.wsu.edu/fac/hewlett/

cultdiv.html). Besides tending to hunting and gathering duties, Aka fathers either held or were within arm's reach of their infant 51 percent of the time over a 24-hour period. They aren't just fair-weather fathers either. As caregivers, observation showed, Aka dads demonstrated an "intimate, affectionate, and helping-out nature."

So if you're searching for a role model during your journey through the first year of fatherhood, you could do a lot worse than the Aka pygmies. They may be small in physical stature by Western standards, but as fathers who take an active interest in caring for their young, they tower above.

Aka fathers wouldn't have had much in common with fathers in Western countries back in the 17th and 18th centuries. For the most part they left childrearing to the dames, instead focusing on providing economic support and meting out discipline. Indeed, in places such as England, France, and the United States, fathers were seen as all-powerful rulers of the family, real Tony Soprano types, minus the Cosa Nostra bloodline.

As such, the relationship between father and offspring could often be distant. With the onset of the Industrial Revolution in the 19th century, the dynamic began to take on a more familiar tinge. Men went to work in factories, leaving their women home during the day to care for the kids.

Here in the 21st century more men seem to be seeing merit in the Aka pygmy approach to fatherhood. More involvement by dads in childrearing is welcomed, especially by the women who otherwise might be bearing more than their fair share of parental responsibilities. Traditional parenting roles have evolved. And so, now, must you. All the better if doing so adds a few extra years to your lifespan.

## MEET YOUR CAVEMENTOR

For a shining example of how gratifying and rewarding the transition from caveman to family man can be, we must turn to one of our own, the estimable **Gronk,** whose personal evolutionary journey from modern throwback to full-fledged *Homo sapiens* status during pregnancy and childbirth (detailed in *The Caveman's Pregnancy Companion,* the predecessor to this book), then into parenthood, qualifies him as a role model of sorts.

## Gronk

Gronk is an example of how a new father overcame—and sometimes reveled in—his troglodyte tendencies to become an exemplary parent and partner, the consummate caregiver for his woman and offspring. Other than being named after an abandoned cement structure in the Rocky Mountains of Colorado, Gronk is an everyman. For within many new fathers, experienced or otherwise, lurks some measure of uncertainty about the unknown—the unknown as it applies to your new arrival, and to you and your woman as parents. On the frontier of fatherhood, even a guy whose feet are firmly rooted in the 21st century will at times exhibit primitive qualities: headscratching, expressions of incomprehension, frustrated ground-pounding of the fists at particularly low points, and elated chest-pounding during especially emotional high points.

It helps to have an experienced guide when entering unfamiliar territory. Drawing from his own experiences as a new dad, Gronk will serve as your oversized, Yeti-like sherpa for the next 12 months, helping you navigate the highs and lows of labor's fourth stage. Here's someone to whom a guy like you can relate: a man who effortlessly mixes modern-day accoutrements with true caveocity, who at one moment can be seen ham-handedly text-messaging a business client and the next deftly fashioning a clay pinchpot to hold his youngster's animal tooth collection.

What's more, Gronk himself is fresh off his own journey through the first phase of fatherhood. His chip-off-the-old-blockhead, Peanut, is named after a lake in which Gronk often swam as a youth. If it weren't for one or two distinctive features, clearly traceable to Gronk's side of the genetic swamp, Peanut's cherubic appearance might rightfully have earned her a place on the label of a baby food jar. But while there are many advantages to having arms of such unusual length, carving out a career in modeling isn't among them.

Let the travails and triumphs of Gronk and Peanut in their respective new roles serve as reference points for the journey on which you are embarking. While the trail they blaze for you is generally well-marked, it is also rife with thrilling downhills, grinding ascents and a host of confusing intersections. At times you likely will beg for some navigational assistance.

## Dr. Brian, Medicine Man

There are limits to the depth of information and advice peers can provide on childrearing, particularly when it comes to health and medical issues. So while it may be constructive to compare notes with your golfing buddies on the distinctions between a corn, a bunion, and a plantar wart, it is wise to defer to an expert on more delicate matters related to the well-being of your baby.

Thankfully there's a doctor in the house who not only understands the healthcare needs of a baby but also can relate those needs in the language of grunts and gestures that most cavemen understand. **Dr. Brian, M.D.,** a practicing, board-certified family doctor, appears throughout the book to shed light on medical issues related to the baby. Hundreds of parents have entrusted Dr. B with the health of their children, from delivery through the first year and beyond. If anyone knows the medical issues parents are likely to confront with their child during labor's fourth stage, it is he. And as for that growth on your foot…given its size, he recommends you see a podiatrist immediately.

## Lots of Help from the Ladies

Let's be frank here: The historic record paints a rather unflattering picture of the male segment of our species. While there certainly are many notable exceptions, some of history's most errant, harebrained schemes are attributable to men, from ancient territorial clashes to religious purges to wars on terror to the manufacture of the Ford Pinto. The damage from such schemes has been immeasurable. Yet somehow the human race has persevered. For that we owe females a big debt of gratitude, for they have provided the yin to the male yang, the Carmella to our Tony, the compassion and perspective to counterbalance a frequent lack-thereof among some members of the male species.

Hercules, Jason, and Perseus would have been lost without Athena, the Greek goddess of wisdom. We too are wise to honor the virtues of the fairer sex. In these pages we celebrate them by fortifying each chapter with insights from the sage residents of our own little Olympus, a group of women we have dubbed the **Caveman's Ad Hoc Female Advisory Council**. We have convened this informal assemblage of professional women to guide, support, and occasionally admonish us during the first year of fatherhood. Each is an expert in some facet of childrearing or baby care, so the info they provide is not to be taken lightly.

# KELLI

is a registered dietician who shares her expertise in postpartum nutrition and diet for both baby and mom.

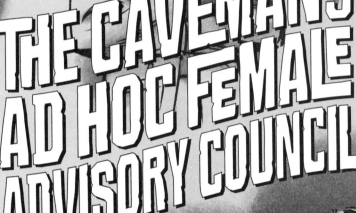

# PAT,

aka the Breast Whisperer, is founder and director of the Breastfeeding Center of Greater Washington, D.C., and one of the country's foremost lactation consultants. She will help unlock the mysteries of the female breast and breastfeeding.

# DESIRAE

is a doula and massage therapist who suggests massage techniques to relax babies and their parents.

# THE CAVEMAN'S AD HOC FEMALE ADVISORY COUNCIL

# STASIA & GINA,

who are writing a book based on their extensive research in the field of the human libido, will weigh in with vital insights on male and female sexual dynamics following the birth of a child.

You have been dealt a pretty sweet hand: the opportunity to partner and procreate with a beautiful woman who now has delivered a tiny angel into your hairy digits. Holding those cards, how can you do anything but go "all in"—to commit wholeheartedly to the discovery of your inner dadness?

In raising a baby and being a father, you're drawing from many of the same primal instincts that have safely guided you to this point in your life. That you are breathing, that you have access to food, clothing, and shelter, that you have managed to land a female partner who is at least your equal in almost every way, and that with her help, input, and occasional instruction, you, like so many males before you, have stumbled upon the secret of human reproduction, are testaments to the power of those instincts. You know what it takes to stand upright in a contemporary 21st-century environment, so you probably have a reasonable grasp of a person's basic human needs. This knowledge of simple life-survival skills will serve as your foundation for raising the little morsel into a fully realized adult human.

In case there's a guy in the crowd who needs a brief refresher course in that area, let's look at the work of Abraham Maslow, a 20th-century pioneer in the field of humanist psychology (and, it appears, a closet caveman in his own right, given the contours of his facial hair and his affinity for studying primates). Maslow, you may recall from your high school or collegiate studies, introduced a system he called the Hierarchy of Needs in the 1940s to explain why human beings act as they do. Using a pyramid to illustrate the system, Maslow theorized that human behavior is shaped by our drive to meet certain needs, from the most basic to the most complex.

Drawing from his extensive observation of people and other primates, Maslow diagrammed a pyramid consisting of five tiers of needs. At the bottom or foundation of the pyramid are basic biological/physiological needs, like food, water, oxygen, sleep, sex, etc. Having met those, people then are driven to satisfy needs in the next tier, which relate to safety, security, and protection. The third tier consists of needs for social "belongingness" and love—family, relationships, and the like. Once those are satisfied, there's the need for esteem, manifested by a drive for achievement, recognition, and status. At the pyramid's pinnacle is the most complex of needs: the drive for self-actualization—personal growth and fulfillment.

The simplest of males may spend a lifetime dwelling near the basement level of Maslow's pyramid; a needs structure resembling a split-level ranch will suffice for them. But for the rest of the human race—your baby included—there are more advanced needs eventually to be met. During your baby's first year, who assumes chief responsibility for fulfilling them from top to bottom? The answer is staring back at you in the mirror.

Yes, as the two heads of your nuclear family, you and your woman are in charge of seeing that your youngster's needs are met. At least for that first year, those needs won't advance much beyond the third tier of Maslow's hierarchy, so as a parent and provider you won't be challenged to scale the heights of the pyramid—*yet*.

## ...THE CAVEDAD MUST READ

Whether you consider Mr. Maslow a genius or a fount of psychobabble, you are responsible for the well-being and development of your offspring. And the handbook for how to meet those needs somehow has found its way into your calloused mitts. Erudite cavemen who are reading the conventional version of this book (versus the all-pictograph, scratch-and-sniff version available at Big & Tall & Hairy specialty shops) should appreciate the intuitive simplicity of its arrangement. In many ways it follows Maslow's hierarchy, with each chapter covering a group of basic human needs that you and your woman, as new parents, will strive to fulfill to protect and nurture your growing youngster. All in all, this trail of narrative crumbs is designed to be fairly intuitive to follow. It is written to a reading level that should be manageable for most branches of the primate family tree, including humans and our close cousins the chimpanzees, who have shown an ability to master sign language vocabularies of several hundred words and arrange them in short sentences.

Best efforts are made to keep the material in these pages well within those cognitive boundaries. Here's a breakdown of the post-partum needs pyramid as it unfolds in the chapters of this book:

**CAPABLE CAREGIVERS**—A baby's best chance to thrive is with well-prepared parents. Chapter 2 sets the tone for all needs-fulfillment activities, providing new papas with the means to mentally and physically equip themselves for the journey at hand.

**FOOD, DIET & NUTRITION**—Your omnivorous offspring likely will drink all of his or her meals early in life but quickly will develop a need for more than that. Chapter 3 reveals how to forage for and prepare the right balance of grains, nuts, vegetation, and game to meet a baby's unique nutritional requirements.

**SHELTER, SAFETY & PROTECTION**—Here in Chapter 4, the caveman caregiver will discover how to identify and fend off threats that might confront a defenseless baby in its new environment outside the womb.

**CLOTHING**—From functionality to fashion sense, there's much a guy must learn about modern attire for babies. Chapter 5 is where to find it all.

**HEALTH & WELLNESS**—The responsibilities that in prehistoric times fell to the clan healer or shaman now are shared by you, your woman, and the healthcare professionals you enlist to protect your youngster's well-being. Get the answers to all your health and medical questions here in Chapter 6.

**SLEEP**—Babies and parents alike need quality sleep. So why do so many seem so sleep-deprived during baby's first year? Chapter 7 investigates the phenomenon and provides cavecouples with the soporific artillery to win the Sleep Wars.

**COMMUNICATION, SOCIALIZATION & STIMULATION**—Now we're advancing a bit in the needs department. From the sound of music to sign language to the first spoken words, Chapter 8 is about empowering the caveman to help his baby make sense of and interact with the world.

**COUPLE & CAVEMAN MAINTENANCE**—At the pinnacle of the first-year pyramid of needs is the preservation of adult identity, intimacy, and sanity during baby's first year. You and your woman have needs too, and failing to fulfill them can take a toll on parents and baby alike. Chapter 9 is full of creative ideas for carving out time for yourselves, even amid one of the busiest times in your lives.

As your partner has reminded you on numerous occasions, you did not actually carry a fetus *in utero* through three trimesters, nor did you endure contractions or push your body to its breaking point to deliver said fetus. Basically you provided the seed and let your woman take it from there, with you as the ever-supportive partner during pregnancy. Now, your seed having grown into a sapling, it seems only fair that you do some heavy lifting of your own. As a fully vested partner in this parenthood venture, it is time to rise to the occasion and fulfill your potential as a yeoman dad.

Your two-fold postpartum mission—and you have no choice but to accept it—is to become a sponge of knowledge, and to apply what you learn in your dual roles as father and partner.

And so, with Gronk as your guide, the journey through the fourth stage of labor begins. Now onto the business of needs fulfillment, not only as it pertains to the baby, but to you and your woman as well.

## The Ten Commandments for New Fathers

For females we are indeed grateful. But without responsible paternal behavior by some male members of the *Homo sapiens* species, the human race might never have survived the Stone Age. Here's the code of responsibility that the cream of the new father crop has been passing down to men of younger generations since well before such notable troglodytes as Charlton Heston and Moses himself walked the earth.

Babies are vulnerable. They need dads who vigilantly look out for their best interests.

The best-equipped dads are those who are on solid ground with their women.

Don't let the pressing responsibilities of parenthood overshadow the amazing moments and emotions life with a baby can conjure.

Do not shy from opportunities to show off thy chip-off-ye-old-block.

In moments of parental indecision or crisis, it's often best to go with what your gut tells you.

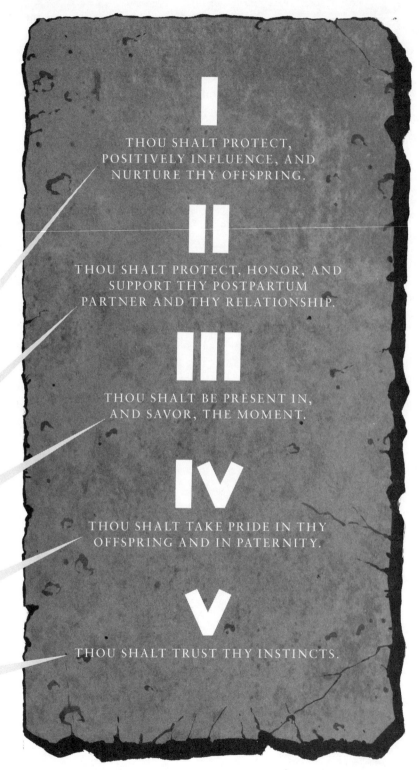

**I**

THOU SHALT PROTECT, POSITIVELY INFLUENCE, AND NURTURE THY OFFSPRING.

**II**

THOU SHALT PROTECT, HONOR, AND SUPPORT THY POSTPARTUM PARTNER AND THY RELATIONSHIP.

**III**

THOU SHALT BE PRESENT IN, AND SAVOR, THE MOMENT.

**IV**

THOU SHALT TAKE PRIDE IN THY OFFSPRING AND IN PATERNITY.

**V**

THOU SHALT TRUST THY INSTINCTS.

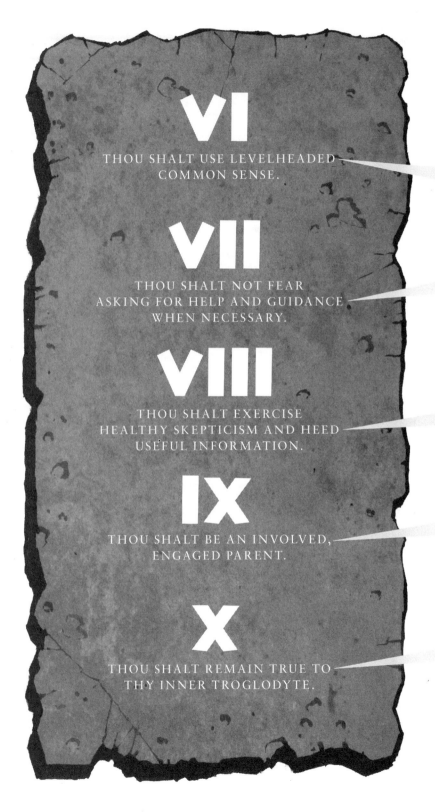

# VI

THOU SHALT USE LEVELHEADED
COMMON SENSE.

The challenges of parenthood can test one's patience. During trying times, let cooler heads prevail. If you cannot count to 10, count to three.

# VII

THOU SHALT NOT FEAR
ASKING FOR HELP AND GUIDANCE
WHEN NECESSARY.

Don't let your pride get in the way of what's best for the caveling. Good advice is out there, from peers, pros, even parents.

# VIII

THOU SHALT EXERCISE
HEALTHY SKEPTICISM AND HEED
USEFUL INFORMATION.

Parenting advice can come at you from all angles. Not all of it is useful and some of it is downright hazardous to the health of your youngster. Consider the source and learn how to filter.

# IX

THOU SHALT BE AN INVOLVED,
ENGAGED PARENT.

Nothing ventured, nothing gained. Leave detached parenting to lesser men.

# X

THOU SHALT REMAIN TRUE TO
THY INNER TROGLODYTE.

Being a responsible father and partner doesn't preclude you from continuing to pursue things that make you who you are. A happier, fulfilled caveman usually makes for a better parent.

# CHAPTER 2

# A WISE, WELL-PREPARED PAPA

## A QUICK PREPARATORY COURSE TO PUT A NEW DAD INTO THE PARENTAL MINDSET

I N THE MID-18TH CENTURY THE DISTINGUISHED SWEDISH botanist, physician, and zoologist Carl von Linné developed a system called *Systema Naturæ* for naming, ranking, and classifying living organisms. In fact, von Linné was so fond of labeling things in Latin that, in true pop star fashion, he gave himself a new name: Carolus Linnaeus.

The basic methodology that the powdered-wig-wearing Linnaeus developed for categorizing plants and animals is still widely used today, as is the name he attached to members of the human species. The zoologist formerly known as von Linné dubbed us all *Homo sapiens*, which from Latin translates to "wise man." Here in the nascent moments of parenthood and on through your tenure as a parent, it is especially important that you and your woman live up to that name. Wisdom, however you accumulate and store it, will serve you well in your efforts to fulfill your baby's needs.

In lumping all humans into the "wise man" category, Linnaeus may have been setting the bar a bit too high for some members of the species, the occasional new dad included. While fledgling fathers may be wise in certain aspects of life, the arrival of a baby can expose a deficit of wisdom in the area of raising a healthy, happy baby. Indeed, you have been called many names during your lifetime: Neanderthal man, simple man, maybe even handyman, Renaissance man or superman. But when it comes to parental and paternal know-how, the wise man moniker might be a bit of a stretch, at least for the time being. As a father, at times you may be an absolute hero and at other times a blatant primitive, your skills rudimentary, your techniques unpolished, your emotions raw, and your confusion evident.

But that is no reason to lose hope. Eventually you, like so many new fathers before you, will accumulate enough knowledge and wisdom as a parent to shed the skins of inexperience and ascend to full *Homo sapiens* status. As far as your baby and woman are concerned, the sooner you get there, the better.

*Grow with Gronk*

What the caveman stands to gain from reading Chapter 2:

- Insight into the mystery that is the neonatal body

- A clue about what lies ahead for him, his woman, and baby in the year ahead

- The acumen to distinguish between sound parenting techniques and potentially ruinous ones

- Keen insight into his woman's postpartum state of mind

- An awareness of the new roles and responsibilities that come with fatherhood

- A knowledge of congenital health issues

- An appreciation for the value of recording the sights and sounds of baby's first year

All that you experienced during pregnancy and childbirth has already put you on the path to enlightenment. But to advance, to evolve from caveman to wise man, you must prepare. Armed with a clue of what might lie ahead for you, your woman, and your baby over the next 12 months, you'll be better equipped to handle any unexpected twists and turns in the path with wisdom and fortitude. But where to find the wisdom to fulfill the destiny Linnaeus envisioned for you as a member of the human race? Much of it will come over time, from your own hands-on experiences as a parent. Some you'll get from observing others in the act of parenting. Some you may have already absorbed long ago when you were on the receiving end of the care your parents and/or guardians provided. Some you will learn on the mean streets. And some you will discover in authoritative information sources, such as this book.

Life with a baby is full of surprises, many of them thrilling and thoroughly enjoyable, some harrowing and perplexing. So, as parents undertaking the enormous responsibility of fulfilling the needs of a largely helpless little human, it's helpful to have a clue about what lurks around the next corner. Who—or what—might your baby look like fresh out of the womb? How do all these moving parts work? What hides between those folds of skin and inside those orifices? What major milestones and key moments are you, your offspring, and your woman destined to encounter over the course of the next year? How much does gender determine how your baby behaves and develops? What can you and your woman do to handle all the new baby-related responsibilities? What parenting techniques are disasters waiting to happen? What are the odds of a baby having congenital health issues? And, amid all these questions, where do you find time to record and document all the amazing stuff happening in your household?

You have questions, curious Cro-Magnon—and in this chapter, you'll find answers to help you become a papa the Aka pygmies would be proud of, a dad who embraces change, expects the unexpected, anticipates the bizarre, rolls with the punches, and rises above challenges. The time has come to get into the parental frame of mind. It's a mindset shaped by unfamiliar emotions that arrive shortly after the newborn does, often with unexpected ferocity. Having just been introduced to this offspring of yours, you may already be awash in feelings, the strength and dimension of which you are unaccustomed to. One is the immediate love you feel for this little one and the other is the sudden sense of responsibility you feel toward your woman and the caveling you created together. This one-two emotional punch is enough to send an uninitiated man reeling.

But your youngster doesn't deserve an invertebrate for a dad. To thrive, the little one needs a papa with a spine, a stand-up guy who expects to persevere and ultimately triumph in his daddy role. Bottom line: Absorbing the best punches parenthood might throw at you requires steel-jawed preparation. That's where this chapter can help. Conditions in the real world can be harsh and the stakes high for new dads who fail to prepare, as our early ape-like ancestors, the australopithecines, may have learned the hard way more than one million years ago, when they crossed paths with their brainier and more adaptable cousins, *Homo erectus* ("upright man"). Evolutionary scholars suggest that once *Homo erectus* became an accomplished hunter, with an ability to make and wield hand-axes and other crude but effective weaponry, the australopithecines with whom they likely co-existed might have become their prey, to the point where they may have been hunted to extinction by their own cousins.

The australopithecines were endowed with massive, equinesque jaws for gnashing hard vegetation. But the fossil evidence paleontologists have pieced together suggests these creatures were more like glass-jawed boxers, unable to absorb the punches the environment kept throwing at them over the course of the Pleistocene epoch. Some 1.2 million years ago, the australopithecines hit the evolutionary canvas, never to rise again, apparently because they could not adapt to new food sources in Africa's changing climate. Instead, they may have become meat for their more resourceful relatives.

There is a lesson in this for new fathers. For throughout human history, it has been the most adaptable species that remain standing and the less prepared ones that often find themselves knocked into oblivion. As a new father and a descendant of *Homo erectus*, you, too, have the capacity to adapt, and you can do so without ever preying upon your own cousins.

# INFANT TOPOGRAPHY & SCATOLOGY

The human body is capable of amazing things. Just ask anyone who has experienced or witnessed childbirth (or seen the work of contortionist Rubber Ritchie). This finely honed mass of sinew, soft tissue, bone, fluid, and miscellaneous cellular formations is a miraculous creation, a constantly chugging, ever-changing organic factory that consumes raw materials, converts them to energy, and expels what it no longer needs as waste.

If on occasion you have been astounded by your own body's processing and production capacities (such as in the aftermath of an evening of Dionysian excess, capped by a 3 a.m. trip to the diner), the newborn baby provides an eminently fascinating study in the workings of the human body. Your baby's bod is especially efficient, often prolific, and at times unpredictable in both its consumption of raw materials and its expulsion of waste. The diagram at right provides insight into the what, where, when, how, and why of an infant's bodily functions, fluids, and other curious physical phenomena you're apt to encounter during the ridiculously long and frequent moments you and your woman spend handling, scrutinizing, and gawking at your offspring, as is any proud parent's unalienable right.

**EXTERIOR COATING:** A little one who emerges *con queso*, skin seemingly laminated in a light, cheesy substance, is coated in **vernix,** which is secreted from the baby's glands for *in utero* skin protection. No other land mammal, not even the apes, produces vernix-coated neonates. But that's no reason to fret about or remove the stuff—it should reabsorb into the skin shortly after birth. Babies (especially those born prematurely) also may come with fine, downy hair called **lanugo** that will disappear over time.

**SKIN COMPLEXION/TONE:** Skin color at birth can be dark red to purple, changing to red as baby adjusts to breathing more air. Redness tends to fade in the first day. A bit of **jaundice**—yellowish tint to the skin—is normal but more than that may require medical attention (as explained in chapter 6).

**MARKINGS:** A small pink or red marking on the eyelids, neck or elsewhere may be what's called a **stork bite** or **salmon patch.** They're harmless and usually fade over time, though they may persist into adulthood and may become more prominent during exertion. Newborns also are prone to **erythema toxicum,** a red rash common on the chest and back that looks like lots of little fleabites. It usually disappears in a few days with no medical intervention. Occurring mostly on the head, a **strawberry hemangioma** is a red, raised or swollen patch that looks a little like mild road rash. It often develops in the first few months of life before fading gradually over a period of months and years. Potentially more serious are **port wine stains,** which don't fade over time and may require treatment later in life. In some instances a port wine stain may become as famous as its bearer (see Mikhail Gorbachev's forehead).

**BREASTS:** Male and female newborns alike may experience swelling of the breasts in the first several days of life; a substance called **witch's milk** may leak from the nipples. It appears as a result of baby still harboring some of Mom's milk-producing hormones and should disappear over days or weeks.

**EXTREMITIES:** Hands and feet may be bluish for several days, which is normal given baby's still-developing blood circulation.

**FACE:** May feature **milia**—small, whitish, hard spots resembling zits. One in five babies also develops **baby acne** (known as acne neonatorum), often on the cheeks and forehead. Each condition tends to fade and/or disappear quickly.

**EYES:** At birth, they're about half the size of an adult's eyes. They may change color over time, particularly among Caucasian babies. Eyes initially can focus only at close range and can detect light and dark but not all colors. They are unable to produce tears for several months.

**NOSE:** Most babies arrive with a keen sense of smell and an olfactory attraction to Mom's milk. A nose that is slightly flattened right after birth as a result of time spent in the birthing canal should soon assume natural shape.

**MOUTH:** Most babies feature an automatic latch-on liplock mechanism to access their chief source of nourishment early in life, the breasts. This prolific orifice also is the source for belches, regurgitation and, in many cases, a great deal of noise.

**EARS:** May be slightly (and temporarily) misshapen from vaginal delivery; typical infant is born with fully developed hearing capability.

**UMBILICUS:** What remains of the umbilical cord after it is cut should begin to dry, darken, and wither before falling off several weeks following birth. What remains is a baby's "innie" or "outie." From a medical standpoint, neither is preferable to the other. There are no known health implications associated with having an innie or an outie belly button (umbilicus). Perhaps you've heard it murmured in the locker room that an outie might in reality be a potentially dangerous small hernia, but according to Dr. Brian, this is pure urban legend. While umbilical hernias do occur, where intestines protrude through a defect in the abdominal wall, they're a much different animal from a plain old outie.

**GENITALS:** Among girls, expect a larger **outer labia** and perhaps a bit of whitish **discharge** or blood-tinged **mucus** from the **vagina** in the first few weeks, as a little girl's genitals might be affected by maternal hormones, as with the breasts. Boys born close to term tend to have a ridged **scrotum** and descended **testicles.** Sometimes the testicles are elevated and thus difficult to locate. In some cases (most commonly with boys born prematurely), one or both of the testes may continue hiding in the abdomen, undescended. Those who are circumcised will have a wound on the **foreskin** of the **penis** that should heal in a week or two.

**BACKSIDE:** Bluish or purplish areas, sometimes called **Mongolian spots,** may occur on the skin of many dark-skinned babies (especially East Asians, East Africans, and Native Americans), mainly on the lower back and buttocks. Caused by concentrations of pigmented cells, they tend to disappear in the first four years of life. Between the cheeks reside the **anus** and **rectum,** through which will pass several waste products, including **meconium,** a sticky, tar-looking substance that constitutes a baby's first bowel movement, and **farts,** which develop naturally from digesting the lactose and proteins contained in milk and formula. The anus is also the insertion point for a **rectal thermometer,** which is the most accurate means to measure a newborn's temperature.

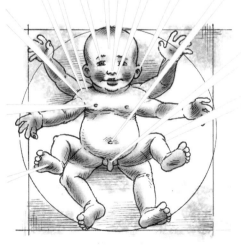

## Bad Head Day

Our first look at a newborn is the culmination of quite a harrowing journey for one so small yet so determined. Before gulping its first breath of air, a gestating fetus must first spend a prolonged period pressed tightly inside a fluid-filled sac, tethered to its mother and battling for space with a big, bloody bag of nutrients (and at least one other fetus, if it's a multiple birth).

When quarters within the womb get too tight, it's time for the bowling-ball-through-a-garden-hose trip down the birthing canal, a muscular tunnel so narrow no light may enter, whose only natural exit is so small its diameter is typically measured in centimeters. After enduring a process that can involve much squeezing, suctioning, shoehorning, cursing, cajoling, and ultimately, in some cases, surgical intervention (an episiotomy or a C-section), the little one makes an appearance.

But before the proud parents can begin identifying family features, they first may need to confirm to themselves that their offspring is indeed human. Being delivered vaginally can make quite an impression on the little one's cranium, as the two soft areas at the top of a baby's head where the skull bones haven't yet grown together, called **fontanels,** allow the bones of the skull to be flexible to accommodate passage through those tight quarters. What you see as a result might startle you. But if members of the attending medical team don't shrink in horror from the sight, that's a good sign your child's appearance is at least somewhere in the realm of normalcy.

Here are some of the common head shapes and hair formations you're apt to see in a nursery full of newborns. Concerned parents, fret not. Fontanels allow the bones of the skull to quickly shift back into position, restoring natural proportions in a matter of hours or days.

The Nixon

the YODA

THE ALBERT EiNSTEiN

The BELDAR...

The GORBY

THE GERRY COONEY

THE GERBER.

THE RINGO

THE BUCKWHEAT

THE JERRY GARCIA

THE EDDIE MUNSTER

THE HOMER SIMPSON

THE DONALD

## SWEEPING GENDERIZATIONS

The contemporary caveman prefers his gender roles cut and dried, like the smoked stuff that hangs in his meat locker. He clings to a world order in which men are hunters and women are gatherers, no in-betweens. But we live in a world where distinctions between the sexes are blurring. There are men named Marilyn and women called Craig. Even the manliest of males do yoga and weep openly during the fourth act of Verdi's *Aida*. They don't just eat quiche, they make it from scratch.

So why let black-and-white attitudes impede a child's progress in a world of endless possibilities? Why not sever yourself from those pink-and-blue gender stereotypes and embrace the egalitarian flexibility that our 21st-century society permits? If you find yourself gravitating to any of the sweeping generalizations below, better catch yourself before you draw your woman's ire—and a spanking.

| BLUE ♂ | PINK ♀ | GRAY AREA |
| --- | --- | --- |
| Tough | Dainty | Girl babies may enjoy mild roughhousing as much as boy babies—and the accidental kick to your groin hurts just as much coming from a girl as it does coming from a boy. |
| Stoic | Emotional | Expressions of emotion are healthy and common among boys and girls alike. And boy babies *do* cry—just as much as girl babies do. |
| Baseball | Barbie | Boys (and men) like playing with dolls, girls (and women) can hit a ball a long way. |
| Dirty | Clean | Crud, crust, dirt, and dust will find your child, regardless of gender. |
| Impervious | Vulnerable | Anyone who's been around infants knows boys and girls are equally susceptible to emotional and physical pain. |
| Time with Daddy | Time with Mommy | Boys need quality time with their mamas, likewise girls with their papas. |
| Pants | Dresses | Here in the heyday of spandex, fashion takes a backseat to comfort. |
| Short hair | Long hair | Nowadays even big, tough football players have ponytails dangling outside their helmets. |
| Silent | Chatty | Verbose babbling isn't a gender-specific trait. |
| Aggressive | Docile | Anyone who believes baby girls are timid pushovers has never lived with one. |
| Rebellious | Compliant | One-year-old girls can throw a tantrum with as much gusto as their male counterparts. |

## LABOR'S FOURTH STAGE:
## YEAR ONE

Baby's first 12 months are likely to provide a dizzying sequence of milestones, momentous events and auspicious beginnings, interspersed with low points that hopefully you will be able to file away as learning experiences. Exactly when all this stuff occurs will vary greatly from baby to baby, so be flexible in your expectations. Some kids may walk at nine or 10 months, others not until they are well past one year old. Some will need a ton of sleep, others not as much. Fine motor skills and speech will come to some young knuckledraggers much quicker than they come to others.

All of this can be a little much for the caveman to get his mind around. Some of the first-year highs and lows you will recall lucidly for the rest of your life, others you will recollect only vaguely, and some you will immediately block from memory. How will it all unfold? The timeline on the next spread provides an inkling.

**MONTH:** 1   2   3   4   5

## baby

MONTH 3:
RAISES HEAD, CHEST WHEN PLACED ON ABDOMEN

FIRST RIDE IN THE JOGGING CHARIOT

DAY 5: FIRST BATH

MONTHS 4–5: FIRST LAUGH

WEEK 2: REMNANTS OF UMBILICAL CORD DROP OFF

2–4 MONTHS: MOVE FROM CRADLE/CO-SLEEPING INTO CRIB

4–6 MONTHS:
EATS FIRST SOLID FOOD
CAPABLE OF SEEING IN FULL COLOR
ROLLS OVER UNASSISTED
NAPS 2–3 TIMES DAILY, 1–2 HRS PER

AVERAGE LENGTH AT ONE MONTH: GIRLS, 21 INCHES, BOYS, 21.5 INCHES

3–4 MONTHS:
FIRST THROUGH-THE-NIGHT SLEEP (BLOCK OF 5+ HOURS)

2–3 MONTHS: FIRST RESPONSIVE SMILE

MONTH 4:
CAN REACH FOR AN OBJECT

AVERAGE MONTHLY GAINS AT 1–3 MONTHS OF AGE: 1.5–2 LBS, 1 INCH

3–6 MONTHS:
EYEBROWS BEGIN TO CREEP TOGETHER
BEGINS TO SUPPORT LEGS WHEN IN STANDING POSITION
CUTS FIRST TOOTH

## PARENTAL

MONTH 2: FIRST POSED FAMILY PORTRAIT

DAY 1: PARADE OF VISITORS TO MEET BABY BEGINS

DAY 1: FIRST TIME CHANGING DIAPER OF OWN OFFSPRING

PARENTS' FIRST NIGHT OUT WITHOUT BABY (MONTHS 4–6)

DAY 10: FIRST PANICKED CALL TO PARENT FOR COPING ADVICE

DAY 10: FIRST PANICKED CALL TO PEDIATRICIAN FOR MEDICAL GUIDANCE

1 MONTH: PARADE OF VISITORS TO MEET BABY SLOWS TO A TRICKLE

## Mom

Month 3: Twelve weeks of parental leave concludes

Week 2: First successful yield from breast pump

Months 2–3: Ready, willing, able to resume sexual intercourse

Week 6: First postpartum work-out (health permitting)

Months 2–4: Postpartum hormonal swings begin to moderate

## DAD

DAY 1: FIRST TIME WITNESSING BABY BOY'S ERECTION

MONTH 3: TWELVE WEEKS OF PARENTAL LEAVE CONCLUDES

MONTH 3: FIRST POSTPARTUM ROUND OF GOLF

DAY 2–3: READY, WILLING, ABLE TO RESUME SEXUAL INTERCOURSE

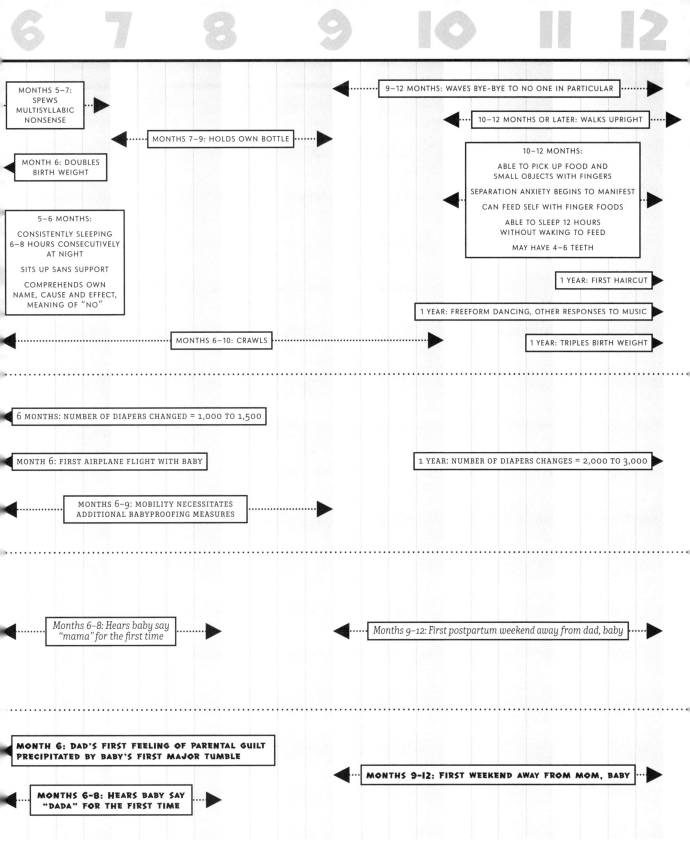

6 7 8 9 10 11 12

MONTHS 5–7: SPEWS MULTISYLLABIC NONSENSE

9–12 MONTHS: WAVES BYE-BYE TO NO ONE IN PARTICULAR

10–12 MONTHS OR LATER: WALKS UPRIGHT

MONTHS 7–9: HOLDS OWN BOTTLE

MONTH 6: DOUBLES BIRTH WEIGHT

10–12 MONTHS:

ABLE TO PICK UP FOOD AND SMALL OBJECTS WITH FINGERS

SEPARATION ANXIETY BEGINS TO MANIFEST

CAN FEED SELF WITH FINGER FOODS

ABLE TO SLEEP 12 HOURS WITHOUT WAKING TO FEED

MAY HAVE 4–6 TEETH

5–6 MONTHS:

CONSISTENTLY SLEEPING 6–8 HOURS CONSECUTIVELY AT NIGHT

SITS UP SANS SUPPORT

COMPREHENDS OWN NAME, CAUSE AND EFFECT, MEANING OF "NO"

1 YEAR: FIRST HAIRCUT

1 YEAR: FREEFORM DANCING, OTHER RESPONSES TO MUSIC

MONTHS 6–10: CRAWLS

1 YEAR: TRIPLES BIRTH WEIGHT

6 MONTHS: NUMBER OF DIAPERS CHANGED = 1,000 TO 1,500

MONTH 6: FIRST AIRPLANE FLIGHT WITH BABY

1 YEAR: NUMBER OF DIAPERS CHANGES = 2,000 TO 3,000

MONTHS 6–9: MOBILITY NECESSITATES ADDITIONAL BABYPROOFING MEASURES

*Months 6–8: Hears baby say "mama" for the first time*

*Months 9–12: First postpartum weekend away from dad, baby*

MONTH 6: DAD'S FIRST FEELING OF PARENTAL GUILT PRECIPITATED BY BABY'S FIRST MAJOR TUMBLE

MONTHS 9-12: FIRST WEEKEND AWAY FROM MOM, BABY

MONTHS 6-8: HEARS BABY SAY "DADA" FOR THE FIRST TIME

## THE PARENTAL PANDORA'S BOX

Desperate times do indeed call for desperate measures. Parents will try just about anything to quiet a colicky infant, lull an overtired, cranky baby to sleep, and soothe an unsettled newborn. And if something works once or twice, they are apt to try it again and again. Why mess with success?

Two words: slippery slope. Don't do something once with a baby that you're not comfortable repeating a hundred or a thousand times. If the means to a particular end is grounded in sound parenting fundamentals, great, you've added a viable weapon to your caregiving arsenal. But just because a technique works once doesn't mean it's worth repeating. In fact, in the scheme of things, certain parenting techniques are merely gimmicks that invite trouble because they place onerous demands on you and/or reinforce behaviors you might just as soon not see perpetuated.

In the infant care arena, these quick-fix tricks are sometimes called "accidental parenting" and they often turn out to cause more trouble than they quell. Some of the most common of these techniques are explained at right. We introduce them early in the book so you have an opportunity to nip them in the bud.

| The Action | What It Addresses |
| --- | --- |
| Using a vehicle to "drive" baby to sleep | Baby's difficulty falling/staying asleep in normal bed-type setting |
| Bolting into baby's room at his/her slightest nighttime or naptime peep | Parent's need to offer comfort, believing it's the best option for quieting baby |
| Sticking only to a few food items baby seemingly really likes to eat | Desire to keep baby in a culinary comfort zone and ensure he/she is eating enough |
| Reluctance to expose baby to certain environments due to risk of contracting an illness | With still-developing immune systems, babies are particularly susceptible to sickness. |
| Using the television to occupy baby so parent can finish unspecified household task uninterrupted | Parent's lack of time to focus on household duties |
| Relying solely on one person to put baby to sleep | If baby usually goes right to sleep when Mom puts her down, why tamper with success? |
| Leaving baby on your bed unattended so parent can perform a household task | Frees parent to accomplish said task unencumbered |
| One parent regularly rides in back seat with fussy baby to offer comfort during car ride | Baby may not like riding in the car, particularly for long trips, prompting him/her to persistently voice displeasure. |
| Letting baby handle household electronic equipment such as phones, remote controls | Parents are constantly searching for items to engage baby's attention |
| Allowing baby to regularly skip naps | Instead of interrupting an errand or a visit in order to keep baby on sleep schedule, parents may opt to keep baby awake and finish what they've started. |

| Why It Works Short-Term | Why It's Perilous Long-Term | Preferable Alternatives |
|---|---|---|
| Motion gets baby to sleep when seemingly nothing else will. And when baby sleeps, so can you. | Perpetuates reliance on vehicle as sleep prop. You'll end up regularly out on the roads at 3 a.m., when even many truckers are sleeping soundly. | A routine that includes means of soothing, winding down baby: reading, singing, rocking, etc. |
| Babies often soothe quickly and easily in the presence of a parent. | Babies who don't learn to soothe themselves may have persistent problems going to/staying asleep. | Wait out noise from baby's bedroom to let baby develop self-soothing ability. |
| Comforting for parents to see baby eating heartily; amusing to watch him/her interact with favorite foods | Baby will not be exposed to a broad range of flavors and textures, limiting his/her culinary horizons and your menu options. Could create a finicky (vs. an adventurous) eater. | Let baby taste lots of different (age- and health-appropriate) foods. If he/she rejects something once, introduce it again. |
| Exposure to fewer "Petri dish" environments can curb the instance of illness. | By limiting your baby's outings, you also are limiting healthy social and environmental interaction. | Germs are everywhere and virtually inescapable. The earlier your baby is exposed to them, the quicker he/she will tend to build immunities. |
| Even the Weather Channel can be riveting viewing for a baby. | It's not called the Idiot Box for nothing. Numerous studies document the negative impact television viewing can have on babies' brains. | Engage baby's attention with a mobile, easy-to-hold toys, music, a disco ball, anything besides the TV. |
| Babies tend to crave routine; they may not fuss if the same person puts them to bed night after night. | Trouble lurks when baby's routine is disrupted and someone "new" must put him/her to bed; detrimental to you having a social life. | Have Dad put baby down some nights and Mom others to get the little one accustomed to variety. |
| Infant can't yet roll over, so should be safe lying slug-like in the middle of a California King mattress. | Eventually baby will learn to roll over; if the first time he/she does so happens while unattended on the bed, prepare to administer first aid, grapple with parental guilt. | Find a safer place to put baby temporarily, such as in a playpen, on a play floormat. |
| Interaction with parent brings peace and quiet to potentially angst-filled infant passenger. | Youngster may grow accustomed to having a parent alongside for backseat entertainment. | Have passenger interact with baby safely from the front seat unless absolutely necessary; provide music, toys, books, etc., to occupy his/her attention. |
| Babies are curious about items they see their parents handling consistently; they are fascinated by all those little buttons and blipping lights. | Handling battery-operated or electrically charged items is potentially harmful to baby and actual item. | Provide baby with access to other less hazardous but still engaging items that entertain with sounds, lights, buttons, and other movable parts. |
| Some babies seem not to be fazed by missing a nap here and there. | Babies thrive on routine and need a lot of sleep. Those whose routines are regularly disrupted may in the long run have less predictable sleep habits. | Make every effort to establish and stick to a sleep routine with baby; well-rested, routine-oriented babies may be better equipped to overcome the occasional (and inevitable) missed nap. |

Their predilection toward traditional gender roles aside, some guys on one occasion or other have dressed up as a woman—and secretly relished the experience. (Wink, wink. Nudge, nudge.) The arrival of a baby brings good news to guys who crave the occasional gender bender, for this is a period in life that demands you put yourself in a woman's shoes. And those shoes belong to the mother of your child. But this is no dress rehearsal for next year's Halloween party (although you may already be pretty amped to model the Paris Hilton costume you've been painstakingly assembling). This is parenthood, and your efforts to walk in a woman's shoes carry a much more serious purpose.

Never has it been so imperative for you to try to understand your partner's point of view. Being a guy limits your capacity to contribute in certain areas of childcare, such as breastfeeding, which means additional responsibilities for the new mom. As a full partner in this parenting venture, the best thing you can do for the ongoing health and well-being of your newly expanded nuclear family and your relationship as a couple is to show you "get it." A guy who gets it is willing and able to pick up slack in other areas of need fulfillment as it pertains to both his woman and his young 'un.

When it comes to fatherhood, the most enlightened, best prepared males are those who keep the best interests of their ladies top of mind, who listen to what their women are saying, grasp what they are experiencing, and know how to act accordingly. Here's where such traits as empathy, sympathy, proactiveness, and an ability to read between the lines become indispensable to the new father. But not every caveman comes equipped with those qualities. Sometimes they must be hammered home, no easy task given the thickness of the male skull.

Straight from mothers' mouths to your eyes come the insight and advice a new dad needs to walk in Mom's shoes with aplomb, however ill-fitting those cherry-red pumps may feel on his feet. Thanks to **Stasia** and **Gina**, new inductees to the Caveman's Ad Hoc Female Advisory Council, for loaning us the shoes. Stay tuned for additional intelligence from these two ladies in later chapters of the book, especially in the sections on breastfeeding and sexual relations.

Their advice to new dads, not to be taken lightly:

*Employ and embrace
your new mantra:*
**Happy Mommy, Happy Family.**

*Remember, we've been
sucked on, pulled on, and
grabbed at while holding
a completely dependent
human being 24/7. We don't
need another baby right
now. Don't whine about work
or how loud our newborn
screams. It's not sexy.*

*Don't ask us if
we feel fat or bloated.*

*Being a good dad is **hot**.
It makes us far more attracted to you.
If you want some action, take the
midnight feeding.*

*If there's a year to
spend money in restaurants,
this is the one.*

*Read up on postpartum
depression. It happens
to a notable percentage
of us in the first year. If
we're experiencing it, we'll
probably deny it. Be aware
of the symptoms and seek
professional advice if
necessary. Left untreated,
it can profoundly and
adversely impact most
facets of life, including our
sex drive.*

*No commentary whatsoever about*

    *(a) how clothes fit;*

    *(b) caloric intake; or*

    *(c) supermodels.*

*Remember, if we're nursing, we're
supposed to eat more than you. So
we're allowed to have a few desserts
here and there free from wisecracks
or passive-aggressive comments like,
"Are you sure you want that, too?"*

*Be high-octane, all the time.
Demonstrate far more energy
than us. Be our rock.*

*30 minutes alone every day with
the newspaper (preferably off-site
at a café with a European vibe)
can go a **long** way. Bear that in
mind. You might get lucky.*

*Please know that we miss reading, we miss our minds, and we miss
stimulating conversation. Don't stop asking us questions about subject
matter Beyond the Babe. If you're working outside the home and we're not,
bring us news from the outside world. The more we dwell on the babe, the
more claustrophobic and possibly martyr-ish we may feel or become. Keep
us thinking outside the box...the schedule box, the crib box, the diaper box,
the grocery-list box. Box us in and watch us wither into asexual Mombots.*

*Three words:*
**coffee in bed.**

We have already debunked the myth that labor comes in three stages. Now it's time to take aim at another traditional view of labor—namely how it is divided in a household where a baby resides.

Division of labor is a concept commonly associated with the Industrial Revolution and the rise of capitalism. But it goes back much further than that, to the days of our early *Homo* ancestors who pioneered the hunter-gatherer way of life. Pushed to the brink of extinction by the unforgiving Ice Age climate of the Upper Paleolithic period, cavedwelling hominids figured out that to sustain themselves and conquer their foes, they needed to divide responsibilities. Their survival depended on vital contributions from both male and female members of the group. Men often were assigned the task of hunting large game and hauling it back to the fieldstone ranch, while women gathered smaller game and plants and, with the help of older children, made clothing and built shelters. Such tasks as collecting firewood, gathering materials for tools and weaponry, and the actual fashioning of those implements, were also shared among clan members.

Slackers who failed to embrace the communal attitude could find themselves evicted from their stone domiciles and ostracized from the group. Left to fend for themselves in the permafrost, these mildly motivated creatures may have migrated to places that were more accepting of their leisurely attitudes. Some found their way to the champagne powder of the Alpine high country. Others wandered onto the Iberian Peninsula, drawn by inviting seas and the gnarly sets they saw breaking off the coast. These knuckledraggers were the prehistoric forebears to the modern-day recreationalists who today populate ski resorts and beach towns around the world.

While becoming a dad does not signal an end to your own recreational pursuits, it may drastically and permanently alter the dynamics that have shaped your lifestyle and the relationship between you and your lady. Change is a positive force in life, but for a Cro-Magnon who has carved out a nice, comfortable existence as a childless person, it doesn't always come easily. The changes you're apt to confront as a new dad are part of a broader personal evolution, a journey of transformation in which you progress (in no particular order) from a me-first mindset as a single person, to a we-first attitude as part of a committed relationship, and now on to a wee-one-first state of mind as a parent on whom a little tykster is depending.

How, then, to divide household duties and need-fulfillment responsibilities between you and your woman? Even today the debate rages: are men innate hunters and women natural-born gatherers? Recent research suggests not. Indeed, based on their study of division of labor in hunter-gatherer societies throughout history, researchers theorize that women on occasion have become successful hunters while men have likewise shown strong skills as gatherers. Their conclusion: "The universal tendency to divide subsistence labor by gender is not solely the result of innate physical or psychological differences between the sexes; much of it has to be learned." (Source: "What's a Mother to Do? The Division of Labor among Neanderthals and Modern Humans in Eurasia," Kuhn, Steven L. and Mary C. Stiner, *Current Anthropology* 47:6.)

These are words to live by for folks like you who must subsist (and coexist) in a contemporary household that's been blessed with a new baby. Learning to divide responsibilities—but not necessarily along traditional gender lines—is key to survival during labor's fourth stage. While the numerous spears and trophies mounted on the walls of your study suggest your prowess as a hunter, at certain times you also will be called upon to demonstrate skills as a gatherer in settings that may be unfamiliar, such as the grocery store produce aisle or the infant and toddler section of a clothing retailer.

A baby is sure to place new demands on your time and energy. There will be times you feel stretched too thin and times you feel obligated to attack the to-do list when all you really want to do is rest. In such a state, the process of determining who does what often boils down to basic egalitarian principles. Sometimes skillset and experience will dictate who takes on a specific task. Let the person with needle and thread skills sew the baby's clothes. Other times it will come down to which partner has the time to perform a given task. Have a few minutes to spare after changing a light bulb in the laundry room? Might as well fold the clothes in the dryer while you're there. In some instances it is a matter of attrition, where a responsibility falls to whomever is least exhausted or merely to whomever happens to be awake when duty calls.

And call it will, persistently and sometimes loudly. There will be times where one parent will feel like he or she is pulling a heavier load of responsibility than the other. The division of labor between you and your woman may in some instances become a divisive force in your household. All you can do is the best you can. As partners in this baby venture of yours, each of you will at times need to take one for the team, to do more than your fair share. Such is life with a baby. Papas who are prepared to contribute in the areas listed below may even discover sides to themselves they never knew existed, including a knack for needlework.

**Childcare.** Caring for a baby can be an all-consuming undertaking. Parents need breaks—time all their own, where what they do isn't dictated by the needs of the little one, however irresistible that baby might be. For your health and sanity as individuals and as a couple, it's worth making the effort to free blocks of time for one another, whether it's to take a nap, read, shop, play golf, fish or sip a latte at the coffee shop. Just an hour or two away can be enough to recharge the batteries. Keep in mind, though, that it's also fun and worthwhile to spend time together as a family unit.

**Nighttime wakings and feedings.** The adult human body is not built to withstand night after night of multiple wee-hour wakings. Unfortunately that may be exactly what parents are subjected to given a newborn's tendency to sleep in short bursts and wake howling for food. There tends to be little synchronization between the body clocks of a newborn and his or her parents. The goal is to get baby to sleep longer periods between feedings, until he or she can actually sleep through the night. But until you reach that point, try developing a schedule in which you and your woman alternate nights or alternate feedings. If baby is hungry, you have a bottle of breast milk (from a supply stored in the refrigerator or freezer) or formula to deliver to the hungry suckling while your woman snoozes peacefully. What you're striving for with such an arrangement is at least one decent night's sleep every other day, or at least a decent block of uninterrupted sleep most nights.

**Meal preparation and clean-up.** There might have been a time in life where cooking meant punching buttons on the microwave, scrounging scraps from the dark recesses of the fridge or adding hot water to a container filled with a mysterious freeze-dried material to get it to reconstitute into something edible. Post-meal clean-up was merely a matter of wiping one's chin and disposing of the empty food container. This approach may have sufficed during the me-first phase of life, when instant appetite gratification often took precedence over taste and nutritional concerns. But with a recently pregnant partner, a new baby, and your own nutritional needs to think about, eating healthily is a high priority. So while mac and cheese and frozen pizzas still can prove useful in a pinch, meal-making takes on a new nutritional emphasis, particularly in addressing the dietary needs of a breastfeeding woman and a baby who has just begun eating solid foods, typically later in the first year. Meal preparation now may require more thought and more effort. Here is where even a culinarily challenged caveman can pitch in by sharing—or even taking over the lion's share of—duties in the kitchen, including both cooking and clean-up. Those efforts will be rewarded with fresher, better tasting, and healthier meals for all concerned. Daunted by the prospect of preparing meals for an entire household? Turn to Chapter 3 for a crash-course to turn the culinary Cro-Magnon into a meal-making maestro.

**Shopping (groceries, etc.).** As part of a modern-day hunter-gatherer household, you may feel more comfortable conferring with the local butcher about a certain cut of meat than you do navigating the towering aisles of big-box bulk retailers or locating a feminine hygiene product in a grocery store. But when your woman has her hands full with other things, you likely will be called upon to demonstrate your range and versatility by serving as a gatherer of household supplies. A good way to get your feet wet in this realm is with highly targeted outings to the grocery store or local farmer's market where you shop for ingredients for a meal you plan to make.

**Laundry doody.** Blow-out, a term you are accustomed to using to describe an especially energetic social gathering, takes on an entirely new and markedly antisocial meaning when applied to the bodily functions of a baby, in which case it describes a bowel movement (or series of movements) so voluminous or explosive that it cannot be contained by a diaper, and so soils the caveling's clothing. The presence of a new fudge factory in the home, one who is prone to such incidents, increases not only the volume but the filth factor associated with household laundry responsibilities. This is especially true for families that opt to use launderable (re-usable) cloth diapers (such as for economic, environmental or dermatological reasons). Regardless of the type of diapers your baby wears, doing the laundry is bound to become a more time-consuming task that demands more attention to detail than the common caveman is used to applying to such an activity. Not only does their minuteness make them difficult for the digitally challenged to separate and fold, they often carry stains that require extra steps unfamiliar to an unseasoned launderer, such as soaking and application of additional cleaning solutions. But don't let that deter you from doing your share of washing and drying. Read and follow directions on the package, and seek advice if necessary, lest you cause your woman consternation by turning once-colorful clothing a dull grayish-beige.

**Upkeep of the home.** "Hire a cleaning person" is one of the most common pieces of advice conveyed by parenting veterans

## Helping Hands, Productive Palms

Finesse and fine motor skills are elusive traits for one so accustomed to handling blunt-force implements. But babies are delicate creatures. Caring for them requires dexterity, digital aptitude, and a soft touch. Here are some of the tasks that require new dads to refine their brutish ways, file down their calluses, and put their opposable thumbs to productive use:

**Diapering**—Proper positioning, hold-and-fold skills are indispensable.

**Insertion of rectal thermometer**—The goal: single-plunge entry (no mulligans), to a depth that yields an accurate reading without tickling the upper digestive tract.

**Support for bobbleheaded baby**—Huge palms provide an ideal cradling spot to support the head during baby's noodle-neck phase.

**Clipping nails**—Trimming nails but not skin is a tall task with a newborn; yelps, blood indicate your technique needs work.

**Trimming hair**—Safety takes precedence over style. The amateur barber must handle scissors with precision and care, mindful that baby's head movements might be unpredictable; practice on doll advisable but no guarantee of future success.

**Ear cleaning**—Use cotton swabs to clean wax after it's out of the canal, but avoid inserting a swab into the ear canal due to a real risk of hurting the ear.

*(continued on next page)*

*(continued from previous page)*

**Bathing**—Resist temptation to overzealously scrub baby's scalp and skin; be sure to support baby such that full head remains well *above* water level.

**Multitasking while holding baby in one arm**—Sure-handed grip and adequate neck support are musts with a one-armed baby hold; exercise extra care when the task brings proximity to high heat, open flame, sharp kitchen implements, power tools, etc.

**Dressing**—If buttons, zippers, clasps, and snaps on adult-sized clothing present a challenge (lifelong struggles with the brassiere are common among troglodytes), grappling with baby clothing can drive a guy to distraction. It's why we cavemen love Velcro.

**Soothing pats, strokes, caresses and massage**—Some of your most therapeutic moments may have come from being manhandled by your "tough love" massage therapist. But softer is better when trying to soothe a baby.

to childrearing rookies. Keeping the home tidy and clean while also maintaining the yard requires effort that many new parents (even those who consider themselves neat freaks) find tough to muster, given all their other baby-related responsibilities. If there's money in the budget to accommodate paying a cleaning person and/or lawncare professional, go for it. If not, the job is at least partially yours. To make it fun and rewarding, turn it into a cardiovascular workout by introducing a speed component to such activities as vacuuming, lawn-mowing, and mopping. To really get those competitive juices flowing, inaugurate your own Household Olympics. How many pounds of weeds can you pull in 30 minutes? Can you beat your woman's personal best time for vacuuming the entire home? Who between the two of you can scrub the bathroom longest without gagging from cleaning solution fumes? There's no limit to the things you can do to make the mundane more exciting.

**Miscellaneous.** More responsibilities to consider in your ongoing division of labor discussions: paying bills, taking baby to the doctor, performing necessary acts of hygiene and grooming on the little one, arranging for babysitting, and coordinating social activities, to name just a few.

## YOU, MR. RECORDING SECRETARY

Not long after the birth of Peanut, Gronk's abstract expressionist urges led him to scrawl geometric representations of his caveling's conception, birth, and early life on the walls of his basement. Was this merely a moronic act of defacing one's own property? Hardly. In fact, with such a gesture Gronk was fulfilling a primal need for self-expression that links modern man to our earliest human ancestors.

It was our ancient forefathers who 75,000 years ago in a cave called Blombos high upon a limestone cliff near the southern tip of the African continent left behind beads made from nassarius shells and ochres engraved with abstract designs. Some believe these artifacts represent the earliest evidence of mankind attempting to express itself through art. Fast forward another 50,000 years to Europe in the Upper Paleolithic period, where *Homo sapiens*, having migrated out of Africa, were showing themselves to be not only accomplished artists but also budding historians, with the ability to record time by marking the bones of slain animals to indicate the passage of days, lunar months, and seasons.

Working in a part of the world that would later produce artists of the beret-wearing, one-eared variety, the European Cro-Magnons were creatively prolific, working in a range of media, from sculpture to painting to etching. Using materials such as hematite and manganese oxide for paint, crudely fashioned sticks for brushes and the mineral formations surrounding them for a canvas, troglodyte *artistes* (circa 15,000–10,000 years ago) left their descendants a huge array of cave paintings in places such as Lascaux in France and Altamira in Spain. Some posit that their work represents attempts to capture and relate noteworthy events—hunting escapades, intertribal clashes, sexual conquests, and the like. Others contend it was painted mostly for ceremonial or religious purposes. Still others theorize that it was merely an outlet for *Homo sapiens* to express their burgeoning creativity, increasing intellect, and more refined communications skills.

All of which demonstrates that we really aren't too far removed from our Cro-Magnon brethren in harboring an innate drive to express ourselves, to record history, and to capture and convey experiences, events, ideas, and emotions so that others might share them. Indeed, those instincts tend to bubble over with the arrival of

a baby. Thankfully, here in the 21st century we have access to a huge variety of powerful technological tools for capturing and storing the sights and sounds associated with the many amazing moments your family stands to experience during your baby's first year. The pace of life tends to accelerate once a baby comes along. Special moments can arise unexpectedly and pass fleetingly, so it helps to have some sort of image-capture device at hand to record them for posterity. That way you'll have memories stored for on-demand access to supplement your own mental images, which at times may get a bit fuzzy. Among the tools and media you may want to consider investing in:

- a digital camera, for quick still photographs you can store, print, e-mail, and archive (some cameras are also capable of taking short movies);

- a digital video camera, to add movement and sound to the equation, and to gain the ability to view and edit home movies on your computer or TV (many digital movie cameras also take stills);

- a 35mm film camera, for old-school types, plus film and a reliable film developer;

- a photo printer, photo paper, and photo albums to produce your own shots and organize them in books;

- a journal, scrapbook, and/or blank book to write down thoughts and store important keepsakes such as *in utero* images of the caveling from the amniocentesis procedure during pregnancy, the wristbands you, your woman, and your little one wore in the hospital, a lock of hair from baby's first haircut, etc.

Wise indeed is the new papa who arms himself with these types of tools, for they will prepare him for that special occasion in the not-too-distant future when he and his little one sit down together to view the photo albums, scrapbooks, and home movies he has been compiling—a sort of recap of baby's first year. Here's a great chance to get sentimental and provide the caveling with a multimedia narrative of how those first 12 months unfolded.

Until that moment presents itself, however, there is much more wisdom for you to accumulate. So let the indoctrination into needs fulfillment continue with a foray into the culinary and dietary responsibilities you face in feeding a fledgling omnivore. *Mangia bene!*

# DR. BRIAN

## What If...?: Straight Talk on Congenital Health Issues

The proof came the last time you attended a family reunion. Staring at you from the other side of the volleyball net were males blessed with features so strikingly similar to yours that it was clear you all shared a common genetic lineage: bushy sloping forehead, hyperactive sweat glands, and a posterior pelt so thick it carries an SPF rating of 100. Given the apparent dominance of the genes that produce these characteristics, it will be next to impossible for any of your offspring to escape inheriting some of those features themselves. But unless a doctor tells you otherwise, these are not considered issues that threaten the health of a newborn.

Matters related to the origins of the family unibrow aside, however, it's common and legitimate for new parents to have questions and concerns about the health of their child at birth. Most parents have at one time or other harbored dark thoughts about their child being born with a congenital health issue.

First some good news to put those paranoid thoughts to rest: an estimated 97 of every 100 babies in the U.S. are born healthy, according to figures from the Centers for Disease Control and Prevention.

Chances are your baby will be as close to perfect as you imagined. The overall 3 percent birth defect rate in the U.S. (worldwide the rate is closer to 6 percent) is known as the background rate or population risk for birth defects. For certain narrower population segments, such as among parents with no family history of birth defects, the rate may be much lower. By the same token, the incidence may be higher among people with a family history of birth defects. Whatever the case, even a small chance is significant enough to warrant at least some discussion between you and your woman about the possibilities and realities associated with newborn health. The reality is that parents have *some* control over whether a child is born with congenital anomalies or congenital abnormalities, also known as birth defects. Alcohol consumed in excess by a pregnant woman is among many of the environmental **teratogens** (agents a pregnant woman may have been exposed to that harm the gestating fetus) that can pass through an expectant mother's system to directly and negatively impact a fetus. Fortunately birth defects caused by environmental factors are extremely rare. So while the "what ifs" certainly are worth thinking and talking about, they're probably not worth dwelling upon, unless medical indications (such as results from an amniocentesis performed during pregnancy) justify doing so.

Birth defects manifest in all cultures, races, and nationalities. They can run the gamut from being so minor they are virtually undetectable to being severe enough to require immediate (and perhaps ongoing) medical attention. What we often don't know is *why* they occur. Indeed, even with huge advances in modern medicine, 70 percent of birth defects still have no known cause. Of the 30 percent that do, most are attributable to environmental teratogens, and, more commonly, genetic factors (inheritance, chromosomal).

More good news to help you sleep better at night: Highly developed countries such as ours are better equipped than ever to treat children with birth defects, thanks to improved diagnosis, care, and prevention. For example, according to the March of Dimes, the U.S. reported a 46 percent drop in infant mortality rates from birth defects from 1980 to 2001. So even if your deepest, darkest fears are realized, my comrades in the medical profession stand ready to provide the best possible treatment.

In addition, there are numerous groups to which parents may turn for information, guidance, and support, including:

- Your local hospital, doctor, church or social organization

- American Academy of Pediatrics, www.aap.org/healthtopics/genetics.cfm

- The March of Dimes, www.marchofdimes.com

- The National Information Center for Children and Youth With Disabilities, www.kidsource.com/NICHCY/

- Parents of Disabled/Ill Children, www.birthdefects.org

- Peace Health, www.peacehealth.org

- Support groups that address a specific birth defect

# CHAPTER 3

# FOOD, DIET & NUTRITION

FROM BREASTFEEDING TO HOMEMADE BABY FOOD, HOW TO FORAGE FOR AND PREPARE NUTRITIOUS FEASTS FOR YOUR FLEDGLING OMNIVORE

T HE CHASE IS ON. BAREFOOTED, CRUSTED IN MUD, SPEAR in hand, Gronk is pursuing a bird across the tundra. It's the same dream every time he eats poultry. The bird he is stalking might be a turkey, chicken, pheasant, duck, or goose—whatever fowl he ate the previous evening invariably reappears as his quarry in the dream. This is no normal bird, though. It is fast, shifty, and imposingly large, easily taller than Big Bird. Panting and salivating, the agile feathered beast eludes the caveman in almost playful fashion, like Muhammad Ali doing the rope-a-dope.

Inevitably the chase leads Gronk and the giant fowl out of the wilderness, toward civilization. The pursuer and his quarry reach a busy street, Gronk several paces behind but losing ground. He reaches into his hip pouch for a stone to hurl at the beast in the hopes of felling or at least slowing it. But before Gronk can cock his arm, the behemoth bird bolts across the street and through a parking lot filled with huge, idling tour buses and pick-up trucks equipped with game hoists and gun racks. It's heading toward the entrance of a restaurant that Gronk recognizes as one of his favorite eating establishments: the Bottomless Trough Buffeteria.

Huffing and puffing like Sylvester chasing a giant Tweety Bird, he tails the fowl into the buffeteria. The bird careens off diners, who, without interrupting their chewing, listlessly lift their heads out of their troughs to see what's causing the ruckus. Gronk launches himself at his quarry. The avian dodges him and collides with a line of diners, who are stationed one beside another in four-point stance above their meals. One by one the heifer-like trough-feeders topple like dominoes. The bird makes a quick move toward the exit but slips on a slick of thick, brown gravy that is spreading across the floor, sending it hurtling toward the imposing buffet spread. Beast meets buffet station with a tremendous crash. The barge-like structure begins to teeter, then tips on its side, its contents spilling and congealing into a steaming blob of gruel.

## Grow with Gronk

What the caveman stands to gain from reading Chapter 3:

- The motivation to eat and live healthier

- The courage to seize control of his family's dining destiny

- A clear understanding of a baby's nutritional needs

- A deep appreciation for the benefits of breastfeeding

- A grasp of how a woman's breasts make milk

- The manliness to become a breastfeeding "lactivist"

- Keen insight about formula as an alternative to breast milk

- An explanation for why he can't make milk

- A clue about when his caveling will grow teeth

- A proven strategy for introducing a baby to solid foods

- The ability to hunt and gather healthy foodstuffs for his family

- The skill to craft home-cooked meals fit for babies and big folks alike

Suddenly Gronk's attention is diverted from the bird by the sound of a whimpering child. Worriedly he scans the room for the source of the distressed sounds. As he searches, the bird stealthily rises and eyes the caveman ominously. Now just several feet behind an unwitting Gronk, it spreads its massive wings and readies its talons to pounce. Here at the Bottomless Trough, hunted has become hunter.

The baby wails. Gronk's eyes snap open. Drenched with perspiration, it takes him a moment to realize it was only a dream and the wail he heard came from Peanut's room.

Maybe it was the tryptophan in the bird (enhanced, perhaps, by the effects of a stiff drink before bed) that makes this dream sequence especially vivid and its aftereffects particularly long-lasting. What lingers is a feeling that his subconscious mind is trying to slip him a message via the disturbing impressions of the Bottomless Trough and its patrons—their listlessness and flabbiness, plus the unnatural odors, gelatinous contours, and gluttonous volume of food on the buffet.

He recalls the figure of the lean, strong hunter chasing the huge fowl—a vision, perhaps, of his own trim figure 10 years prior, before he discovered places like the Trough. He remembers noticing that some of the diners in his dream bore a striking resemblance to members of his own family and friends. Maybe, he thinks, this recurring dream is sending him a message that with the arrival of his new baby, Peanut, it's time to confront the buffet beast head-on by re-examining his diet and health. And while he's at it, why not spearhead a household-wide effort to eat more nutritiously? For now that he's a dad, one of his responsibilities is to help the caveling grow strong and smart with a healthy, appropriate diet. The last thing the little one needs for a nutritional role model is a guy who lives huddled in a culinary cave, ignorant to the many benefits he can bring to his family by infusing their diets with fresh, nutrition-packed meals that actually taste good.

Today, Gronk decides, he's going to do some research and make some lifestyle changes. It's out with all-you-care-to-eat, in with a healthy, balanced, and sensibly portioned diet. Maybe he'll surprise his woman by dragging some fresh meat and produce back to the stone domicile and turning them into a fabulous dinner. Peanut may be exclusively breastfeeding for now, but eventually her teeth and digestive system will be equipped to handle solid foods. And when they are, Gronk will be ready.

What should you and your woman know about breastfeeding? Beyond breast milk and formula, how prepared are you to meet your caveling's dietary needs? When the baby starts transitioning from breast milk to solids, or when your woman politely asks you to cook dinner, will you be ready to deliver something other than take-out, just-add-water or microwave vittles? All you need to know to evolve from a gastronomic git into a skilled *Homo sapiens* chef is right here in this chapter.

## HERE'S TO GOOD HEALTH— AND HARA HACHI BU

As his household's protector, one of the caveman's most pressing duties is ridding his surroundings of potential baby hazards, from the sharp objects in his spear collection to toxic substances in the home (for more on those responsibilities, see Chapter 4, addressing the need for shelter, safety, and protection).

Don't forget to take stock of your cabinets, fridge, and pantry, for there may reside a major threat to your little one's health—substances we loosely call "food" that when consumed (once the baby is systemically strong enough and dentally equipped to do so) may lead the caveling down a dark path toward obesity, diabetes, and heart disease. We Americans are fatter than ever, largely because of our growing affection for calorie-dense but nutrient-deficient foods, such as those commonly found at establishments like the Bottomless Trough Buffeteria. Horrifying but true: the average American purchased fast food 16 days of each month between January and September of 2007, according to the consumer tracking group Sandelman & Associates.

That kind of food usually is inexpensive, easy to find, addicting in nature, served in huge portions, and marketed heavily by big business. Exacerbating the food problem is the tendency for city planning agencies to cater to our addiction to the automobile at the expense of walkers, cyclists, and mass transit riders. All of which stacks the odds against the caveman and his clan being able to live an active, healthy lifestyle.

That doesn't mean you are powerless against these forces. In fact, as a new dad it is well within your power—and incumbent upon you—to act as a positive role model by helping the members of your family dodge the dangers associated with obesity and a sedentary lifestyle. It wouldn't hurt if we all took a step back and adopted some of the eating and exercise practices of our prehistoric forebears. While human genetic make-up has changed little over the past four million years, our diet has evolved dramatically. The Paleolithic diet consisted largely of fruits, nuts, and vegetables, supplemented with meat and fish. Whatever meat people ate was usually lean because the animals spent much of their time trying to elude the knuckle-draggers who stalked them.

At the other end of the spear, all the exercise involved in stalking kept hunter-gatherers lean, too. In pre-agricultural societies, humans necessarily exercised to obtain their nutrition, following game herds and fashioning tools and weapons to kill and butcher whatever they managed to catch. Before milling began some 10,000 years ago, the carbohydrates people ate were mostly complex in make-up, containing important dietary fiber. Fossil evidence shows that our ancient ancestors were indeed lean specimens, with strong bones, and in the case of Neanderthals, especially muscular bodies reminiscent of those a passer-by might glimpse during a stroll along Venice Beach.

In setting a dietary tone for the postpartum household, we could also take a cue from some of our 21st-century contemporaries. The South Pacific island of Okinawa, part of Japan, may safely be called the healthiest place on earth. It is home to the world's highest per-capita population of centenarians (six times as many centenarians per 100,000 people as in the U.S.). Okinawans live 97 percent of their lives in a disability-free state, compared to 91 percent among Americans. Rates of heart disease and breast cancer there are less than a quarter of what they are in the U.S. All this despite not being an especially affluent area.

Have the Okinawans stumbled on the fountain of health? In a way, they have. They eat a low-fat diet that's rich in vegetables. According to Dr. Bradley Willcox, author of *The Okinawa Program*, their diets are "low in calories and high in nutrient density…with high antioxidant loads." Furthermore, Okinawans somehow have learned not to overstuff themselves at mealtimes, instead choosing to stop eating when they are about 80 percent full. They call this secret to eating "hara hachi bu," which translates to "eat until you are eight parts full." As Dr. Willcox explains, the Okinawans "ended up being healthy all their lives...Coupled with physical activity, farming, and fishing, you have the right recipe for longevity."

The good news is that the Okinawans don't have a patent on that recipe, which includes lots of servings of whole grains instead of the refined grains we Americans tend to consume in mass quantities in things like white bread, cookies, cakes, and white rice. Whole-grain foods like brown rice and whole-wheat bread contain unrefined carbohydrates that provide nutrients essential to the health of the human brain, central nervous system, and muscles, while also helping ward off heart disease, diabetes, and cancer.

To be a dad who is healthy enough to play vigorously with his children and grandchildren throughout a long life, we advocate taking a page out of the Okinawan and Paleolithic playbooks. Eat a varied diet, with lots of fruits and veggies, low-fat and whole-grain foods, but cut way back on things made from refined sugars and carbs. Add regular (or at least somewhat frequent) exercise to the mix. And try to stick to the principle of hara hachi bu.

Those dietary guidelines are especially relevant to breastfeeding moms, given the milk pass-through factor (explained later in this chapter). And they become directly relevant to a baby when he or she makes the transition from breastfeeding to solid foods, whenever that occurs. It will take time for your little one to learn to hunt and gather healthy stuff for his or her own meals, so it's your job as parents to know exactly what the baby needs to grow and develop during the first year, then to feed the offspring accordingly.

A baby's overall requirement for calories is determined by his or her size, rate of growth, activity, and energy level. Generally speaking, though, a caveling's caloric needs per pound of body weight are higher during the first year of life than at any other time.

For the first **four to six months of life**, breast or formula feeding can provide sufficient calories all by itself. Those calories come from protein, fat, and carbohydrates. **Protein** is a basic part of every cell. A baby's body relies heavily on it to grow in the first two months of life. As doughy as an infant may look, don't skimp on **fat**, a key source of essential fatty acids. It is important that fat constitute about 40–50 percent of caloric intake during infancy. **Carbs**, primarily lactose, are a baby's principle source of dietary energy. As for **liquids**, there is adequate water in breast milk or formula to meet a baby's requirements, at least through the first six months. No need to supplement water until solid foods have been introduced. By regularly consuming adequate amounts of breast milk from a well-nourished mom or iron-fortified formula, a baby should get plenty of the **vitamins** and **minerals** he or she needs.

## THE BREAST OF TIMES: A MAN'S GUIDE TO MILK SOURCES

In the modern world we're faced with choices every day. Paper or plastic? Premium or regular octane? Over or under? Lasik or specs? Over-easy or scrambled? Boxers or Comanche-style? Dylan or Neil? Apple or PC? Foreign or domestic? Guy or girl on top? XM or Sirius?

Most of these decisions aren't make or break, nor are they black and white, right or wrong. But the decision you and your woman face about what to feed your newborn is not one to take lightly, for it can impact your little one for a lifetime. Breast milk, formula or a combination of the two? A caveman might naturally be inclined to favor breast milk, mainly because he likes its packaging. The goal of this section is to engorge your mind with all the info a cavecouple needs to make a well-informed decision on a very important issue.

Might as well be up-front with everyone: we are breast men as much as we are cavemen. That is, we support breasts in general and, more specifically, their right to supply milk to babies. We also wholeheartedly support the women who are attached to these breasts, particularly when it comes to the practice of breastfeeding. We appreciate the physical (and psychological) benefits feeding from the breast offers to babies, their moms, families, and society at large. We sing the praises of the breast and breastfeeding! If we could do it, we would.

But we recognize the demands breastfeeding places on a woman, and we realize that it isn't something all women do for long periods of time. For some, medical/physical issues might prevent it. Others choose to discontinue it within weeks or months of baby being born, for a huge variety of reasons, most of them very personal.

From the spectator's perspective, it's easy for a guy to urge a woman to "Go ahead and breastfeed." But it is also hard to ignore the substantial upsides associated with it from a health and development perspective. The case for breastfeeding is so over-whelmingly strong, we can't help but recommend that new moms at least try it and, better yet, do it for as long as they see fit. Ultimately, the breastfeeding strategy comes down to the woman who owns the breasts, with substantial feedback from the breastfeeding caveling and some from the caveman, too.

Our ancestral mothers never had to choose between providing their young with breast milk and today's chief alternative to it, formula. From the earliest humans right up through the middle of the 20th century, breast milk, even when provided by a wet nurse (a stand-in breastfeeder), was the exclusive food source for infants. Wet nurses in fact have played a crucial role throughout history. Since breastfeeding may work as a contraceptive method for women, a queen who wanted to keep squeezing out potential heirs in rapid-fire fashion would enlist wet nurses to breastfeed her young so she could start trying to conceive again ASAP.

If there is a perfect food for a baby, it is breast milk. The World Health Organization recommends that a child breastfeed for at least two years, a duration it says is justified because so many children around the world contract diarrhea illnesses from contaminated water used in making formula. Two years of breastfeeding might seem like a long time to some of us. Even as we tout the virtues of breastfeeding, we acknowledge that the thought of a child looking his mother in the eye and verbally ordering his own breast milk makes some folks uneasy.

If two years seems a stretch, the breastfeeding policies of groups like the American Academy of Pediatrics and the American Academy of Family Physicians might seem more practical. Each group advocates that babies (with a few rare exceptions) be *exclusively* breastfed for at least six months. Exclusive breastfeeding (defined as an infant's consumption of human milk, with no supplementation of any type, including water) has been shown to provide improved protection against a whole host of diseases. The many other perks associated with breastfeeding are provided in the text on the next page.

Right out of the chute, babies may start reaping the benefits of the breast. The first milk a new mom produces is called **colostrum** and it is ideally suited to the needs of a newborn, with a high concentration of antibodies, especially IgA, which helps protect the lungs, throat, and intestines. Colostrum also helps "seal" permeable newborn intestines to prevent harmful substances from penetrating them. In addition, it contains a high concentration of **lactoferrin,** an iron-binding protein (not found in infant formula) that, among other things, works to limit the availability of iron to bacteria in the intestines, thus affecting which healthy bacteria will thrive in a baby's gut.

Besides being lower in fat and higher in proteins and carbo-hydrates than milk a breastfeeding woman will produce later, colostrum is easy for a baby to digest. It has a laxative effect, help-ing an infant pass his or her first bowel movements and helping prevent newborn jaundice by keeping the little one's system mov-ing along. Moms typically will make colostrum, or transitional milk, for two weeks or less. By continuing to breastfeed well beyond that point, women set themselves up to deliver all sorts of benefits to their little diners, themselves, and their families.

## BENEFITS OF BREASTFEEDING

### For Moms

- Can stimulate oxytocin production to help prevent postpartum bleeding and bring uterus back down to pre-pregnancy proportions.

- Positive psychological effects, perhaps reducing incidence of postpartum depression.

- Quicker return to pre-pregnancy body—breastfeeding saps a woman of 500 calories a day.

- Reduces risk of breast and ovarian cancer, osteoporosis, risks associated with heart disease.

- Stimulates bonding between mother and baby. Hormones released during breastfeeding strengthen a mother's nurturing feelings toward her child. One study demonstrated that breastfeeding mothers touch their infants more frequently, suggesting that the benefits of breastfeeding extend past feeding times. Other research has shown that mothers who breastfeed exhibit more physiological and social responsiveness toward their infants.

### For Babies

- Contains perfect amounts of fat, carbohydrates, and protein for a baby's development.

- May reduce the risk of Sudden Infant Death Syndrome (see page 186).

- Contains DHA and ARA, fatty acids important to development of the brain and retina.

- Contains vitamins, minerals, digestive enzymes, hormones, and antibodies from the mother that help the baby to resist infection.

- Breast milk is easily digestible, with special enzymes for optimal nutrient absorption.

- Reduces the risk of heart disease in adulthood, according to recent research, which found that adults who had been breastfed exhibited a lower-than-average body mass index and higher-than-average levels of the so-called "good" HDL cholesterol. Both of these factors protect against cardiovascular disease.

- Has been shown to increase IQ.

- Breastfeeding has been shown to lower baby's risk of developing many diseases, including allergies, asthma and wheezing, autoimmune thyroid disease, diabetes, eczema, gastrointestinal diseases such as Crohn's, Celiac disease, diarrhea illnesses, ear infection, Hodgkin's lymphoma, meningitis, multiple sclerosis, obesity, respiratory infection, rheumatoid arthritis, sleep apnea, and urinary tract infection.

- Suckling promotes proper development of teeth and speech organs.

- It's immediately available, at just the right temperature for a baby.

## To Family & Society

- Reduces demand for energy and other resources required to produce and transport man-made feeding products (formula, etc.).

- Saves cash by sparing parents the cost of formula. All told, breast milk costs about half as much as formula, figuring in investments in breast pumps, nursing bras, and other items needed for breastfeeding moms. It also reduces the health care tab. Kaiser Permanente, one of the country's largest HMOs, determined that infants who were breastfed for a minimum of six months had $1,435 less in health care claims than their formula-fed contemporaries. Stick the savings in a college fund.

- Results in fewer sick days for parents. Since breastfed babies are statistically healthier than their formula-fed peers, the parents of breastfed babies spend less time at home caring for a sick youth.

- Reduces the burden on landfills (it requires no retail packaging).

- Serves as a form of contraception (though not 100 percent reliable, as detailed on page 246), helping curb population growth and demand on finite global resources.

## BABY'S (AND MAN'S) BREAST FRIEND

Human females are blessed (some might say cursed) with the largest breast-to-body-size ratio of any mammal, a phenomenon that anthropologists, evolutionary biologists, zoologists, and fraternity brothers have been racking their brains about for years. The human female breast is a wondrous milk production and delivery system, disguised as a beautiful, tear-shaped body part that has made generations of males stand at attention. The breast of a lactating woman includes six basic parts:

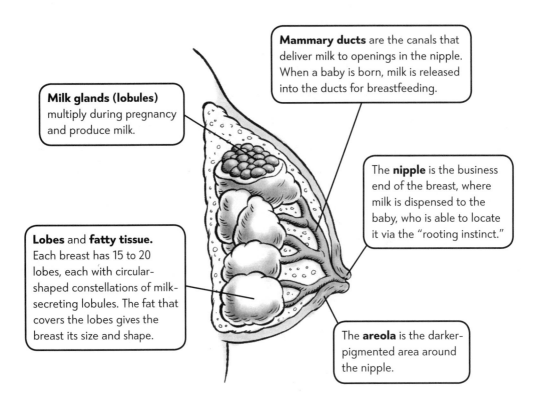

**Mammary ducts** are the canals that deliver milk to openings in the nipple. When a baby is born, milk is released into the ducts for breastfeeding.

**Milk glands (lobules)** multiply during pregnancy and produce milk.

The **nipple** is the business end of the breast, where milk is dispensed to the baby, who is able to locate it via the "rooting instinct."

**Lobes** and **fatty tissue.** Each breast has 15 to 20 lobes, each with circular-shaped constellations of milk-secreting lobules. The fat that covers the lobes gives the breast its size and shape.

The **areola** is the darker-pigmented area around the nipple.

## THE MAMMARIAN MAINLINE

Straight from mom to baby, with some filtering, is how many substances travel once ingested by a breastfeeding woman. No worries, generally speaking, if the woman is taking in healthy, non-toxic stuff. But if she's putting substances into her body that aren't good for a baby, bad news travels fast.

A woman's body makes breast milk from nutrients present in her bloodstream and bodily stores, including proteins, fats, vitamins, and minerals. There's a real difference between stuff that, when passed along via breast milk, poses genuine health risks to babies and stuff that merely makes a caveling uncomfortable, gassy, and noisy. The main dietary contributors to infant gas are:

1. Dairy protein in Mom's diet. Those that "slip" through breast milk can be difficult for some babies' systems to break down. If, especially during the first three months of breastfeeding, your baby seems especially gassy in relation to the amount of dairy Mom eats, she may want to go off dairy for a while to see if her consumption is causing the baby gassiness. If your baby is having severe gastrointestinal problems that may be impacting development, talk with a doctor.

2. Fast let-down. When Mom's milk "lets down," the baby can choke, gasp, and swallow air. Those air bubbles have to come out somehow and can cause distress as they work their way toward an exit.

3. Too much lactose from breast milk. The composition of breast milk changes as the baby nurses. It begins watery and high in carbohydrates (lactose), then gradually becomes higher in protein and finally fat. If a baby tends to only nurse for a short time each session, or tends to switch breasts frequently, he or she may be getting too much lactose and not enough protein or fat. This overload of sugar can cause gas in some babies. To remedy the problem, don your "lactivist" hat and suggest she nurse on only one side until that side is "empty" to give the suckling a balance of lactose, protein, and fat.

The gas will pass, but the health issues a baby can experience from other substances passed along in the breast milk of a nursing mother may not resolve themselves so easily. Here are a few your woman should avoid:

## Food for Thought

The La Leche League's philosophy on breastfeeding, baby nutrition, and health. Cavemen, take note of #8 in particular:

1. Mothering through breastfeeding is the most natural and effective way of understanding and satisfying the needs of the baby.

2. Mother and baby need to be together early and often to establish a satisfying relationship and an adequate milk supply.

3. In the early years, the baby has an intense need to be with his mother, which is as basic as his need for food.

4. Breast milk is the superior infant food.

5. For the healthy, full-term baby, breast milk is the only food necessary until the baby shows signs of needing solids, about the middle of the first year after birth.

6. Ideally, the breastfeeding relationship will continue until the baby outgrows the need.

7. Alert and active participation by the mother in childbirth is a help in getting breastfeeding off to a good start.

8. *Breastfeeding is enhanced and the nursing couple sustained by the loving support, help, and companionship of the baby's father. A father's unique relationship with his baby is an important element in the child's development from early infancy.*

*(continued on next page)*

(continued from previous page)

9. Good nutrition means eating a well-balanced and varied diet of foods in as close to their natural state as possible.

10. From infancy on, children need loving guidance which reflects acceptance of their capabilities and sensitivity to their feelings.

For more info, visit the La Leche League website at http://www.llli.org.

**Nicotine:** Nicotine that accumulates in the bloodstream may also enter breast milk. The risks it poses to the baby depend on the amount of nicotine in mother's blood. Heavy-smoking moms who breastfeed may see reduced milk production and gastrointestinal problems in the baby. However, smoking cigarettes does not mean a woman shouldn't breastfeed. It is probably healthier for a baby to breastfeed from a mother who smokes than to be formula-fed.

**Medications:** Medications may pass from the bloodstream into breast milk. Most medications are safe with breastfeeding, but to be on the safe side, we recommend that a lactating woman ask her doctor about medications before she takes them.

**Medicinal herbs:** Without the benefit of a huge body of research on the subject, there's a likelihood that a small percentage of medicinal herbs ingested by a mom enter her breast milk. Again, a breastfeeding woman should ask her doctor before taking medicinal herbs.

**Vitamins and minerals:** Vitamins and minerals can be found in natural food sources and supplements. Both the baby and Mom need them to thrive. While it is a good idea for Mom to continue taking a prenatal vitamin while breastfeeding, she should consult a doctor before adding other individual vitamins or minerals to the mix.

**Caffeine:** In most cases, there's no harm in Mom consuming moderate amounts of caffeinated beverage, since so little of it is transmitted to the baby. Drinking pots of trucker-grade joe at one time is another matter altogether for mother and child alike, since caffeine can accumulate in babies before they hit 3–4 months of age. After that, their bodies can begin to process it better.

## SECRETS OF THE BREAST WHISPERER

After spending seemingly all day, every day, with a suckling attached to her bosom, a breastfeeding mom is apt to be bursting with insight and information she'd like to share with her caveman about what's going on with her breasts. Thankfully she has a willing pupil in the new dad, who himself is bursting with curiosity about the process, the product, and the transformation of his woman's breasts from playthings to food producers.

To shed light on matters of the breast, with which new fathers must become familiar, we enlist the help of vastly experienced lactation consultant Pat Shelly, IBCLC, RN, MA, director of the Breast-feeding Center for Greater Washington. She's called the Breast Whisperer for good reason.

**KNOW THE BENEFITS OF BREASTFEEDING.** They're numerous, and they're spelled out in the chart earlier in this chapter. The more enlightened a caveman is about breastfeeding, the better equipped he'll be to support his woman in the effort.

**TAKE BREASTFEEDING SERIOUSLY.** Pre-baby, a woman's success in meeting life goals may have been measured according to similar factors as men: professional achievement, community service, fulfillment in relationships, etc. By contrast, as a new, primal, and thoroughly female experience, breastfeeding brings a new paradigm. Her reaction to it may vary from thrilled to shocked. Much may ride on the success she has with breastfeeding. It is her first project as a mother, one that can be all-consuming. Success can breed self-confidence; struggles can lead to supreme frustration.

**KNOW WHEN TO CALL UPON A SPECIALIST FOR HELP.** If frustration about breastfeeding difficulties sets in and the two of you—your woman in particular—feel strongly about sticking to the mother's milk feeding program, it might be time to call a lactation consultant. The lactation consultant is an unheralded but potentially major player on the postpartum healthcare team. Look for a consultant who's been certified by the International Board of Certified Lactation Consultants and/or has an "RLC" after their name, which denotes board certification. If the two of you decide to use a consultant, offer support by attending the appointments, paying attention, and taking notes.

**SHE'S "HORMONAL."** You better believe it! Lactating women have high levels of prolactin, the principle hormone stimulating milk production, or lactogenesis. One potential effect of having high prolactin levels in her body is a difficulty concentrating. If she tends to trail off mid-sentence more than usual, you can blame…uh… Anyway, there's also a hormone called oxytocin that not only triggers milk let-down, it's important in stimulating bonding and maternal behavior in a female. This may manifest as intense, protective behavior. Oxytocin is also a catalyst to uterine contractions during childbirth, so some women may have "after pains" (pelvic pain) from breastfeeding. So it stands to reason that breastfeeding shortly after giving birth might make the uterus contract more quickly, decreasing maternal bleeding.

**BECOME A LACTIVIST.** Guys can offer a helping hand in breastfeeding, not to hold the actual breast or the baby's head during feeding sessions but rather to use their palms for back rubs (the Breast Whisperer says they help milk flow/production). But more important than that, his support can help a struggling breastfeeder through her frustrations. Your lactivism can really make a difference. Even with the evidence weighing so heavily in favor of breastfeeding, more than 70 percent of babies are formula-fed by the time they reach three months of age. If you both favor the breast, there are ways the lactivist (you) can sway things in that direction:

- Relieve your woman of some daily chores so she can pump in peace.

- Help her to feel comfortable breastfeeding anywhere. (*Ignore the morons who would have her feed the baby in the bathroom. They wouldn't settle for eating their steak in the john!*)

- Take a breastfeeding class with your woman.

- You can't make milk (as Dr. Brian explains on page 61) but you can wash bottles and help in the handling and storage of pumped milk.

- Handle bottle-feeding the baby with breast milk, as needed.

- Handle burping the baby and related clean-up.

- Change the baby's diaper before and after feedings.

- Take the breast pump for a test drive yourself to see how it handles.

- Encourage her, support her, and enjoy the view.

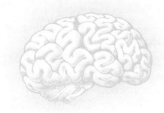

## Inside Mommy's Mind: Installment 2

New Caveman Ad Hoc Female Advisory Council members Gina and Stasia offer us guys indispensable advice for helping lactating ladies:

> The most incredible thing you can possibly do for us at night is get out of bed when the babe cries, bring the baby to us in bed **and** (this is the crucial step) bring the baby *back* to the bassinet or cradle when we're done nursing. Do this at least once a night until we're done with middle-of-the-night feedings. Remember that we're bearing the responsibility the other two to six times each and every night, not to mention the 12 times each day. You can do the full round-trip once. If the baby is taking a bottle, you know the drill; it involves not waking us up. **Just this once.**

> Serve us ice water often and every time we're nursing. We're always thirsty. We're told that if we don't drink, like, 10,000 ounces of water a day, our milk production slows. We get really bummed out when our milk production slows. It's maternal, elemental.

> Hand us the TV remote, especially when we're tethered to the Boppy pillow or otherwise have no free hands or ambulatory capabilities, which is often.

## A BREASTFEEDING PRIMER FOR LACTIVISTS

Like a baby who prefers getting milk right from Mom's bosom, anyone with a discerning eye for good breastfeeding information would prefer to get theirs right from the source rather than secondhand from some troglodyte who's never owned his own breasts, let alone produced an ounce of milk in his life. To get the essentials for a successful breastfeeding campaign, we turn to CAHFAC member Kelli, an experienced breastfeeding mom who also happens to be an expert in infant diet and nutrition.

**Ready, aim, fire.** Follow these steps to help your woman find breastfeeding bliss:

1. Gather a healthy snack and drink for Mom, plus anything else she might want within reach, such as a telephone, book or the TV remote.

2. Even if your little angel baby is screaming to be fed, take a moment to help her get in proper feeding position. She should sit in a place that offers good back support. Suggest she try different leg positions, such as elevated on an ottoman, on a stool, hanging down or folded in front.

3. Grab a firm pillow (some are made specifically for breastfeeding) for her lap to keep the baby at a comfortable breastfeeding elevation.

4. Place the baby on the pillow in whatever breastfeeding position is most comfortable for supplier and suckling.

5. She should bring baby to her breast, not the other way around. Notice her posture; good back support and posture reduce her risk of back and shoulder aches.

6. Encourage her to brush the baby's cheek or lips with her nipple to get the baby to open wide. If the little one needs encouragement, your woman can use her thumb or finger to pull down on his or her chin while placing him or her on the breast.

7. Make sure the baby latches on to the entire areola, not just the nipple. Most nipple trauma is caused by the baby only latching on to the nipple.

8. Now it's time to take aim. Your lady should point her nipple toward the roof of the baby's mouth (which by now should be wide open), allowing the diner to latch onto the entire areola. Baby's

lips should both be flared outward (think of fish lips) and neither one should be pursed (folded under). If one is pursed, Mom can simply break the suction by inserting her pinkie into the corner of the baby's mouth, then pulling him or her away. Now try again!

**Troubleshooting.** Breastfeeding doesn't come automatically or easily for many women. It's a learning process for mom and baby alike. Here are a few tips a caveman might find handy for helping his woman overcome common breastfeeding challenges:

- **Her milk hasn't come in!** It usually takes three to five days after delivery for a woman's milk to arrive at the outlet. Don't fret if it doesn't come in immediately. She'll be feeding the baby colostrum until it does. Later, to increase yield and speed up milk delivery, she can use a breast pump after each feeding.

- **Her nipples are sore!** As she learns to breastfeed, and especially before her milk comes in, her nipples may become sore. If this happens, be sure she's using the positioning and latch-on techniques mentioned above. Provide her with pure lanolin cream as needed if her nipples become dry or cracked.

- **Engorgement!** At different phases of breastfeeding (i.e., when her milk first comes in), her breasts may become engorged. Happy day for you, right?! Warm compresses or a warm shower can get her milk flowing before she expresses. Then, she can use hand expression, a breast pump and/or breastfeeding to relieve some of the pressure. Lastly, have cold compresses ready after expression and nursing to ease any discomfort.

**Why a woman may not breastfeed her baby.** Here are some of the most common obstacles to a sustained breastfeeding campaign:

- **Health reasons.** Several conditions might prevent a new mom from breastfeeding, among them a past injury that hampers function of the milk ducts, hormonal deficiencies, the presence of an infectious disease like HIV (which could be transmitted to the baby) or chemotherapy for cancer (a contraindication to breastfeeding since it involves powerful drugs that could transfer to the baby).

- **Work and time constraints.** Commitments to jobs or other children make the time-intensive process untenable for some moms. Some women who plan to take only a few weeks pregnancy/postpartum leave from work may not want to start something they cannot continue, mindful of the effect stopping feeding might have on the baby and her. Also, work-related travel requirements could take a woman away from the baby too frequently to make breastfeeding a feasible endeavor.

- **Pain.** Breastfeeding can cause cracked and painful nipples. After childbirth, some moms get fed up with pain.

- **Revulsion toward the process.** Some women simply don't like the concept or the practice of their body serving as a perpetually on-call food source.

- **Sexual/body image issues.** Some women think if they offer their breasts to their infant as a means of nourishment that it takes the polish off the apple, neutralizing their perceived sexiness. At least that's what we've heard from some women. Others worry breastfeeding will cause the breasts to sag and thus be less attractive. Studies (borne out in field research conducted by the very single Dr. Brian) have shown, however, that any breast sag results more from pregnancy itself than breastfeeding.

- **Anxiety.** She may have a fear of failure—that she'll have problems feeding or won't produce enough nourishment for the baby. Others may find it too complicated to worry about when a bottle seems so easy.

- **Societal/cultural influences.** Whether it's views expressed by friends and family or disapproving looks from strangers, some women might feel external pressure not to breastfeed.

- **Lack of knowledge.** Some women aren't aware of the many compelling benefits that breastfeeding brings.

- **Misinformation about risks to the baby.** Some mothers stop breastfeeding because they have a fever or are taking a medicine. Rarely are these reasons to stop breastfeeding.

## THE BREAST PUMP: MODERN CONVENIENCE FROM A MEDIEVAL CONTRAPTION

Back in the 1920s, one of our troglodyte brethren, a chess-playing mechanical engineer named Edward Lasker, invented and patented a human breast pump that he adapted from a model made for bovines, an achievement that earns him a place in the Cultivated Caveman Crevasse of Fame.

For a lighthearted chuckle during a particularly stressful parenting moment, the thought of your woman hooked up to a device

# DR. BRIAN

## Why Men Can't Make Milk

Having seen the intimacy shared by Mom and baby during breastfeeding, it's not unusual for new dads to feel a bit envious. We have nipples; why can't we put them to constructive use, too, like the Dayak fruit bat, the only male mammal known to produce milk?

One reason men aren't destined to nurse like male fruit bats is anatomical: we cannot produce milk like females because we don't develop mammary glands. There's a chance a baby boy might make milk, however. Male and female babies are born with their main milk ducts intact, so the gland that produces milk is there in the male. It remains undeveloped unless stimulated by female hormones such as estrogen and oxytocin, which, when passed from mother to newborn male, may prompt his nipples to produce a substance called "witch's milk" for a short time. Otherwise, nipples are just one of those sexually neutral pieces of equipment we're all blessed with, like lips, lungs, and butt cheeks.

The other chief hurdle to male milk production is a developmental and hormonal one. Guys actually do start growing breasts; *in utero* they develop similarly to a girl's. In truth, we all start off as females, at least until the Y chromosome kicks in and makes us male. Come puberty, however, male and female chests usually part ways. That's when girls' breasts are stimulated to grow, mainly by their bodies producing the hormone estrogen. This development is known as thelarche.

Men's breasts, by contrast, are stimulated to grow by hot dogs, pizza, and beer. This consumption-related development is called gynecomastia, known in locker-room lingo as "man boobs." It is true that adolescent boys can develop noticeable breast tissue. But this usually resolves within a couple of years. In most instances, however, the phenomenon known as male breast enlargement will not resolve itself. The only known treatments are obvious ones: weight loss through diet and aerobic exercise, and exercising the pectoralis (chest) muscles with push-ups, bench presses, and the like.

We can't make milk, but we can speculate. Let's look at the pros and cons of the male-as-milkmaker scenario:

## Top 10 reasons men shouldn't lactate (or own their own set of breasts):

10. Can't master the reach-around to unlatch and remove bra

9. Makes prized tanktop collection obsolete

8. Hard to aim pee at toilet—can't see over own rack

7. Breast engorgement throws off golf swing

6. Milk tastes like cigars

5. Baby can't find nipple through thick chest hair

4. Self-suckling threatens baby's milk supply

3. Baby's precious milk wasted in squirt fights with buddies

2. Embarrassing catcalls from workmates

1. Crotch starts feeling attention-starved

## And the Top 10 reasons they should:

10. Men more apt to make eye contact in conversations with women

9. New employment opportunities for guys in lingerie, wet nursing

8. Non-dairy creamer no longer necessary

7. Catalyst to miraculous gains in bra, seatbelt fit, and functionality

6. Handy place to nestle a beer

5. Gives men with breasts an outlet besides sumo wrestling

4. Reduction in rubbernecking-related traffic accidents

3. A new twist on the "There once was a man from Nantucket…" limerick

2. A perfect complement to the man-gina

1. Finally qualified to get that job at Hooters

designed to extract milk from her breasts always produces a smile. That's not to diminish the value of the breast pump, aka the lactation station, a device either manual or motorized that many women rely upon to build a household supply of stored breast milk. The milk it produces may be stored at room temperature for up to 10 hours, kept in the fridge for up to a week or stored in the freezer for up to six months.

One reason moms and lactivist dads like the breast pump is that it gives people other than Mom the ability to deliver breast milk to a baby via a bottle. That's particularly handy because it can free a sleep-starved woman from overnight feeding duties. It's also useful in increasing a mother's milk production. Since production is a matter of supply and demand, the more she feeds and pumps, the more milk her body will try to make.

Use the comparison-shopping skills you developed in purchasing your high-definition TV, car or lawnmower to help your lady evaluate breast pumps. Some pumps operate manually, which may require considerable effort, while others are powered by electricity, working automatically so that the woman's hands are free to hold a book, text message or eat an apple. While we appreciate the primitive nature of manual models, convenience makes us lean toward the more advanced electric units. In that category, a **dual pump** tends to be more efficient than a single pump apparatus because it works both breasts at once like ravenous newborn twins, cutting pumping time in half. A new dual pump can be had for anywhere from about $100 to $350, and used ones for much cheaper (if the milk source doesn't mind using a broken-in model). Most mothers who plan to pump regularly go the dual pump route. **Hospital-grade pumps** are the best pumps available, but you'll pay more for them.

Using a dual pump, a typical milk extraction session might last 10 to 20 minutes. The process may make a woman feel bovine, so praise and reassurance from the caveman certainly can encourage her to overcome those feelings for the good of the caveling.

When it comes to protecting the baby's best interests, some moms "pump and dump" their milk, particularly to avoid passing a substance such as alcohol on to the youngster. Say you and your woman have followed our advice to get a babysitter and head out together for a night on the town, minus the caveling (see Chapter 9). After a glass of wine over dinner, she wonders whether it would be wise to rid her body of the milk most likely to contain traces of the alcohol she consumed—to pump it, then dump it down the drain.

For some, it's an approach worth considering. While alcohol does pass into breast milk, it does so in small amounts and for a short duration. It leaves the body as it is metabolized. The level of alcohol in breast milk directly correlates to the amount of alcohol in the bloodstream. While the American Academy of Pediatrics Committee on Drugs and Chemicals and Human Milk has indicated that alcohol consumption and breastfeeding aren't mutually exclusive, it's up to the cavecouple—and mainly the breastfeeding woman herself—to decide whether to mix breastfeeding and alcohol consumption. Many women elect not to drink alcohol at all until they're done breastfeeding altogether. If your woman demands solidarity, you may have to curb your alcohol intake as well. There's one way for a guy to shed some of his own pregnancy weight.

## THE SCOOP ON FORMULA

Formula. Chemists, mathematicians, and auto racing fans know the word, and so do parents. This is the product that many moms and dads provide their tiny progeny as a replacement for, or in addition to, breast milk. Usually available in powdered, just-add-liquid form, formula is a safe, sound alternative to breast milk. It can't match mother's milk in beneficial content, but it will adequately meet a baby's nutritional needs. Many parents swear by formula and feed a lot of it to their infants. Indeed, formula is a convenient and oftentimes necessary component in helping to nourish our population's littlest bodies.

The formula industry is regulated by the U.S. Food and Drug Administration, which often follows recommendations by the American Academy of Pediatrics Committee on Nutrition. The FDA requires all baby formula to contain nutrients found in breast milk to ensure the closest approximation to the real thing. When shopping, look for formula products that are iron-fortified. The following must be included in all formulas produced in the U.S.:

- Protein (typically from cow's milk or soy)
- Fat
- Linoleic acid
- Vitamins: A, C, D, E, K, Thiamin (B1), Riboflavin (B2), B6, B12

## Surplus Milk Belongs in the Bank

Some breastfeeding women become such prolific producers that they end up with more milk than they and their babies know what to do with. Perhaps it is time to visit the bank. The surplus can be donated to any of 11 milk banks scattered across North America, which may use it for a variety of worthy causes, such as to feed premature babies in hospital neonatal intensive care units, and to furnish breast milk to families that are unable to breastfeed children for medical reasons. Banked milk may even end up in far-flung places like Africa to help curb the spread of HIV/AIDS, which can be passed to babies through breast milk. Milk banks are supplied by donors who have been certified according to guidelines prescribed by the U.S. Food and Drug Administration and the Centers for Disease Control and Prevention.

- Niacin

- Folic acid

- Pantothenic acid

- Calcium

- Metals: magnesium, iron, zinc, manganese, copper

- Phosphorus

- Iodine

- Sodium chloride

- Potassium

- Soy formulas may also include Biotin, Choline, and Inositol

Let's take a trip down mammary lane for a look at the origins of formula. In 1867, Justus von Liebig, a German chemist, developed the world's first commercial infant formula. Clearly stronger at scientific reasoning than marketing, he named his product Liebig's Soluble Food for Babies. The relative success of this product quickly gave rise to competitors such as Mellin's Infant Food, Ridge's Food for Infants, and Nestle's Milk. Basically they were similar to formulas of today, as well as the stuff the astronauts drink: flavored, powdered nutrients to which one adds water to make a beverage.

At the dawn of the 20th century in the United States, most infants were breastfed, although many received some formula feeding as well. Evaporated milk products became widely available at low prices, and several clinical studies observed that babies who were fed evaporated milk formula thrived as well as breastfed babies. These studies, plus the affordable price of evaporated milk and the availability of the home icebox, initiated a tremendous rise in the use of evaporated milk formulas. In the late 1920s, Similac was released, coining a word to describe a product that was designed to be "similar to lactation." Since the 1940s, advances in processing techniques, such as homogenization, have greatly improved the ways imitation dairy products, like formula, are made. By 1950, over half of all babies in the U.S. were reared on commercial milk formula. Heavy marketing by formula companies ensued through the 1960s, including marketing campaigns that provided free or inexpensive product to hospitals and pediatricians' offices. By the early 1970s, more than 75 percent of Americans were fed formula, spurring an industry that now produces revenues well in excess of $3 billion a year in the U.S. alone. Dairy is a big business, and so is imitation dairy.

To maintain its strong foothold, the formula industry introduces itself to many new parents via the goodie bags that hospitals hand out to fledgling moms and dads as they head home with their new addition. It's nice to give folks free stuff, but the bottom line is that such a practice may work against the worthy cause of breastfeeding. Compounding the controversy surrounding the marketing of formula, many poor mothers try to stretch their formula supply by using less formula powder than is necessary. As a result, some infants receive inadequate nutrition from weak solutions of formula.

The reality is, though, that formula, when handled and consumed the right way, is a viable, if less than perfect, source of nutrition for babies.

## HOW FORMULA STACKS UP

Like all species, we're here to perpetuate our genetic strengths and hopefully do what is best for our children. Study after study shows that breastfeeding is best for kids, mothers, families, and society in general. The American Academy of Pediatrics, the American Dietetic Association, the American Academy of Family Physicians, the World Health Organization, and virtually every other major medical body weighing in on the subject agree that mothers should breastfeed exclusively for at least the first six months of life. But breastfeeding for that amount of time or longer isn't feasible for every new mom. Enter formula, which stacks up as the second-best choice for nourishing a baby. There should be no guilt associated with providing it to a little one.

Still, what makes formula second-best to milk from the breast? Let's weigh a few key factors:

- Breastfed babies tend to feed more often than bottle-fed babies because the fats and proteins in breast milk are more easily broken down than the fats and proteins in formula, so they are absorbed and used more quickly. Therefore breastfed babies may have fewer digestive troubles than bottle-fed babies. On the other side of the coin, there's the convenience factor from less frequent feedings with formula.

- Since babies tend not to absorb fats in formula as well, formula-fed babies may have more unpleasant-smelling bowel movements. (We challenge readers to find us one that smells pleasant; we'll send a prize to those who do.)

- Lipids such as DHA and ARA are found in breast milk but not in many formulas. These long-chain fatty acids are important structural building blocks for the brain and retina.

## THE BIG TRANSITION: SOLID ADVICE ON INTRODUCING SOLID FOODS

For the first months of your baby's life, you may feel like a third-string quarterback carrying a clipboard on the sidelines, more spectator than participant in the food provision aspect of infant needs fulfillment. But when your baby is ready to ingest more than breast milk or formula, you and your woman better be prepared to fill his or her proverbial feedbag with the substance and nutrition to fuel that hardworking, fast-developing little bod.

First, a few words preaching restraint. Parents, resist the temptation to introduce solids too early, since this has been associated with a higher incidence of food allergies. Also, babies don't develop good coordination for swallowing solids until four to six months, so feeding them solid food too early might mean a higher risk of choking. Remember, too, that babies don't *need* anything besides breast milk or infant formula for at least six months, so there is no hurry.

How will you know the time is ripe to introduce solids? All babies develop differently and some will show interest in solid foods earlier than others. If your caveling can hold his or her head up, shows interest in what you're eating, and/or seems hungry between regular feedings, he or she is probably ready to try some solid food.

When introducing solids, start conservatively, one food at a time. Provide a single new food to the little one exclusively for five to seven days before adding another new food so you can isolate the cause of any allergic reaction or toleration issue. Begin with small bites, a teaspoon or so at a time, slowly building to a tablespoon at a time.

Many babies' introduction to the wonderful world of solids comes in the form of a relatively plain product, such as infant cereal. Rice cereal is a good place to start. It's easily digestible, it can be made with breast milk or formula as the liquid component, it is often fortified with iron and it is highly non-allergenic. You can

start with just one or two tablespoons once a day before or after a normal breastfeeding. Try to be consistent with the time of day and order of eating. Next add a cereal feeding to follow one or two more breastfeeding sessions.

Once your baby adjusts to cereal, vegetables can be introduced next, followed by fruits, then meats. Again, take it slowly, one food at a time, in very small bites and portions. That guards against allergic reactions, which occur when the body's natural defense system incorrectly perceives certain foods as harmful and overreacts to the "invasion" by producing a rash, explosive gas, and other symptoms. If you suspect a food allergy, eliminate the potential culprit from baby's diet for two weeks. Most food allergies come from peanut butter, eggs, cow's milk, soy, shellfish, and wheat products.

Expose your baby to lots of different foods—always following developmentally appropriate nutritional guidelines, of course. Early exposure to a broad array of food tastes and textures paves the way for better, more adventurous eating habits later. Complementary foods rich in iron can be introduced gradually beginning around six months of age (pre-term and low-birth-weight babies likely will need iron supplementation prior to that). By about eight months of age, and after the baby shows an ability to digest single-

# DR. BRIAN

## When Will Baby's Grin Turn Toothy?

The peace and quiet that typically prevails in Gronk's rock abode during breastfeeding time suddenly is shattered by a scream. The caveman bolts from his workshop, where he has been whittling sticks, into Peanut's room to see what's amiss.

There sits his woman, grimace on her face, one breast fully exposed, holding Peanut at arm's length as if the cherub were a rabid animal. The yelp that brought this suckling session to a halt came from Mom, not baby. Tender as her nipple already is from all the feeding, it has been victimized by Peanut's attempt to test her newly emerged first tooth. For the nipple, it's a matter of being in the wrong place at the wrong time.

Toothiness may be an issue for some nursing moms. But who can blame babies for wanting to test the choppers that sprout from their gums with regularity throughout the first and second year of life. A baby's primary teeth begin to form in utero around the 16th week of pregnancy and are almost completely formed underneath the surface of the gums at birth. The first tooth usually erupts through the gum some time between the fourth and 12th month, with the lower teeth typically growing out before the upper teeth.

From that point, babies tend to cut an average of about one tooth per month. While tooth development differs from kid to kid, the first tooth to erupt is usually the central incisor in the middle-front position on the lower gum, followed by the second central incisor on the lower jaw. Then may come the four upper incisors, followed by the first four molars, the remaining bottom two lateral incisors, and the cuspids. Sometime around the age of two, he or she should get the last of his or her 20 primary teeth, the four second molars.

There's a good reason the emergence of a tooth is called "eruption," for teething can turn a baby's mouth into a drool-spraying orifice of pain and soreness. For relief, you can provide acetaminophen, ibuprofen or teething gels (infant formulas for each) as directed. But more than that stuff, the little one might appreciate something to ruminate on, like a pacifier, a teething ring, even a cool spoon or cold, wet washcloth. Babies who are battling teething and already have an adequate number of choppers to chew things might appreciate a teething biscuit to chew on. No need to buy them at a store when you can whip them up in the comfort of your own kitchen, using the following flavorful recipe.

Some store-bought teething biscuits contain high fructose corn syrup, while certain recipes for homemade biscuits call for lots of sugar and eggs, a possible allergen. This recipe is lower on sugar, egg-free, easy, and guaranteed to keep junior gumming away. Keep in mind, teething biscuits may crumble in the little one's mouth, the pieces presenting a potential choking hazard. So never leave your little one unattended while he or she is enjoying one.

**SERVING SIZE:** 12 biscuits

**RATING (LEVEL OF DIFFICULTY):** Homo habilis (see explanation of recipe rating system on page 77)

**ESTIMATED PREP AND COOK TIME:** 30–40 minutes

**NEED FIRE?** Yes—oven

**GATHER:**

1 cup flour

1 cup dry infant rice cereal with bananas (or other flavored or unflavored infant cereal)

3 tablespoons cooking oil

Ice water

## DIRECTIONS

Preheat oven to 425°F.

In a mixer or food processor, combine flour and cereal.

Gradually incorporate oil.

Mix ¼-cup ice water at a time until dough begins to form a ball and pull away from the bowl.

Roll out to the thickness of a thick cracker on a floured surface and cut into desired shapes.

Bake on an ungreased cookie sheet, 10–12 minutes or until lightly brown. Cool completely before providing to caveling.

grain cereals, vegetables, and fruits with no problem, you can start adding other foods such as:

- at eight to 10 months, mixed grain cereals, cheese cubes, finger foods, strained and pureed meat, chicken, beans, cottage cheese, plain yogurt, cooked egg yolk, and tofu; then,

- at 10 to 12 months, mashed and chopped foods from the family meal.

The introduction of solids is also a good time to add a cup to the little one's eating tool belt. Try a sippy cup with handles and a small amount of water. If the cup has an internal plastic stopper in the spout, take it out so he or she learns to drink from a cup instead of simply sucking on something new. There may be a mess, but the little one should learn to drink from a cup like a champ in no time!

A few more pointers to consider in building your infant menu:

- Don't worry about restricting baby's intake of fat and cholesterol. Little ones need calories, fat, and cholesterol to develop mentally and physically.

- Practice spoonfeeding so your baby gets practice with this crucial utensil.

- Don't worry too much about providing a healthy baby with extra liquids other than breast milk or formula, except to provide water on very hot days. A supplemental drink of water also may be needed when solid food is first introduced.

- **Avoid** foods that expose babies to health risks. Don't feed a child **seafood, peanuts, nut butters** or **tree nuts** before age 2 or 3. Don't feed a baby **eggs, citrus fruits** and **juices, cow's milk** or **honey** until after his or her first birthday. Whole cow's milk contains so much protein, sodium, and potassium that it can cause stress to an infant's immature kidneys. The proteins and fats are harder for an infant to digest and absorb than the ones in breast milk. Also, some infants are allergic to cow's milk (and other dairy products). Avoid foods that pose a choking hazard, such as **seeds, popcorn, whole berries** and **whole grapes, raw veggies, meat sticks, hot dogs,** etc.

- Steer clear of salt or sugar when making homemade baby foods. For example, avoid using canned foods to make baby food; they tend to contain large amounts of salt and sugar.

- Always wash and peel fruits and vegetables and be sure to remove seeds or pits before providing the pieces of produce to a

## Feeding Guide for the First Year

| Item | 4 to 6 Months | 7 Months | 8 Months |
| --- | --- | --- | --- |
| **Breastfeeding or Formula** | 4 to 6 feedings per day or 28 to 32 oz. per day | 3 to 5 feedings per day or 30 to 32 oz. per day | 3 to 5 feedings per day or 30 to 32 oz. per day |
| **Dry Infant Cereal with Iron** | 3 to 5 tbsp. single grain iron fortified cereal mixed with formula | 3 to 5 tbsp. single grain iron fortified cereal mixed with formula | 5 to 8 tbsp. single grain cereal mixed with formula |
| **Fruits** | 1 to 2 tbsp., plain, strained/ 1 to 2 times per day | 2 to 3 tbsp., plain, strained/ 2 times per day | 2 to 3 tbsp., strained or soft mashed/2 times per day |
| **Vegetables** | 1 to 2 tbsp., plain, strained/ 1 to 2 times per day | 2 to 3 tbsp., plain, strained/ 2 times per day | 2 to 3 tbsp., strained, mashed, soft/2 times per day |
| **Meats and Protein Foods** | | 1 to 2 tbsp., strained/ 2 times per day | 1 to 2 tbsp., strained/ 2 times per day |
| **Juices, Vitamin C Fortified** | | 2 to 4 oz. from a cup | 2 to 4 oz. from a cup |
| **Starches** | | | |
| **Snacks** | | Arrowroot cookies, toast, crackers | Arrowroot cookies, toast, crackers, plain yogurt |
| **Development** | Make first cereal feedings very soupy and thicken slowly. | Start finger foods and cup. | Formula intake decreases; solid foods in diet increase. |

| 9 Months | 10 to 12 Months |
| --- | --- |
| 3 to 5 feedings per day or 30 to 32 oz. per day | 3 to 4 feedings per day or 24 to 30 oz. per day |
| 5 to 8 tbsp. any variety mixed with formula per day | 5 to 8 tbsp. any variety mixed with formula per day |
| 2 to 4 tbsp., strained or soft mashed/2 times per day | 2 to 4 tbsp., mashed or strained, cooked/2 times per day |
| 2 to 4 tbsp., mashed, soft, bite-sized pieces/2 times per day | 2 to 4 tbsp., mashed, soft, bite-sized pieces/2 times per day |
| 2 to 3 tbsp. tender, chopped/2 times per day | 2 to 3 tbsp., finely chopped, table meats, fish without bones, mild cheese/2 times per day |
| 2 to 6 oz. from a cup | 2 to 6 oz. from a cup |
| | ¼–½ cup mashed potatoes, macaroni, spaghetti, bread/2 times per day |
| Arrowroot cookies, assorted finger foods, cookies, toast, crackers, plain yogurt, cooked green beans | Arrowroot cookies, assorted finger foods, cookies, toast, crackers, plain yogurt, cooked green beans, cottage cheese, ice cream, pudding, dry cereal |
| Eating more table foods. Make sure diet has good variety. | Baby may change to table food. Baby will feed himself/herself and use a spoon and cup. |

**Beware the Juice (No, We're Not Talking O.J. Simpson)**

The juice isn't just bad for ballplayers; too much of it can have negative consequences for a baby. One look at Barry Bonds and one might conclude that steroids inflate statistics, head size, and ego, with all sorts of other unsavory side-effects. A similarly negative connection might be drawn between babies and fruit juice. While juice is often deemed to be a natural, healthy drink, it has very little nutritional value to babies. Juice can cause your little one:

- to have loose stools;

- to develop an aversion to less-sweet foods, including whole fruits and veggies;

- to be deprived of nutrients from other foods because all he or she wants is juice;

- to consume excess calories through the toddler years that may lead to excess weight gain;

- to develop tooth decay from too much sugar on developing teeth, especially when consumed via a bottle (big no-no!).

- No need to swear off juice altogether, however. A baby may drink it, but only in moderation and only after accepting a variety of foods into his or her diet. Here are a few guidelines:

  Only use 100 percent juice, not fruit "punch" mixes or fruit "drinks."

  Limit juice intake to 4 ounces per day or less.

  Mix water with juice to decrease its sweetness.

caveling. Take special care with fruits and vegetables that come into contact with the ground; they may contain botulism spores that cause food poisoning.

- Avoid the "clean your plate" edict. The goal is to teach a child to eat as much as he or she needs to feel sated.
- Expect baby to exhibit a pickier palate starting around age 1.

Things change considerably for many babies' diets later in the first year, as shown in the American Academy of Pediatrics feeding guide on the previous pages. With the caveling perhaps having a few teeth in place, with the time now appearing ripe to adapt the breastfeed-or-bust campaign to accommodate other, non-liquid nutrition sources, and with the caveman having gained a working knowledge of the kinds of foods that are and are not suitable for a baby, the stage is set for him to take another evolutionary step, this one into a part of the home, the kitchen, that he previously used more for consumption than creation. Trapped inside you is a meal-making machine just waiting to bust out. So toss the clipboard and strap on your helmet. Time to get in the game!

## A HOW-TO GUIDE TO MODERN HUNTING & GATHERING

Vegetation grew so plentifully on the open steppes of Europe during prehistoric times that it was more than enough to sustain huge populations of herbivorous mammals. Here in the 21st century, the shelves at the supermarket, local grocer's, farmer's market, butcher shop, and specialty food store hold more than enough stuff to satisfy the nutritional needs, varied palates, and raging appetites of just about anyone, young and old, herbivore, carnivore, and omnivore alike. And unlike the hunter-gatherers who inhabited the steppes in Paleolithic times, one needn't spend most of his waking hours foraging for it, tracking it, slaughtering it, butchering it, and preparing it. The foods and ingredients he doesn't grow himself usually are readily available at a local retail outlet.

Among the many evolutionary opportunities that fatherhood presents, the chance to shoulder more of the household's hunting, gathering, and meal-production responsibilities is one of the most compelling. If you like to eat stuff that tastes good and prefer that the substances you shovel into your body also be healthful, that's all the selfish motivation you need to undertake a journey of culinary discovery. Factor in the benefits you bring to your baby and your woman by serving them healthy meals and it's a slam dunk! As a partner in the baby venture, it is only fair that you embrace those responsibilities, if for no other reason than to relieve your woman of kitchen duty when she's too cooked to cook.

The journey starts with proper hunting and gathering techniques—an ability to locate the right ingredients for the meals the cavecook will be preparing. Guys for whom the grocery store or market is unfamiliar territory need merely to follow a few basic guidelines to fill their chariots with good-for-you goods.

## Do...

- make out a shopping list and remember to bring it with you to the store.

- bring your own bags (or bladders) for carrying groceries home, if feasible.

- keep your food purchases fresh and local when possible; patronizing independent suppliers and shops may cost a bit more, but the quality can be better.

- make friends with the local butcher; as two carcass-worshipping, cleaver-wielding cavemen, you should have plenty to talk about.

- read labels and look for foods that offer nutritional value, not just junk calories. Think Okinawans.

- leave plenty of room for foods in their natural, unprocessed state, such as fruits and vegetables.

- ask uniformed store personnel for help locating an item you can't find.

- shop the frozen section last. You don't want that stuff thawing during your shopping spree.

- buy a little something for your honey. Good choices include a small piece of premium chocolate, or, if there are healthy flowers at the market, a small mixed bouquet.

- recognize the budgetary benefits that eating home-cooked meals provides; eating out gets expensive.

## Do Not...

- take a bite from a piece of produce, then return it to the bin.

- fondle the meat too vigorously.

- invest in "baked goods" with shelf lives stretching into the next decade.

- purchase pre-sliced fruit or mushrooms unless you plan to use them promptly.

- allow yourself to be observed by store personnel and patrons with your nose buried in a block of cheese.

- go to the store hungry, lest you end up with a carriage full of junk food and a pocket full of candy wrappers.

- hop the deli counter and use the meat slicer to cut your own.

- get in line for express checkout with hundreds of items in your chariot.

- use the produce watering sprinklers for bathing purposes.

- argue heatedly with a fellow troglodyte shopper over who gets to catch the rotisserie drippings.

- demand free raw meat samples from the butcher. That's a deli thing.

- slip a bag of frozen peas into your pants to cool off the "boys."

- don a white lab coat with an "Apprentice Butcher" nametag and frighten shoppers by wielding a bloody saw.

- loiter in the feminine hygiene section, exclaiming, "Somebody's friend is visiting."

- ride your shopping cart skateboard-like down the aisle.

## PROTECT AND SERVE

Members of the *Homo sapiens* species weren't too far removed from their cavedwelling days when, in the 5th century B.C., the Grecian Hippocrates, whom we now recognize as the father of modern medicine, began espousing his health care philosophies. "Do no harm," Hippocrates said. Those words still resonate here in the 21st century, particularly as they apply to a troglodyte's kitchen and meal-making habits.

Your culinary evolution begins with a Hippocratic-type lesson in the three Do No Harm principles of caveman cooking. As well-meaning as your efforts to take charge of your family's dining destiny are, you're bound to do more damage than good if you don't follow these basic rules of safe food handling and kitchen behavior. So place your hand on a stack of cookbooks and swear to adhere to the following, and to always wear a hairnet:

1. **Do no harm to those you serve.** Always follow safe food-handling practices. That means:

    - thawing food properly by keeping it in the refrigerator or under cold running water. Don't let food thaw at room temperature and never thaw meat on racks above fresh foods, which can be contaminated if meat juice drips on them.

    - diligently keeping hands clean. Wash your mitts (and dry them with a clean towel) after using the bathroom and after handling raw meat, raw poultry or raw seafood.

    - taking measures to avoid cross-contamination. Don't use the knife or the cutting board you used to cut raw meat/poultry/seafood to cut other stuff without washing them thoroughly.

    - cooking to doneness. Undercooked meat can pose health dangers to a breastfeeding mom and baby.

2. **Do no harm to thyself.** The thought of preparing a killer meal all by yourself has you pretty amped. But don't get careless in your enthusiasm; always exercise caution when using knives and other sharp kitchen implements. You don't want to interrupt meal preparations to locate a missing digit in the goulash, to douse a fire on your scalp or to remove a hunk of your own skin from the food processor blade.

3. **Do no harm to your relationship.** Providing your woman with a day off from dinner duty doesn't mean leaving her with a pile of post-meal dishes. Avoid exasperating her by staying ahead of the mess—cleaning, drying, and putting away whatever you've used in meal preparation as you go, then, after everyone has eaten, doing the remaining dishes.

## Arming the Cavecook

Behind every well-prepared meal is a well-equipped kitchen. Here's a list of implements for a caveman cook to include in his arsenal:

Apron (cavemen love the blood-red "Psycho Griller" apron, available at www.cultivatedcaveman.com)

Basting brush (crucial grilling tool)

Colander

Cutting board(s)

Electric mixer

Food processor

Garlic press

Grilling screens (crucial grilling tool)

Hairnet (for you heavy shedders)

Knives, well-sharpened

Measuring spoons, measuring cup(s)

Meat thermometer (we like digital, instant-read types)

Nonstick skillet/pans

Oven mitt(s)

Pulverizing tool (meat hammer, etc.)

Rolling pin

Sheet pans/baking sheets

Skewers (crucial grilling tool)

Spatula (crucial grilling tool)

Spray bottle

Tongs (crucial grilling tool)

Wire rack

Wire whisk

## ABOUT THE RECIPES

Evolution has left the contemporary caveman sitting pretty. He has a mastery of fire and a host of ways to harness it to suit his purposes. He has access to tools and implements whose utility surpasses anything Otzi the Iceman ever imagined. And all it takes is a trip to the market for him to find a bounty of fresh ingredients suitable for the human diet, from nuts, berries and other vegetation to grains, meat, and many, many more healthy sources of sustenance.

What he might not have is the ability to put them all together into actual dishes people will want to eat—and benefit from doing so. From homemade baby food recipes that require little more than cutting and pulverizing to more intricate meals that bring additional skills to bear, we've collected a range of recipes built to satisfy the palate as well as the nutritional needs of the folks with whom you share your cave, baby and mom included.

### Degree of difficulty

Good cooks aren't born, they're made. Some cavemen in the crowd may need lots of hand-holding as they evolve from primitive to Prudhommian in the kitchen; others already know how to throw their weight around in the meal-making department. The recipes in this section cater to people at both ends of the spectrum and everyone in between. Each recipe is rated on a scale of simplicity represented by four caveman characters. The more upright the character, the more "evolved" the recipe.

Recipes labeled with a knuckledragger are the easiest to prepare, while those bearing the fully upright *Homo sapiens* character are the most advanced, though still relatively straightforward to execute. Use the following thumbnails to determine which recipes correspond to your place on the evolutionary arc:
Other recipe elements:

- **Need Fire?** indicates whether the recipe requires ingredients to be cooked over a flame or heat source.

- **Hunt** specifies any meat required for the recipe.

- **Gather** specifies other non-meat ingredients needed for the recipe.

## RECIPES

### Gourmet Gummables: Homemade Baby Food

The timing couldn't be better for a fledgling caveman cook: his first stabs at becoming competent in the kitchen coinciding with the caveling's first forays into solid food. Having grown accustomed to cereal, it's time for the baby to graduate to vittles with a little more pizzazz. Here's a golden opportunity for the new dad to cut his teeth in the kitchen by preparing some tasty homemade mush for the little one, starting with pureed veggies, then moving on to fruits and later, meats (see the section on transitioning to solid foods earlier in the chapter for more detailed food introduction strategies).

Not only does homemade baby food tend to be cheaper than the store-bought stuff, it's fresher, tastier, and just as healthy. It's also ideal for toothless types, from the very young to the very old. For the cook and consumer alike, this is about as primitive as it gets—perfect for the gastronomic greenhorn. So grab a camera, role out the tarpaulin, alert the dog, and start the bath—this is going to get messy.

The **Knuckledragger** is what his name implies, someone whose hands have been used mainly for personal propulsion and a bit of grooming but almost never for food preparation. He's an absolute beginner in the kitchen.

The more evolved but still very primitive **Neanderthal** has a limited grasp of kitchen tools and food preparation but needs lots of help to overcome his culinary clumsiness.

***Homo habilis*** (handy man) represents a male who, with a little more polish and seasoning, is on his way to being fully self-sufficient in the kitchen.

At the top of the culinary food chain stands the ***Homo sapiens***, a guy who not only does his own hunting and gathering but can also execute a high-touch meal with aplomb.

## Do the Math

To measure up in the kitchen, a caveman must be able to measure ingredients and, when called upon, to convert those measurements from one unit to another. Keep this conversion chart handy and you'll spare yourself much head-scratching—and your diners much gagging.

### Basic U.S. Conversions

1 tablespoon (tbsp) = 3 teaspoons (tsp) = 1/16 cup

2 tablespoons = 1/8 cup = 1 ounce (oz)

4 tablespoons = 1/4 cup

5 tablespoons + 1 teaspoon = 1/3 cup

8 tablespoons = 1/2 cup

10 tablespoons + 2 teaspoons = 2/3 cup

12 tablespoons = 3/4 cup

1 cup = 48 teaspoons

1 cup = 16 tablespoons

1 cup = 8 fluid ounces (fl oz)

1 pint (pt) = 2 cups

1 quart (qt) = 2 pints

1 quart = 4 cups

4 quarts = 1 gallon (gal)

16 ounces (oz) = 1 pound (lb)

### U.S. to Metric Conversions

1/5 teaspoon = 1 milliliter

1 ounce = 28 grams

1 teaspoon = 5 milliliter

1 pound = 454 grams

## BASIC VEGETABLE PUREE

*Vegetables should be an early staple in the caveling's solid diet. Eventually you can create blended vegetable medleys, but not before you ensure that all veggies in the combination have been previously offered with no allergic reaction. For this simple recipe, we recommend trying sweet potatoes, carrots or peas, and branching out from there.*

**SERVES:** 8 ice-cube-sized portions

**RATING:** Knuckledragger

**ESTIMATED PREP AND COOK TIME:** 5 minutes

**NEED FIRE?** No

**GATHER:**

○ 1 cup cooked (steamed or microwaved) fresh or frozen vegetables

○ 4–8 tablespoons of cooking liquid, breast milk or formula

Slice veggies into pieces small enough to fit into a blender or food processor.

Put vegetables and liquid into your chosen appliance and puree until smooth.

Serve immediately or freeze in a covered ice cube tray for easy portioning.

# PRIMITIVE FRUIT PUREE

*This banana recipe should please the little primates in the crowd. Don't be afraid to shake the trees and comb the bushes for other fruits to use.*

**SERVES:** 2 baby-sized portions

**RATING:** Knuckledragger

**ESTIMATED PREP AND COOK TIME:** 2 minutes

**NEED FIRE?** No

**GATHER:**

○ 1 ripe or almost ripe banana

Strip down to your tank top. Peel the banana. Grab your favorite kitchen pulverizing tool and mash the banana like you mean it, until it's more liquid than solid. Finito!

1 tablespoon = 15 milliliter

1 fluid ounce = 30 milliliter

1 cup = 237 milliliter

2 cups (1 pint) = 473 milliliter

4 cups (1 quart) = 0.95 liter

4 quarts (1 gallon) = 3.8 liters

Cooking temperature: to convert Fahrenheit (F) to Celsius (C): $0.555 \times (°F - 32)$

## Metric to U.S. Conversions

1 milliliter = ⅕ teaspoon

1 gram = 0.035 ounce

5 milliliter = 1 teaspoon

15 milliliter = 1 tablespoon

100 milliliter = 3.4 fluid ounce

1 kilogram = 2.205 lb = 35 ounces

240 milliliter = 1 cup

1 liter = 34 fluid ounces = 4.2 cups = 2.1 pints = 1.06 quarts = 0.26 gallon

0.946 liters = 1 quart

0.454 kilograms = 1 pound

1 kilogram = 2.205 pounds

Cooking temperature: to convert Celsius to Fahrenheit: $1.8 \times (°C + 32)$

SOURCE: UNITED STATES DEPT. OF AGRICULTURE (USDA)

## CHICKEN & PEACHES
## A LA CAVELING

*This one is fit for members of the 9- to 12-month-old crowd
who have a few teeth in their heads and who previously have
been introduced to peaches and to chicken, without signs of
allergic reaction.*

**SERVES:** 4–6 baby-sized portions

**RATING:** Neanderthal

**ESTIMATED PREP AND COOK TIME:** Very little prep; 40 minutes to cook
rice (start cooking chicken when rice cooking time is down to 10 minutes)

**NEED FIRE?** Yes, stove top

**HUNT:**

- ○ ½ cup boneless chicken, cubed

**GATHER:**

- ○ ¼ cup cooked brown rice

- ○ 1 ripe, washed, and pitted peach, flesh only

- ○ 1 tablespoon peach or apple juice

- ○ 2 tablespoons breast milk, formula, plain or peach yogurt

Start by cooking the brown rice as directed on the package (allow
time—brown rice takes a while). Cook the chicken cubes in a
pan with water. Mix all ingredients together and chop in a food
processor or blender, leaving some lumpiness.

# CREAMED CHICKEN & POTATO

*Another soft-serve delight for a baby who's approaching the first birthday.*

**SERVES:** 2 baby-sized portions

**RATING:** Neanderthal

**ESTIMATED PREP AND COOK TIME:** Very little prep; 30 minutes to cook chicken and potato

**NEED FIRE?** Yes, stove top

**HUNT:**

- ○ ¼ cup cooked boneless chicken, shredded

**GATHER:**

- ○ 2 teaspoons sweet butter or margarine
- ○ 1 teaspoon unbleached flour
- ○ ¼ cup cooking liquid (water you used to cook chicken in)
- ○ ¼ potato, boiled or baked and cut into small cubes
- ○ 1 tablespoon grated white cheddar cheese

Cook the chicken in a pan with water, reserving some of the water for later. Shred the chicken. Melt butter in another small, heavy pan over low heat. Stir in flour and blend well. Add 2 to 3 tablespoons of cooking liquid from the chicken pan and stir until smooth.

Cook over low heat until mixture begins to thicken, then add shredded chicken and potato cubes and stir for 2 to 3 minutes more, until heated through.

Add cheese, and if you like, any well-cooked vegetable (peas, carrots, cauliflower, etc.) to add nutritional value.

## Grow Your Own, Green Thumb

The first agricultural revolution came about 10,000 years ago, ushering in a golden age of bountiful food- and livestock-raising that coaxed people out of their caves to form vibrant farming and trading communities. You can start your own little agricultural revolution at home and show off your green (opposable) thumb by growing your own fresh produce. The veggies, fruits, and herbs you raise in your own plot can serve as fresh, healthful ingredients for the meals and snacks you make for you, your woman, and the caveling. Few activities are as primitively satisfying as nurturing a seed or seedling you planted into a mature, harvestable plant. Gardening is an option even for someone who lives in an urban setting and/or lacks a patch of dirt to sow. All you need is a hospitable climate, a garden container large enough to accommodate a plant as it grows, some good quality soil, water, sunshine, and TLC.

That look in your baby's eye as you sink your teeth into a succulent, savory piece of meat is called *longing*. The string of noises that spews from his or her mouth loosely translates as, "Dad, I appreciate the mashed peas, but that meat smells mighty good." Once the caveling has a proven ability to gnash and swallow solid food without choking, the caveman chef can kill two birds with one stone by creating meals fit for little and big folks alike.

Cooking one meal for baby and another one entirely for you and your woman is inconvenient, time-consuming and not the best precedent to set for the future. Savvy chefs know how to adapt a meal so it's fit for every generation represented at the dinner table. Not only will you avoid the "separate vittles for littles" approach, you'll be laying the groundwork for an important family dining ritual. Here are a few to set the tone—delicious meals for baby that adapt directly into crowd-pleasers for more mature humans.

*Roasted Butternut Squash for Baby*
*(6–7 months of age or older) becomes...*

## CREAMY ROASTED BUTTERNUT SQUASH SOUP

*for the Rest of the Clan*

........................................................................

**SERVES:** For baby, 10–12 servings; for clan, 4–6 servings
........................................................................

**RATING:** *Homo sapiens*
(less evolved types risk serious bodily harm peeling squash)
........................................................................

**ESTIMATED PREP AND COOK TIME:** 45 minutes
........................................................................

**NEED FIRE?** Yes, stove top
........................................................................

**GATHER:**

○ 3 pounds butternut squash, peeled and cut into chunks

○ 4 tablespoons butter

- ○ 2 tablespoons butter
- ○ 2 Granny Smith apples, peeled, cored, and chopped
- ○ 1 large onion, roughly chopped
- ○ Salt and freshly ground pepper to taste
- ○ 4 cups chicken or vegetable stock
- ○ ½ cup white wine
- ○ 1 teaspoon fresh tarragon leaves or ½ teaspoon dried
- ○ 1 cup cream
- ○ Chopped parsley or chives for garnish

Place the squash in a steamer above a couple of inches of water (because winter squash is so porous, we recommend cooking it above the water, rather than in it). Cover and cook until the squash is tender, about 25 minutes.

While the squash is still hot, place it in a food processor with the 4-tablespoon allocation of butter and process until smooth.

Baby's meal is now complete.

Set aside half the mashed squash for the little one and reserve in a covered ice tray.

Place the 2-tablespoon allocation of butter in a large, deep saucepan; turn heat to medium. When butter melts, add the remaining squash, apples, and onion. Cook until the onion softens, about 5–10 minutes. Season with salt and pepper to taste.

Add the stock, wine, and tarragon and bring to a boil. Let it cook for 10 minutes.

Blend soup with a handheld immersion blender.

Stir in the cream and serve with garnish.

**Note:** The possibilities with this type of recipe are endless; some good baby food combinations that are ideal for folding into soups include mushroom and barley, potato and carrots, vegetables and beef, and white bean and ham. You get the idea.

*Mashed Potato and Ground Beef for Baby (9–10 months and older) becomes...*

# DELICIOUS SHEPHERD'S PIE

*for the Rest of the Clan*

**SERVES:** For baby, 10 portions; for the rest of the clan, 4–6 portions

**RATING:** *Homo habilis*

**ESTIMATED PREP AND COOK TIME:** 1 hour

**NEED FIRE?** Yes, stove top and oven

**HUNT:**

○ 1.5 pounds lean ground beef

**GATHER:**

○ 2.5 pounds Russet or Yukon Gold potatoes, peeled and cut into similar size pieces

○ 2 cups chicken stock

○ 3 tablespoons butter

○ 2 tablespoons sour cream

And for the Shepherd's Pie:

○ Salt and pepper

○ 1 large onion, diced

○ 3 cloves garlic, minced

○ 2 carrots, thinly cut

○ 2 pieces of celery, thinly cut

○ ¼ cup red wine (optional)

○ 2 tablespoons butter

○ Fresh chopped parsley for garnish

In large pot, boil potato until soft, drain and return to pot (why dirty another?).

Add stock, butter, and sour cream then mash (best done while grunting). Reserve about one-quarter of the mashed potatoes for the baby's meal.

In a large skillet, brown the ground beef. Reserve about one-quarter of the ground beef for baby's meal.

Combine beef and potatoes reserved for baby's meal and pulse in a food processor. Baby's meal is now ready to serve.

In a large skillet, melt 1 tablespoon of butter over medium heat. Add onion, garlic, carrots, and celery; cook for 5 minutes, stirring occasionally. Season with salt and pepper.

Add wine to vegetable mixture and let it cook for 2 to 3 minutes.

Stir in ground beef to the skillet, season with salt and pepper.

**Note:** Experiment with any fresh or dried herbs you like to use. This dish holds up well with additional flavors.

Put ground beef mixture in an oven-proof container, set oven to broil, and raise oven rack to top level.

Slice remaining butter and put butter pats on top of potato.

Broil uncovered until potato turns golden brown.

Serve and garnish with fresh parsley.

## FEED (& ROMANCE) THE FEEDER

Pregnancy may have prevented your woman from eating certain foods and ingredients. Here in the postpartum period, she can bust free of those culinary constraints, even if she's breastfeeding. Now is a good time to let her in on the health secrets of the Okinawans. Not only does the meal described below follow some of their dietary tenets, it also can serve as the food component of a romantic evening at home with your woman. Just add ambience (torches or candlelight, strolling minstrels or other tasteful music selections). Dessert might consist of a reciprocal massage, performed in front of the fire on a piece of faux animal pelt.

# HALIBUT SIMMERED IN GINGER AND SOY BROTH

*Spear a big fish and let diners reap the health and flavor benefits.*

**SERVES:** 4

**RATING:** *Homo habilis*

**ESTIMATED PREP AND COOK TIME:** 20 minutes

**NEED FIRE?** Yes, stove top

**HUNT:**

- ○ 1.5–2 pounds Pacific halibut steaks (2 large steaks)

**GATHER:**

- ○ 1 tablespoon peanut oil or vegetable oil
- ○ 2 tablespoons minced garlic
- ○ 2 tablespoons fresh ginger, minced or grated
- ○ 1 teaspoon dark sesame oil
- ○ 3 tablespoons soy sauce
- ○ ½ cup low sodium vegetable or chicken stock
- ○ ¼ cup scallions, minced

Heat a large non-stick skillet over medium-high heat for 3 minutes. Add the oil and turn the heat to high.

Add the fish to the pan and cook for 1.5 to 2 minutes per side.

Turn the heat to medium-low. Sprinkle the garlic and ginger around the perimeter of the fish, then drizzle the sesame oil over it. Add the soy sauce and stock to the skillet and cover.

Cook for 5 minutes and remove the lid. With the fish still in the pan turn heat to high to reduce the liquid by about half (this should only take a minute or two).

Serve the fish over rice with the sauce spooned over it. Garnish with scallions.

# MISO CORNY SOUP

*A slight twist on an Asian classic. Today, miso and tofu can be found in many grocery stores.*

**SERVES:** 6–8

**RATING:** *Homo sapiens*

**ESTIMATED PREP AND COOK TIME:** 50 minutes—
10 minutes to prep, 40 minutes to cook

**NEED FIRE?** Yes, stove top

**GATHER:**

- ○ 4 shallots, minced
- ○ 2-inch piece fresh ginger, peeled and sliced
- ○ 2 tablespoons vegetable oil
- ○ 2 tablespoons all-purpose flour
- ○ 1 quart chicken stock
- ○ 4 cups water
- ○ ¼ cup miso paste
- ○ 3 tablespoons soy sauce
- ○ Sugar (granulated), to taste (about 1 tablespoon)
- ○ 1 teaspoon dark sesame oil
- ○ Dash chili flakes
- ○ 5 ounces frozen corn kernels
- ○ 1 package firm tofu
- ○ ½ cup frozen peas
- ○ Salt and white pepper to taste

In a large saucepan, sauté shallots and ginger in the oil.

Stir in flour and cook while stirring for 2 to 3 minutes.

Whisk in stock and water.

Add miso paste, soy sauce, sugar, sesame oil, and chili flakes.

Bring to a simmer and cook 20 minutes. Add corn and tofu and cook 10 minutes longer. Add frozen peas and cook until they're warmed through.

Season to taste with salt and white pepper.

## STEAMED ASPARAGUS WITH ROASTED RED PEPPER VINAIGRETTE DRESSING

**SERVES:** 4

**RATING:** Knuckledragger

**ESTIMATED PREP AND COOK TIME:** 10 minutes

**NEED FIRE?** Yes, stove top (or microwave steamer)

**GATHER:**

- ○ 1.5 pounds asparagus
- ○ ¼ cup jarred roasted red peppers
- ○ 1 tablespoon red wine vinegar
- ○ 2 medium garlic cloves, pressed through a garlic press
- ○ 6 tablespoons extra virgin olive oil
- ○ Salt and black pepper, to taste

Steam the asparagus until it bends slightly in the hand.

Blend the peppers, vinegar, garlic and olive oil in a food processor or blender for the dressing.

Scrape the dressing into a small bowl and add salt and pepper.

Arrange the steamed asparagus on a platter and drizzle with the dressing. Can be served warm or at room temperature.

## ULTRA-MODERN MEALS WITH A PRIMITIVE TWIST

Half a million years ago, before mankind tamed fire, hominids ate mostly raw vegetation and wild game. This involved constant foraging and endless chewing, which may explain the densely muscled jaws sported by our prehistoric ancestors.

Once humans learned to cook, everything changed. The heat in cooking breaks down the fibrous collagen in meat and the stringy fibers in plants, making chewing easier. Cooking with fire gave us the means to consume way more calories in far less time. Eventually, according to anthropologists, this led to greater brain activity and larger brains, better health, smaller teeth and jaws, and a more upright gait.

There's a good reason some of the methods pioneered by early humans have endured even today: They are not only practical but produce fabulously tasty meals! About 300,000 years ago, our ancestors developed the capacity to cook tough meats and vegetables in liquid, a practice called braising. Also in this era of culinary enlightenment, people began to cook what they hunted and gathered over open flame. Eventually they began fashioning earthenware pots to hold the stuff they wanted to cook over fire. The recipes that follow allow a caveman to get back to his culinary roots in style.

## BEER BRAISED PORK LOIN

*Few cooking techniques capture the flavors of a nice piece of meat as well as braising. The braising process usually begins by searing the food to create a flavorful crust on the meat. Then liquid is added and the dish is covered and cooked "low and slow"—at a low temperature, for a long period of time.*

*When done with the proper liquids (stocks, beer or wine) and the right aromatics (root vegetables and herbs), braising carries more flavor than boiling or stewing and doesn't dry out or burn food the way roasting can.*

............................................................

**Healthy Habits for Her to Drop Pregnancy Poundage**

The package has dropped. A few days later, the new mom looks in the mirror, sees a still-protruding abdomen and wonders why she still looks pregnant.

Bite your tongue, caveman. This isn't the best time to come up with a clever comment about mom's figure. The weight will come off, but it will take time. A weightloss rate of 1 to 2 lbs. per week is healthy for most new moms; rapid weight loss can leave her malnourished and fatigued. To stay healthy, lose weight, and feel good, she can:

**Breastfeed.** It burns up to 500 calories per day, similar to running for an hour!

**Eat often**—five or six small, healthy meals per day rather than three larger ones.

**Drink plenty of fluids.** Breastfeeding requires women to consume about 32 extra ounces of fluid each day. Dehydration can lead to poor digestion, headaches, fatigue, and an inability to lose weight efficiently.

**Resume an exercise routine** once her doctor approves. Recent studies show there's no substance to claims that exercise by a breastfeeding mom infuses her milk with extra lactic acid, causing babies to consume less.

**Sleep as much as possible.** Some recent studies correlate mom's weight loss with adequate sleep.

**RATING:** Neanderthal

**NEED FIRE?** Yes, conventional or Dutch oven

**HUNT:**

○ 1 pork loin roast (about 5 pounds)

**GATHER:**

○ 3 cups chopped onion

○ 5 carrots, diced

○ 12 ounces dark beer

○ 2 teaspoons salt

○ ¼ teaspoon pepper

○ 1 bay leaf

○ 4 whole cloves

○ Kosher salt and freshly ground pepper, as needed

Brown the pork loin (which you have seasoned generously with salt and pepper) on both sides by roasting it in hot oil in a large Dutch oven or roasting pan, about 10 minutes. Drain all but 3 tablespoons of cooking liquid from the pan.

Sauté onions and add carrots until they are softened; stir in beer, salt, pepper, bay leaf, and whole cloves. Return pork to pan or Dutch oven and cover tightly with lid or aluminum foil.

Bake at 350°F for 2 hours or until pork is tender. Place pork loin on a serving platter and cover with foil to keep it warm.

Pour cooking liquid (the 3 tablespoons you reserved earlier) from pan into a large bowl; skim off fat and remove bay leaf.

Place cooking liquid with vegetables into a blender; cover and process at low speed until smooth.

Pour processed beer sauce into a saucepan. Bring to a boil, stirring often. Spoon sauce over sliced pork to serve.

# TANDOORI CHICKEN

*This dish originated in India, where it is traditionally cooked in a type of oven called a tandoor, then served with rice and/or naan (a recipe for which follows). Here it is adapted for preparation on your favorite flame source, the BBQ grill. The chicken is marinated in a yogurt seasoned with a variety of ingredients. Turmeric gives the final product a yellow-orange color.*

**SERVES:** 4

**RATING:** *Homo habilis*

**ESTIMATED PREP AND COOK TIME:** 10 minutes prep; 2–5 hours to marinate; 20 minutes cooking time.

**NEED FIRE?** Yes, from a BBQ grill

**HUNT:**

- ○ 1.5 pounds boneless chicken breasts and/or thighs

**GATHER:**

- ○ ½ cup plain yogurt
- ○ 1 tablespoon vegetable oil
- ○ 2 tablespoons lemon juice
- ○ 2 cloves of garlic, minced
- ○ 1-inch piece of fresh ginger, minced
- ○ 1 teaspoon ground cumin
- ○ 1 teaspoon red chili powder
- ○ 1 teaspoon paprika
- ○ 1 teaspoon salt
- ○ ½ teaspoon turmeric
- ○ ½ teaspoon ground cardamom

Mix together yogurt, oil, lemon juice, garlic, ginger and spices.

Make diagonal slashes in the chicken meat to allow marinade to penetrate better. Pour yogurt mixture over chicken.

Put chicken in plastic Ziploc-type bag and marinate it for at least 3 hours in the fridge.

Preheat grill and brush the grilling surface with a little cooking oil to keep chicken from sticking.

Grill chicken until cooked through (to an internal temperature of 170°F), turning once at estimated midway point.

Serve hot with basmati rice or naan (see below).

## NAAN

*This Indian flatbread is similar to Middle Eastern pita bread. It's traditionally cooked in a tandoor oven. Making this delicious bread appeals to a caveman's sporting nature, for it requires kneading, twisting, and punching the dough, then hurling it onto an open flame source—in this case your own barbecue grill. If you do happen to have access to a tandoor, feel free to use it.*

**RATING:** *Homo sapiens*

**ESTIMATED PREP AND COOK TIME:** 90 minutes total, including 70 minutes prep and rising time; 20 minutes attending the grill.

**NEED FIRE?** Yes, from a BBQ grill

**GATHER:**

- ○ 1 package active dry yeast (0.25 oz. package)
- ○ 1 cup warm water
- ○ ¼ cup white sugar
- ○ 3 tablespoons milk
- ○ 1 egg, beaten

- ○ 2 teaspoons salt
- ○ 4 ½ cups bread flour
- ○ 2 teaspoons minced garlic (optional)
- ○ ¼ cup butter, melted butter

In a large bowl, dissolve yeast in warm water. Let stand about 10 minutes, until frothy. Stir in sugar, milk, egg, salt, and enough flour to make a soft dough. Knead for 6 to 8 minutes on a lightly floured surface, or until smooth. Place dough in a well-oiled bowl, cover with a damp cloth and set aside to rise. Let rise for about 1 hour, until the dough has doubled in size.

Punch down dough and knead in garlic. Pinch off small handfuls of dough about the size of a golf ball. Roll dough pieces into balls, then place balls on a tray. Cover balls with a towel and allow them to rise until doubled in size, about 30 minutes.

During the second rising, preheat grill to high heat.

At grill side, roll one ball of dough out into a thin, flat circle, approximately ⅜-inch thick. Lightly oil the grill. Place dough circle on grill and cook for 2 to 3 minutes on one side, until puffy and lightly browned. Brush uncooked side with butter, and turn over. Brush cooked side with butter and cook another 2 to 4 minutes, so both sides are now lightly browned. Remove from grill and continue the process for remaining pieces of dough.

## The Legend of the Ghost Chili

Natives of the hilly Changpool region in northeastern India call it the "bhut jolokia"—the ghost chili. And for good reason, because it's downright scary how hot this pepper is—so spicy, in fact, that the *Guinness Book of World Records* has declared it "the hottest of all spices."

Just how hot is this thumb-sized chili? A bit of classic Tabasco sauce measures 2,500 to 5,000 Scoville units, while typical habanero peppers may score in the 150,000 to 300,000 range. The heat factor for the ghost chili: 1,001,304 Scoville units, almost twice that of the next-hottest pepper ever measured. Even a morsel of the bhut jolokia is enough to make a sauce so hot it's virtually inedible. It's probably a good thing for timid-tongued Westerners that specimens of this legendary pepper aren't yet available outside its native land.

# CHAPTER 4

# SHELTER, SAFETY & PROTECTION

GIVING A DEFENSELESS BABY THE MEANS TO SURVIVE OUTSIDE THE WOMB

TODAY, THE TURQUOISE WATERS OF THE MEDITERRANEAN Sea, its palm-lined pebble beaches, and the famous Côte d'Azur nightlife are just a few of the reasons people flock to the idyllic seaside town of Nice in the south of France. Here on the French Riviera, troglodytes from around the world can be observed attempting to blend into the resort environment in a variety of ways, be it sunning their hides on the beach in French-cut bathing suits, admiring the masterpieces hanging in Le Musée Matisse de Nice, or shambling down the promenade at sunset with their female companions.

Males of their ilk have been drawn to Nice since prehistoric times. It is even said the town itself was named by one of our Cro-Magnon ancestors who, upon surveying the area and its shimmering bay for the first time following a long journey southward on foot from his rock shelter near Les Eyzies, exclaimed, "Nice!"

While it is impossible to prove the verity of that account, thanks to such modern fossil-dating technologies as thermoluminescence and electronic spin resonance, we do know for certain that people have come to the site that is now Nice for at least the last 400,000 years. In fact, a place called Terra Amata, perched high above the Mediterranean Sea overlooking the Bay of Nice, houses the archeological remains of a site believed to have been used by early nomadic *Homo sapiens*, including the first evidence of human-constructed shelters. This was beachfront property at the time. And the huts built there were made from saplings, stones, and perhaps animal hides. There is also evidence of a fire ring, charcoal, animal bones and stone tools (though visitors would be hard-pressed to find signs of the settlement today; reportedly, it is buried beneath the foundation of an apartment building).

It took time and considerable head-scratching, but eventually our ever-resourceful ancestors figured out a few things: one, that they could raise plants and animals for sustenance; two, that with their newfound agricultural savvy, they could sustain themselves

## Grow with Gronk

What the caveman stands to gain from reading Chapter 4:

- An appreciation for his role as his little one's provider and protector—and his fallibility in that role

- A working knowledge of the babyproofing process, indoors and out

- The power to identify environmental risks that could endanger a baby's health

- An understanding of vehicle safety protocol as it applies to a baby

- The know-how to bring harmony to a household with pets and babies

- A working knowledge of key baby-related gear and how to assemble it

- The skill to set up a nursery that's just right for a baby

- The smarts to evaluate childcare options and assemble a strong childcare team

- An appreciation for his right to be a stay-at-home dad, and the doors it can open for him

- The skills to survive a weekend of solo parenting minus Mommy without leading a nomadic hunter-gatherer existence. Having squatters' rights to a choice camp spot on the Bay of Nice for part of the year, was, well, *nice*, but the constant quest for edible foliage, nuts, berries, and animal flesh was tiring. As the icy Paleolithic period yielded to the Mesolithic climatic thaw and then to the agricultural revolution of the balmier Neolithic period, it gradually dawned on these enlightened farmers that they could settle into permanent communities and homes. No longer would they need to roll up their hides, dismantle their huts, collect their goats, and head for more fertile hunting and gathering territory when the spot on which they had been squatting could no longer supply their subsistence needs. This was, after all, the "New" Stone Age. Now they could build structures that had some degree of permanence to meet their basic need for shelter.

Once the architectural light bulb was illuminated, the possibilities were endless. Mankind began building villages of clustered huts made from materials such as stone, wood, the bones of large animals like wooly mammoths, even bricks made of mud—domiciles that ultimately had more staying power than many of the dwellings we rely upon for shelter here in the 21st century. Archeological excavation of Neolithic home sites has yielded a wealth of insight into the lifestyles these people led after liberating themselves from the nomadic, hand-to-mouth, I'll-build-me-a-lean-to-if-I-can't-find-a-cave existence. They raised livestock, they grew and harvested crops, they staked claim to property, and they coupled. Evidence even suggests that some Stone-age males were polygamists, with the husband living in one house and his wives and children inhabiting other surrounding structures.

While this Neolithic idea of a nuclear family survives only in isolated pockets of the world (such as in the Four Corners region of the U.S., as depicted in the "Big Love" series on cable TV), the need for parents to furnish shelter for their little ones is as strong today as it was in the Fertile Crescent in 7,000 B.C. One of your most important responsibilities as a new parent is to provide the proverbial roof over your baby's head—preferably one free of bats, stalactites, persistent leaks, and other potential hazards. From the indoor living space, nursery, and yard to the automobile and all the toys and baby gear with which your youngster is apt to come into contact during the first year of life, the goal is to furnish the little one with an environment that is safe and secure but not sterile, one that encourages healthy indoor and outdoor interaction and exploration without exposure to unusual peril.

This chapter explores the challenges, as well as the creative opportunities, that come with fulfilling a child's basic need for shelter, safety and protection. In it, you will discover the means to shield your offspring from disease, predators, environmental dangers and other hazards both anticipated and unforeseen. You will also learn how to sniff out trouble before your baby encounters it and to handle it quickly and decisively when it does arise. For much of these first 12 months, you and your partner will be your baby's first line of defense in a world in which he or she arrives as a largely helpless little critter. Besides your own impressive physical attributes—19-inch neck, sleeve-busting guns, body fat percentage in the high 30s—the arsenal to which you have access as a defender of the caveling is considerable:

Even with all this weaponry at your disposal, do not expect to be infallible as a protector. There will be chinks in your parental armor. Your child will occasionally contract an illness, sustain bumps and bruises, ingest non-food items, and otherwise endanger his or her physical well-being through various means, some so absurd and farfetched you could never have anticipated them. For the most part, these incidents are like a ding on a new car; they will happen, they make you cringe when they do, but they usually don't cause any real damage.

## PREPARING YOUR LAIR

Babyproofing—turning a home into a safe environment for a tiny human who eventually will grow into a highly curious and ambitious, if not initially capable, crawler, walker, and climber—wasn't an especially common practice in a Cro-Magnon household where one was apt to come across animal droppings, open fires, hunting weaponry, and various organisms that thrive in a dark, dank environment. Lifespans were too short and predators too close at hand back in those days to worry about such trifling threats.

Assuming most of those potential hazards are absent from the modern-day household, new dads here in the 21st century have an inherent edge over their troglodyte ancestors in the babyproofing department. In all likelihood, you will not have to account for the possibility of a hungry saber-toothed tiger crashing into your cave.

- **Common sense**—hear the smoke alarm, hustle to get baby, woman, and you out of the home. Saving your "mature" magazine collection is secondary.

- **Keen instincts**—"something tells me I shouldn't let the little one approach that snarling pit bull."

- **Anticipation**—now that baby can crawl, time to barricade the stairwell with babyproof gates.

- **Cat-quick reflexes**—blocking a baby boy's urine stream in mid-flight requires lightning-fast reactions.

- **A cool demeanor under pressure**—baby projectile-vomits in a restaurant, dad catches most of it in his mitts then calmly asks the server for his bill.

- **Healthy habits**—good hygiene (regular bathing, hand-washing, etc.) keeps bacteria and germs at bay; good nutrition and sleep habits equip baby to grow stronger and fend off illness.

- **Safety tools**—smoke alarms (at least one on each level of a home), fire extinguisher(s), baby gate(s); babyproof cabinet and drawer latches, electric plug covers, etc.

The safety measures you take when your caveling is still an immobile mini-manatee will go a long way toward protecting the little one from harm—and you from charges of reckless endangerment.

**Indoors.** Watching your child endure pain is one of the most excruciating but inescapable realities of parenthood. As a parent, you will likely witness many agonizing moments as the caveling begins gaining mobility and investigating the eye-opening possibilities that self-propulsion offers.

It's normal for babies to take their lumps as they seek to familiarize themselves with their own personal space, their surroundings and the workings of their appendages. They have a hard enough time staying in one piece without facing any additional hazards in a home that hasn't been adequately fortified for the onslaught of an ever-curious, highly motivated, and increasingly capable small one. And because babies don't belong to a union, they expect you, the household Norma Rae (or James Hoffa, Jr.), to fight for their right to safe living conditions.

Babyproofing a home is all about anticipation. What potentially harmful household items might a resourceful little human gain access to by crawling, walking, climbing or simply by opening a drawer or cabinet? Things like medicines, household cleaners, small items that present a potential choking hazard, and your tomahawk collection need to be safely stowed out of reach, behind childproof doors. Once mobile, babies have a unique homing mechanism that empowers them to zero in on things you'd prefer they not handle for their own safety and/or the safety of the item. The secret to successful babyproofing: keep those items out of the "hot zone," the area encompassing anything within range of the child. Range in this case tends to expand as the baby gets older, bigger, braver, stronger, more coordinated and thus more capable of climbing and balancing, qualities some of us have been fortunate enough to inherit from the primates.

Now is the time to take preventive steps by:

- locking away any weaponry in the house, including your prized decorative nunchucks

- finding safe places for items such as pots, planters, picture frames, and vases that, if tipped over, could be a danger to a helpless newborn; anything tippy is a health menace

- setting aside valuables and breakables that might be in reach once the little one becomes upright

- stowing away anything with poisonous or potentially hazardous ingredients, including household cleaning supplies, meds, and magic brownies

- shoring up kitchen drawers and cabinets with babyproof latches, perhaps leaving accessible one or two containing non-threatening pots and pans so the baby can make some noise

- outfitting toilets and the oven/stove with childproof mechanisms, keeping in mind they must not be so complicated they prevent cavemen from gaining access to these very necessary pieces of equipment

- plugging electric outlets with babyproof covers

- safely hiding dangling electrical cords and other items that could trip a fledgling walker or a parent holding a baby (people not holding babies don't matter)

- having your home tested for the presence of such potentially harmful substances as radon, asbestos, lead paint, and dirty bombs

- covering or reupholstering any furniture you would prefer not to have soiled by spilled beverage, vomit, sticky little hands or smeared food.

**Outdoors.** Your days of purposely setting billowing yard fires, hosting lawn dart tournaments, and indiscriminate chain-sawing of the hedgerow at all hours of the day and night are over. If your home has a yard, it also should be hazard-proofed. That means:

- safely storing items with potentially harmful ingredients—paints, primers, stains, strippers (not that kind), antifreeze, motor oil, etc.; rule of thumb: keep anything emblazoned with a skull and crossbones *way* out of reach

- stowing away power tools, lawn equipment, and whatever other sharp or blunt implements you tended to leave around before baby came along

- covering the hot tub with a childproof cover

- mending holes in fences to head off potential escape routes for the stealth crawler/walker

- ensuring gates and other potential exits are childproof

- temporarily deactivating hearths, kilns, chimineas, and the pit you use to smoke pigs.

# DR. BRIAN

*Troglodyte
Environmental
Troubleshooter*

Is thunder a meteorological phenomenon or the sound of the gods expressing anger toward their earthly minions? Are the ceramic gargoyles in your garden truly inanimate objects or have they been leering at you maliciously and tracking your movements across the backyard? The most effective baby-proofers are those who can separate real threat from imagined—and who have the imagination to recognize that even something colorless, odorless or microscopic can threaten the health of a human being.

Threat assessment is a key part of the baby-proofing process. In prepping your home for a little lad or lass, the ability to identify and address true health hazards, and to avoid getting worked up about things that in reality pose no hazard, will serve you well.

## Warranting Immediate Action

**Asbestos:** It is unhealthy to breathe in the minute particles of this evil material, which back in the day could be found in a wide variety of household, commercial, and industrial materials, from roof shingles and insulation to floor tiles and ductwork. If your abode was built only recently, there's probably no reason for concern. But if you have an older domicile, have it tested for asbestos, because prolonged exposure to particles of the stuff has been linked to cancer and lung disease. If asbestos is detected, **do not** try to deal with it yourself. For the good of your family's lives and lungs, get a trained, certified asbestos abatement expert to take care of it. For more info about how to identify asbestos and when to remove it, visit the U.S. Environmental Protection Agency's asbestos web page at www.epa.gov/oppt/asbestos.

**Combustion gases:** As primitive man discovered, where there is fire there is smoke. Nowadays, common household appliances and items that use combustion, including fireplaces, portable kerosene heaters, and stoves, also may produce exhaust containing gases such as carbon monoxide, oxides of nitrogen, and sulfur dioxide. Exposure to these gases can cause flu-like symptoms, respiratory illness, and, in extremely rare instances, even death. So, a few rules of thumb apply: Never use unvented combustion appliances indoors. Use an exhaust hood over a gas stove. Have chimneys and furnaces cleaned annually. Consider putting a portable gas detection device (similar to a smoke detector) in your home, near any appliances that could potentially emit harmful gases (your own buttocks excluded). See to it that utilities such as the furnace and water heater are properly vented.

**Lead paint:** The world would be a less contaminated place if we'd only stuck to the largely harmless media used by Cro-Magnon cavepainters. Instead, mankind began putting lead in paint and lots of other stuff before it finally dawned on us that this was a highly toxic material. Indeed, according to the EPA, lead may have a range of undesirable health effects, from behavioral problems and learning disabilities to seizures and death. Kids six and under are most susceptible to it because their bodies are growing quickly. As with asbestos, older homes are likelier than new ones to have a problem, such as peeling lead-based paint. If you suspect the presence of lead in your home, you may want to get it and the kid(s) tested (after conferring with your pediatrician or family doc, of course). Levels of lead in the blood tend to increase sharply in babies 6 to 12 months of age, and tend to peak at 18 to 24 months of age, according to the EPA. If lead is present in a child, it can be detected with a simple blood test. Meanwhile, in-home tests can determine whether any potentially harmful sources of lead, including paint, are present. Again, it's wise to leave testing and removal to qualified professionals. For more info, visit www.epa.gov/oppt/lead/, call the National Lead Information Center at 1-800-424-LEAD or visit the NLIC site at www.epa.gov/lead/pubs/nlic.htm.

**Radon:** Like your own emissions, this odorless invisible gas is silent but potentially deadly. Exposure to it increases the risk of lung cancer, especially for smokers. Tests for the presence of radon are inexpensive, so you have no excuse not to administer one in your home. Call the

National Radon Hotline at 1-800-SOS-RADON or the EPA's Radon Fix-It Program at 1-800-644-6999 for advice on how to deal with the problem.

**Secondhand tobacco smoke:** If you're a smoker and you're reading this, the habit hasn't killed you yet. But eventually, if you keep it up, not only might it send you to a dirt nap, it also could pose a mighty health risk to anyone who regularly comes into contact with the polluting crud you exhale. Long-term exposure to secondhand tobacco smoke increases risks for lung cancer, respiratory infections, and perhaps heart disease. So if you must light up, do so outside where the only one breathing the toxic stuff is you.

## Also Be Wary of:

**Urban smog:** The soot and gases that spew from power plants, cars, buses, trucks, and off-road equipment don't just harm the environment, they can be hazardous to the health of a baby who is regularly exposed to high levels of them. Indeed, research suggests prolonged exposure to certain pollutants in the air can cause or worsen respiratory problems, such as asthma. The air quality in some urban areas can be so poor that on certain days health authorities urge people with respiratory problems to remain indoors.

**The water you drink:** The water supply here in America is among the safest in the world. But in isolated areas, water quality has been an issue. If you're the curious or paranoid sort, call the EPA's Drinking Water Hotline at 1-800-426-4791 or visit www.epa.gov/safewater/dwhealth. html to learn more about the quality of the water you and your family are drinking. The EPA also recommends that people who rely on private wells have their water tested annually for nitrate and bacteria. Depending on location, it also may be worthwhile to test for pesticides, organic chemicals, and the like.

**Mold and other allergens:** Cavedwellers know the pitfalls of living in porous, damp places. Here in the 21st century, absorbent materials that are frequently exposed to moisture may grow molds and other organisms that can cause allergies and illness. Fixing leaks and areas where there are signs of a moisture problem can keep mold away. If fixing the problem is beyond your capabilities, a good first stop for more info is www.epa.gov/mold. If any old caveman can have his own page on My Space, why can't a microorganism have its own EPA web location?

## Don't Sweat About:

**Cell phones and other handheld communications devices:.** Thus far, the only direct threat to human health posed by cell phones is the very real talk-and-drive menace. However, there is no solid evidence linking normal exposure to and usage of these items to health problems. Stay tuned, though. Recent research has found that prolonged exposure to microwaves emitted by some cell phones killed brain cells in laboratory rats. Here's what the U.S. Food and Drug Administration has to say on the matter: "It is generally agreed that further research is needed to determine what effects actually occur and whether they are dangerous to people." If you're curious, visit the FDA's site at www.fda.gov/cellphones/qa.html.

**Microwave ovens:** The FDA assures us that microwave energy will not leak from a microwave oven that is in good condition. That's a good thing, because exposure to a high level of microwave radiation can cook body tissue. As the FDA acknowledges, "Less is known about what happens to people exposed to low levels of microwaves." Just to be safe, the agency requires manufacturers to certify that their microwave oven products meet a strict radiation safety standard. However, beware damaged microwave ovens, which may present a risk of microwave energy leaks.

**High-voltage power lines:** Most likely it's a severe case of bedhead, not proximity to powerlines, that is causing your baby's hair to stand on end. Again, there is no medical evidence to suggest that living near power lines causes health problems. Extensive study of the issue found no link between the two.

**Computer monitors:** Allowing a baby to stare into a computer screen for hours on end cannot be a healthy thing. But merely having a baby nearby while you stare into the computer screen for hours on end shouldn't pose any threat to the child's health. While most computer monitors do give off x-radiation, the emission levels are so low they're not considered a health threat. Just in case, the FDA holds manufacturers to strict standards for x-ray emissions.

## THE FAMILY CHARIOT

Someday when you are deep into the fourth stage of labor, one of your parental responsibilities might be to teach a teenager to operate a motor vehicle in a safe manner. By that time, your teaching vehicle probably won't be anything like the vehicle Gronk practiced with (a 1982 Renault Le Car that today sits rusting on blocks in his driveway) but could be a hybrid car that plugs into a basic household electric wall outlet to refuel, or one that runs on a hydrogen-fed fuel cell instead of a gasoline-swilling internal-combustion engine.

No sense in losing sleep over the distant inevitability of your offspring operating a motor vehicle when before you is the more immediate (and significantly less terrifying) issue of making your automobile safe for a baby. Here evolution has been working in your favor, for the vehicles of today are equipped with several key safety features that weren't present in the cars we rode in as infants, nor in those in which we took driving lessons as teenagers. The vehicles of yore may have been built like tanks but they offered little in the way of other protective features outside of their lap belts, which work well as bottle openers but not especially well as safety devices compared to what's available today. The vehicles of today not only are better engineered to withstand the impact of a crash, they come with features such as airbags, full seatbelts, and a system called LATCH (Lower Anchors and Tethers for Children) designed specifically to make it easier for the digitally challenged to properly install a child safety seat.

Your dog might appreciate the freedom to roam the backseat and hang its head out the window to catch bugs at high speeds (no loose animals in the auto with a baby onboard, remember), but the rules are different for human passengers, particularly the littlest ones. The law requires that a child *always* be properly restrained when riding in a motor vehicle. Here, it makes sense to be a law-abiding citizen, for motor vehicle crashes are the single largest cause of child fatalities in the U.S., killing more than 1,800 youngsters age 14 and under each year and injuring another 280,000.

Babies are especially vulnerable in auto accidents because they have heads that are disproportionately large, rib cages that cannot adequately protect their internal organs, and bones, ligaments, and muscles that haven't fully developed. Even babies blessed with

an unusually large brow ridge are still susceptible to injury in a vehicle, especially if they are not properly restrained. That's why they need specially designed child safety seats in which they will ride facing backwards for at least the first year of life. These days, the American Academy of Pediatrics recommends that children ride in rear-facing child safety seats as long as possible—and at least until they are 12 months old *and* weigh 20 pounds or more, at which point they can ride in a carseat facing front. Keeping a baby pointing backwards until at least age 1 makes your tiny passenger less susceptible to a major spinal cord injury.

Here, courtesy of the National Highway Traffic Safety Administration, are passenger safety tips to help you protect your most precious cargo:

1. Infants should ride in rear-facing child safety seats in the backseat until at least age 1 and at least 20 pounds.

2. If under age 1, but more than 20 pounds, infants should ride in a child safety seat approved for heavier babies and remain rear-facing until at least age 1. Best practice states that children should ride rear-facing until they reach the upper weight or height limits of the safety seat.

3. Never place a rear-facing infant seat in front of a passenger air bag.

4. Once children outgrow their rear-facing child safety seats (typically over age 1 and heavier than 20 pounds), they should ride in a forward-facing child safety seat until they reach the upper weight (usually 40 pounds) or height limits of the seat.

5. Once children outgrow forward-facing child safety seats, they should ride in the backseat in booster seats until they are at

## Cast Your Own
## Safety Net

Here are a few websites to find additional info on carseats and their manufacturers, installation and safety tips, product recalls, crash test ratings, and other general issues related to passenger safety:

- American Academy of Pediatrics, www.aap.org/family/carseatguide.htm

- Automotive Coalition for Traffic Safety, www.actsinc.org

- Car-safety.org, www.car-safety.org

- Center for Auto Safety, www.autosafety.org

- Insurance Industry for Highway Safety, www.iihs.org

- National Highway Traffic Safety Administration, www.nhtsa.gov

- NHTSA car safety site, www.safercar.gov

- Seatcheck.org, www.seatcheck.org

least 8 years old, unless they are 4 feet 9 inches tall, at which point they should fit properly in a seat belt.

6. After outgrowing a booster seat, children under age 13 should always use a seat belt and ride in the backseat. Remember, kids of all ages are safest when properly restrained in the backseat.

7. Old/used child safety seats should not be used unless you are certain they have never been in a crash and you have all the parts (including instructions). Seats that are six years old or older should be discarded and never used.

8. Prior to installation, always read the vehicle owner's manual *and* the instructions that come with the child safety seat.

9. It is important to remember that the "best" child safety seat is the one that correctly fits the child and the vehicle, and is used correctly every time. In other words, the most expensive seat isn't necessarily the most ideal for your situation.

10. Get your child's safety seat checked by an expert. The NHTSA provides a state-by-state listing of car seat installation safety inspection stations online at: www.nhtsa.dot.gov/people/injury/childps/CPSFittingStations/CPSinspection.htm. Or call 1–866-SEAT-CHECK.

The first of September, 2002, has become a holiday of sorts for cavemen who share a tendency to struggle with any installation process more complex than plug-and-play. From that day forward, federal law has required that all cars, minivans, and light trucks manufactured for sale in the U.S. be equipped with the LATCH system. This is a huge blessing for anyone who has sweated and sworn profusely in the backseat of a car trying to properly install a carseat in a pre-LATCH-era vehicle.

The LATCH system provides at least two sets of car seat anchor bars located where the back and seat cushions of the backseat meet. LATCH-equipped car seats are designed to easily attach to these anchors, with little or no finesse required of the installer. The system also includes a top anchor mounted somewhere behind the backseat of the vehicle, to which the carseat's tether strap can be attached. The top anchor typically comes into play once a child is ready for a forward-facing seat.

Thanks to LATCH, there's no longer a need to use vehicle seat belts to anchor a child safety seat, although child safety seats today are designed to accommodate seat belt anchoring in the rear-facing position in vehicles without the LATCH system. Indeed, there's no reason to start shopping for a new vehicle simply because the one you currently drive lacks LATCH. Who are we to discriminate against older autos, coming from families that once relied upon extinct but fondly remembered vehicles such as the Gremlin, the Pacer, the Fiesta, and the Olds Vista Cruiser sta-wag? A carseat might not work in these vehicles (mostly because there are very few surviving specimens of these vehicles) but when one has been properly installed in a more modern vehicle with a contemporary seat belt that's in good working order, it should be just as safe as one properly installed with LATCH.

Where to put the carseat—behind the driver, behind the front passenger or in the center of the backseat? Any position in the rear is safe. However, safety experts say the center is the *safest* position for a carseat as long as it can be installed properly there. Still, many vehicles lack LATCH anchors in the center backseat position. If that's the case, and the carseat anchors work well in the center using the seatbelts, then that may be the safest option, provided the installation conforms to specifications in the vehicle and carseat owner's manuals. Even the old-fashioned lap belt/bottle opener is considered fine for anchoring infant seats.

Most vehicles made since 1989 have factory locations for the installation of a tether anchor, and beginning with the 2000 model year, most have tether anchors installed at the factory. However, unless you have one of the few types of rear-facing seats that call for using the tether, this feature won't come into play until the caveling becomes a forward-facing passenger.

Automobile safety also entails keeping your vehicle stocked with an emergency kit and free from cargo that could present a risk to passengers—items such as loose bowling balls, ski poles, and the like. In the emergency kit, you will need items such as jumper cables, a flashlight, a blanket, flares, matches or a lighter, and a spare tire and jack or tire inflation kit.

## ANIMAL HOUSE

Contemporary cavemen are no strangers to the phrase "raised by wolves," having heard parents, roommates—virtually everyone with whom they have cohabitated—mutter it in condemnation of the overall disgustingness of their personal space and housekeeping habits. But way back in the Upper Paleolithic period, such a phrase would not have been much of an exaggeration, as children from that era apparently were raised *with* wolves.

In fact, soon after humans domesticated themselves, they began opening their homes to four-legged companions. As far back as 15,000 to 20,000 years ago, evidence suggests early *Homo sapiens* were beginning to share their stony abodes with canines—both wolves and dogs. With parents often out of the cave on hunting and gathering errands, perhaps the concept of human babies being raised by wolves wasn't so far-fetched. In later prehistoric cultures, such as those of ancient Egypt, Greece, and Rome, people kept dogs (*canis lupus familiaris*—thanks again, Linnaeus) and felines (*felis silvestris catus*) as pets.

From dogs and cats to birds, fish, and rodents, pets are now part of many modern families. And, as such, they, too, must adjust to the presence of a new human in the household. Indeed, as much as your life changes with a baby onboard, an adjustment period is also in store for your pet amid shifting routines and household dynamics. Fluffy or Fido might act a bit confused and stressed out when the animal discovers it has been supplanted in the household pecking order and must conform to new rules.

As creatures of habit, dogs and cats may find their routines disrupted and their home turf invaded with the arrival of a baby. Like you, they may have to cope with less (and more frequently disrupted) sleep, less free time for walks and exercise, and generally less time in which they are the focal point for attention. Had you asked your dog or cat to weigh in on the prospect of adding a baby to the household, you might have heard barks or meows of protest. But in the end, as four-legged animals that don't have much say in whether their human companions opt to have kids of the two-legged variety, they must adapt. And with your help, adapt they can.

Early on, the onus is on your dog to adapt to the little one, with your guidance. But ultimately, establishing harmony in a household with pets and babies is a two-way street. Once your baby begins understanding language, it's time to start teaching the lad or lass some guidelines for interacting with the dog or cat, such as staying away from the animal when it's eating and avoiding pulling, poking, and other forms of rough handling. The goal is to get your baby and your animal to co-exist peacefully, even if your pet isn't clamoring to spend time with the baby in the beginning. Here are some suggestions for preparing and acclimating your pet for the realities of the postpartum era:

- **Start enforcing new rules now.** Well before the baby is born, get your pet into household safety mode. If it's a dog, brush up on obedience skills. Establish off-limits areas—couch, beds, etc.— where the animal shouldn't jump because it might endanger the baby. Quit playing fetch indoors. Relocate the animal's sleeping spot if necessary to accommodate the little one. If you anticipate not having time to walk the dog twice a day once the baby arrives, start the hound on a once-a-day walk schedule.

- **Visit the vet** with your pet to confirm the animal is in good health and its vaccinations are current.

- **Trim your pet's nails** (or have a groomer do so) to prevent scratches.

- **Provide a preview.** Have friends bring their babies to your place for a visit (provided the parents are amenable) so the canine can meet the youngster, under your close supervision of course. Reward the dog for positive interactions with treats and loving attention.

- **Cater to their curiosity.** Let your pet familiarize itself with the baby's nursery, clothes, toys, and baby-related items such as the stroller before the little one arrives home. Cats in particular are likely to be curious about all the new stuff flowing into your home before and after the birth.

- **Redirect the animal's energies** and attentions from behaviors like jumping, nibbling, and roughhousing to pursuits that pose less danger to a baby, such as gnawing a chew toy or fetching a stick.

- **Become a pain in your pet's rear.** Once the baby in your home becomes mobile, your pet becomes susceptible to poking, grabbing, lunging, and other generally unpredictable, meddlesome and infantile behavior. Occasionally subjecting your animal to that kind of treatment (without causing it pain, obviously) might help prepare it for those moments of confrontation—although the best policy is to be vigilant in keeping baby and pet out of harm's way by taking steps to prevent those kinds of interactions before they occur.

- **Offer an olfactory introduction.** After the birth, let your animal take a whiff of the new arrival's blanket or an article of his or her clothing before you bring the youngster home for good. Praise the animal around this new smell. Once home, let your pet investigate the newcomer, showering the animal with praise for positive interactions with the infant.

- **Avoid neglect.** Give your dog or cat a long, loving greeting when you first bring baby home, then try to carve time out of your hectic schedule each day to focus on the pet. Animals who aren't getting adequate attention can become quite a nuisance.

- **Foster camaraderie.** Involve your pet in activities with the child. Take the hound with you on walks with the baby. Let the baby observe as you play with kitty.

- **Don't tolerate bad behavior.** Consult with a pet behavior specialist immediately if your pet shows any sign of aggression toward the baby.

## MATERIAL GUY

By the time your kid actually makes an appearance *ex utero*, chances are you and your woman, driven by that unusual pregnancy phenomenon known as the nesting instinct, will have already accumulated a considerable array of equipment and items, many of which are unfamiliar and a bit intimidating to the uninitiated knuckledragger.

Some of this stuff you and your partner will purchase new or find secondhand, some will land in your laps as hand-me-downs, some will come into your possession as gifts and (once you've felt the pangs of baby gear sticker shock) some you may even make with your own hands, like the mobile that now hangs above Peanut's crib, which Gronk fashioned himself from dried fruit pits, pinecones, and fish bones.

Your cave may be bursting with baby-related equipment. Your job is to see that all of it is properly assembled or installed and generally safe for a small human. That entails reading and following assembly and operating instructions to the best of your ability, asking for help and translation if necessary. Don't yield to the temptation to use glue when the instructions call for screws. Here are some of the core items to which these safety general guidelines apply:

- ☐ **Cradle**

- ☐ **Crib** (permanent)

- ☐ **Crib** (portable, may also function as a playpen)

- ☐ **Diaper changing table**

- ☐ **Used diaper storage container**

- ☐ **Stroller**

- ☐ **Baby jogger**

- ☐ **Baby backpack** and/or chest pack

- ☐ **Carseat** and related mounting equipment

- ☐ **Rocking chair**

- ☐ **Bounce chair**, interactive saucer or other combination exercise/containment instrument

- ☐ **Baby gate**

- ☐ **Breast pump** (more on this intriguing apparatus in Chapter 3, in the must-read section on breastfeeding)

## ROOMINATIONS ON THE NURSERY

If space in his contemporary manmade permanent shelter permits, opportunity knocks for the caveman to unleash his creative animal by designing and decorating a nursery for the new arrival, a room that's safe but comfortable, interactive but not overstimulating, playful but functional. Here is your chance to rediscover the lost art of cavepainting in a modern setting while showing the world you have an eye for interior decoration and a desire to make an early aesthetic impression on your offspring.

A nursery should come with a few basic elements: a relatively noise-free location within the home, preferably out of earshot of the place where you and your buddies convene for *a capella* practice; finished floor, walls, and ceilings (fieldstone probably not a good finishing choice); soft, forgiving floor covering (high-piled, rugrat-swallowing shag carpet not a great idea either); at least one childproof window to the outside world; the means to heat and cool as conditions dictate; and, space for a crib.

Beyond those fundamental requirements, the sky is the limit when it comes to decorating and furnishing your baby's personal space. This is a place where your baby will spend considerable time with you, your woman, and perhaps other caregivers, so make it inviting. A few tips to awaken the home decorator in you:

- **Integrate elements from nature into the design scheme.** Solid primary and secondary colors are fine for walls, curtains, carpeting, and the like, but risqué troglodyte artists aren't shy about exploring less conventional decorative flourishes. Stencils of butterflys, pterodactyls, flowers or other non-threatening creatures are nice features. For a true taste of the exotic, try painting an entire wall of the room in the pattern of an animal pelt, such as a cheetah's, zebra's or cow's. If you're not fully satisfied with the results, you can always repaint.

- **Use light-filtering window dressings.** Bathing the baby's room with direct, blazing sunlight is fine for wakeful times of day, but you want the ability to block out at least some of that light at bedtime.

- **Make the crib comfy.** A well-rested baby usually means a happier baby, which translates into happier parents. Thus, you want a sleeping environment where the baby wants to spend time, but one that also is conducive to long periods of slumber. Here you walk a fine line. On one hand, a baby appreciates having creature comforts, such as a favorite blankie and stuffed animals, in there, plus perhaps a mobile overhead, for these are items whose familiarity can be soothing to a restless or fitful baby. On the other hand, turning the crib into an infant funhouse invites wakefulness when a baby should be catching Zs.

    Safety is also an issue in your selection of cribs. For you modern-day *Homo habilis* (Latin translation: handy man) types, we suggest you resist the temptation to fashion one on your own with barbed wire, plywood, and wooden stakes. You want something durable, functional, and non-hazardous that will both contain and offer comfortable space to a hopefully horizontal child. Look for one you can adjust to fit the changing propor-

# DR. BRIAN

*C'mon Baby,*
*Do the Locomotion*

A newborn horse foal may stand and walk within hours of birth. Thankfully for human babies and parents alike, little humans aren't born with either ability. They may be noisy, active, excretory machines, but at least for their first few months of life they are unable to self-propel. Fortunately, that gives parents time to prepare for the transportation evolution their children will undergo and all the excitement that comes with it. Mother Nature has been kind enough to build time into baby's first year for parents to prepare mentally and physically for the demanding job of life-and-limb-saver. Every bit of progress a child makes along the mobility spectrum presents new challenges for the people entrusted with protecting his or her well-being. As baby moves from the early head raise and limb flail to the twist and roll, then the six-point launch position, the crawl, the supported walk, and finally the first official unassisted walking steps, the parental alert level must rise right in step.

While each baby develops on its own schedule, a typical one might evolve into an upright human according to the following schedule:

**Month 2:** Baby uses his or her own strength to raise the head and upper torso, if only for brief periods.

**Months 3 to 6:** Even this early, particularly precocious youths might exhibit an ability to pull themselves forward on their bellies using their arms.

**Months 7 to 10:** Here's when baby might be able to rise to hands and knees and rock back and forth, willing but still not yet able to crawl.

**Months 9 to 12:** Sometime during this period the youngster likely will learn to overcome inertia and propel forward by crawling.

**Months 9 to 12:** The ability to rise to a vertical standing position, using an item like a table as a prop, should come around this time.

**Months 10 to 16:** Once able to achieve the upright position, it's time for baby to take those first wobbly steps. Have a camera and an icepack ready.

## Taking Leave: Know Your Rights

When it comes to progressive, pro-family parenting policies, we could learn a thing or two from the Brits. Not only is the British government planning to increase the period of *paid* parental leave from six months to a full year effective in 2009, it also intends to allow new moms and dads to divide that leave between them. So if one parent returns to work before the child's first birthday, the other parent can take paid leave for the balance of that first year.

The British policy makes Uncle Sam's family leave rules look positively prehistoric. The Family and Medical Leave Act that became law in the U.S. in 1993 requires employers of 50 or more people to allow employees, male and female, to take up to 12 weeks of unpaid leave for the birth or adoption of a child. Under the law, employers must maintain all benefits at current levels during a person's leave and must guarantee that a person who takes parental leave can return to his or her former position or one that is at least comparable in pay and benefits.

The FMLA does not require an employer to pay a person during leave, although it does allow an employee to use paid vacation and/or sick time for some or all of the FMLA leave period. To be eligible for FMLA leave, a person must have worked for an employer for at least 12 months, logging at least 1,250 hours during that time. If you meet those requirements (and have not exhausted your FMLA leave entitlement for the year), your employer cannot legally deny

tions and physical skills of your baby. See the American Academy of Pediatrics website at www.aap.org/family/inffurn.htm for more info.

- **Rock-a-bye baby.** Few things are as soothing to a small child—or to an accompanying parent—as being gently held and rocked. The rocking chair provides an ideal venue for unwinding a baby prior to sleep with stories and a lullaby from a big, hairy baritone. It's always wise to periodically lubricate the chair so squeaks don't disrupt a baby on the verge of sleep.

- As with a rocking chair and crib or cradle, you also can find a safe, solid, secondhand **changing table** at a yard sale or used furniture shop. Even ones that show signs of wear can be restored with a bit of elbow grease and refinishing prowess. You're looking for a stout table with a washable changing surface (given the prevalence of spray, spatter, smear, and leaks to which it will be exposed), plus plenty of space for storing items such as wipes, diapers, and creams so they are within reach during those instances when you will be restraining a flailing baby with one hand while the other is desperately clutching for something with which to wipe wayward poo.

- Other items to consider adding to the mix: colorful art/wall decorations; glow-in-the-dark stars/celestial bodies; a plant or two; floor pillows and/or a beanbag chair; photos of friends/relatives/pets.

## HOW TO SHARE THE CARE?

Babies are born unable to feed themselves, clean themselves, protect themselves or propel themselves. They should eventually gain autonomy in those areas, but until they do, those responsibilities fall largely on the shoulders of their primary caregivers: you, your woman, and whomever else you might invite into the caveling's close supervisory circle.

Members of the caveling's supervisory team will play a key role in meeting the baby's need for shelter, safety, and protection. So who exactly will be part of the team? Will it just be you and your woman, with occasional help from friends, family or another trusted and capable person? Will one parent be the primary supervising caregiver while the other works to bring home the proverbial salted pork strips? If so, who will the stay-at-home parent be? Will you stick to the traditional mom-stays-home-while-dad-wins-bread formula or do the opposite? If both parents will be working, how to find a skilled and trustworthy parental stand-in? These are just a few of the caregiving questions that confront new parents as they weigh what's best for their little one and themselves for the short term and the long term.

The caregiving challenges parents face seldom have black-and-white solutions. Decisions about who takes care of "the precious" are highly personal and rarely easy or simple. They often involve personal sacrifice. Finances weigh heavily, but so do less quantifiable considerations, such as the needs of the baby and your own values, priorities, goals, and emotional needs. Entrusting the well-being of your baby to a third party, even for a few hours a week, can be heartwrenching for a parent. You and your woman might feel strongly enough about staying home to nurture the baby full-time that you opt to forgo a second household income for the opportunity to be a stay-at-home parent (SAHP). However, many couples might not have that choice. Both might want to continue working, or they might need to do so to make ends meet financially, in which case they may look to enlist the services of:

you leave, as long as you provided the employer at least 30 days advance notice of your intention to take time off.

Some states have their own family leave laws to augment the FMLA, with more liberal, parent-friendly benefits and requirements. To find out more, start with a visit to the U.S. Department of Labor's website at www.dol.gov/esa/whd/fmla/index.htm. It's also worth checking with the labor department in your state.

- an unpaid (but nonetheless greatly appreciated) **volunteer caregiver**, such as one of the baby's grandparents or a trusted friend. If a friend or relative is willing and able to spend significant time caring for your child, this is a route certainly worth considering. To assess their preparedness, have them take the F.A.T., on page 5 in Chapter 1. Take extra measures to maintain the integrity of the F.A.T. when administering the test to mothers-in-law, who have been known to go to any lengths to spend more time with a grandchild.

- a paid **nanny/babysitter** who comes to your home to care for the youngster while you and your woman are working. Look for one who not only can pass the F.A.T. with flying colors, but who comes with strong qualifications and references. Given the amount of time this person could be spending with your offspring, finding a good nanny is a screening process not to be taken lightly.

- an **au pair**, a young foreign person (usually a female) who cares for children in return for room and board and the opportunity to live in a different culture. In the U.S., you can find an au pair

via any one of 12 agencies approved by the State Department. To be eligible, candidates must be in the 18 to 26 age range, have at least 200 hours of professional or practical childcare experience (if they will be caring for a child under two years of age), commit to a full year's stay, and be prepared to provide up to 45 hours of childcare per week. They must have completed their secondary school education, be proficient in spoken English, and come with no criminal record. Some Hugh Hefner-type cavemen may have their own qualifications for (and fantasies about) the kind of au pair they'd like to have around the house, but don't let those delusions get in the way of hiring the most competent person for the job. More info can be found on the State Department website at http://exchanges.state.gov/education/jexchanges/private/aupair.htm.

- a **daycare facility** that is equipped to handle kids less than a year old. In this case you likely will be putting your baby in the hands of a group of caregivers who also will be seeing to the needs of other children. As with nannies and au pairs, don't choose a daycare facility for the caveling without thorough due diligence.

## STAY-AT-HOMEBOY

Even grown men need role models. If as a new father you look to the animal kingdom for yours, you could do a lot worse than the male emu. Dads who model themselves after the world's second-largest bird, *Dromaius novaehollandiae*, could become some of the most progressive papas out there. The most dedicated emu-lators might even seriously consider putting their careers on hold to become stay-at-home dads.

Emus are flightless birds, so little wonder that males in the species are among the most grounded fathers one could find. They take full responsibility for the incubation and care of offspring. In doing so, they make considerable sacrifices. During the 56-day incubation period, for example, a male emu doesn't eat, drink or defecate. All he does is mind the nest, standing watch over some 15 to 25 eggs. When they hatch, the male aggressively protects the chicks, driving female emus away, and attacking anything else that dares approach, including humans. He stays with the chicks and if he encounters a lost chick from another brood, welcomes the wayward little one into his group as long as it is smaller than his own offspring. Then, after about a half-year, the emu young begin to separate from their fathers and the cycle begins anew.

## Alone with the Kid(s)

Enduring the rigors of pregnancy, childbirth, and co-habitation with a caveman has earned your woman a premium-quality hall pass. Sensitive new dads realize this and act accordingly, extending to their women an invitation to take a child-free weekend someplace where they can leave behind their responsibilities, like a spa, the home of an out-of-town friend or the motel down the road.

Surprise! Your woman has pounced on the offer, having apparently determined that she can indeed survive a day or two apart from caveling and caveman. Now the onus is on you to ensure that the two of you can survive her short-term absence. While your woman's willingness to leave is on the surface an implied endorsement by her of your parenting capabilities and survival skills, there is no shame in feeling anxiety and trepidation about the prospect of single parenting, even if it is only for a couple of days. Here are a few tips to get you through the experience with as few calls to Mom (your baby's or your own) and as few visits to the ER as possible:

- embrace the experience as an opportunity to bond one-on-one with the baby. After the weekend, you, not Mommy, might be the first person baby calls for in the morning

- book a few baby-centric social activities, such as a play date or an outing to a zoo or children's museum, petting zoo, etc., with other parents and kids

*(continued on next page)*

*(continued from previous page)*

- incorporate the little one into your own activities—a trip to the grocery store, yardwork, even a visit to a buddy's house to catch a football game. Babies don't belong at such places as casinos, target ranges or NASCAR events, so steer clear of those.

- keep baby active; tiring the little one improves the chance for solid sleep, which in turn will provide you with solid downtime

- find a babysitter to give you a break. You've earned a few hours to yourself, so if you have a trusted babysitter, book some time

- if you don't go the babysitter route, have some friends over after you've put baby to bed; invite the loud guy at your own risk

- if baby has a routine, do your best to stick to it; disrupting it could make for an angst-filled few days

- see that the child and the house are in the same condition when your woman returns as when she left. Not only does this instill confidence in your parenting and housekeeping capabilities, it earns you valuable cred for when the time comes to raise the subject of your annual guys' trip to Las Vegas.

With gender roles shifting, cultural barriers crumbling and traditional views of parenting becoming obsolete, the door has never been more wide open for men to take a more active parental supervisory role. Not only are more fathers becoming active participants in everyday childcare, more also are embracing the role of primary caregiver at least on a temporary basis. And they're doing so without compromising or tarnishing their masculinity. In fact, stay-at-home dads earn extra points from women on the studliness scale for embracing a role from which many men still cower. It may seem like a sacrifice to put one's career on hold in order to stay home with a baby, but many men who have done it say the benefits are immeasurable, far outweighing the drawbacks.

According to recent study findings (published, not coincidentally, by a dad, Dr. Aaron Rochlen from the University of Texas; to his caveman friends he's Doc Rock), the vast majority of stay-at-home dads (SAHDS) were employed prior to taking on their new role. And a large share—about 70 percent—are relatively well-educated, with a bachelor's degree or higher. Overall, the SAHDS surveyed reported average to moderately high levels of life satisfaction and psychological well-being, levels comparable to if not slightly higher than those of non-SAHDS. Further, according to Doc Rock's research, the more progressive-minded and flexible they are about gender roles, the likelier they are to be content with and fulfilled by their stay-at-home duties.

Dads who are intrigued by the possibilities of becoming a SAHD might consider the following potential fringe benefits of the job:

**Perk 1:** A hands-on opportunity to mold a young mind and positively influence the life of a young one virtually from the beginning.

**Perk 2:** The rare up-close chance to watch a baby's mental and physical development, moment-to-moment, day-to-day.

**Perk 3:** The opportunity to set oneself apart from most other male *Homo sapiens*, who lack either the fiber or the means to embrace the SAHD role.

**Perk 4:** The chance to meet new people—SAHMS, fellow SAHDS, and various other caregivers—and gain entrée to circles not typically penetrated by cavemen.

**Perk 5:** The ability to take a detour off the conventional career path and gain perspective on one's priorities in life.

**Perk 6:** The opportunity to leave the rat race behind and see what life is like answering to a baby instead of a boss.

**Perk 7:** Keen insight into a caregiving world largely dominated by females and a greater appreciation of what it takes to walk in shoes historically worn mostly by women.

**Perk 8:** The chance to develop or refine aspects of oneself that have previously been neglected, untapped or dormant, such as nurturing skills, housekeeping techniques, organizational and culinary skills, patience, and singing voice.

## BIG-BOY REALITIES & RESPONSIBILITIES

One of your duties as a new dad is to periodically visit the Parental War Room. This is the strategic command center where you and your woman will consider the "What ifs?"

Abstract thought might not be a caveman's sharpest weapon, but it will serve him well in the War Room when it comes time to envision worst-case scenarios and to put in place the necessary protections and precautionary measures to ensure the well-being of an offspring in case the unthinkable happens and tragedy befalls you and/or your woman.

There are morbid possibilities that you nevertheless must account for as a responsible parent, however remote they may seem. That means looking into:

- a **life insurance policy** that will provide for members of your family should you die. Term life policies tend to be cheaper, but permanent policies (such as whole life or universal life) usually provide more comprehensive coverage. Talk to an insurance agent or financial advisor about what might work best in your situation.

- a **disability insurance policy** to cover you and your family should you or your woman be disabled and unable to work to generate income.

- a **will** specifying in clear, legally airtight terms how your assets will be divided and who will become guardians of your kid(s) should you and your woman die.

Not exactly an uplifting note on which to end a chapter. But rather than dwell on such dark thoughts, let's instead move on to the lighter side of needs fulfillment: baby clothing and fashion—now those are subjects to pique a primitive's curiosity.

# CHAPTER 5

# CLOTHING

GOING WHERE FEW
MEN DARE GO: BEYOND
THE LOINCLOTH, TO
THE FRONTIER OF BABY
FASHION (AND THE REALM
OF WARDROBE WISDOM)

E VEN AFTER REPEATED VIEWINGS OF ALL 80 VINTAGE *Star Trek* episodes, plus each of the subsequent movie sequels, the closet Trekkie has never ceased to be amazed by Captain James Tiberius Kirk and his ability to attract females, human and alien alike. The chiseled physique, the cool demeanor under fire, the vast emotional range, the fierce sense of justice, the phaser skills, and the musical talent (we challenge you to find someone who does a better version of "Lucy in the Sky With Diamonds")—Kirk had the entire package.

Above all, Kirk, played by the alpha troglodyte William Shatner, had the right threads. His outfits were formfitting but not so restrictive they hampered the maneuverability necessary to physically dismantle a rival Klingon when the need arose. They were comfortable and functional enough to keep his body temperature just right, even after beaming down onto the surface of an unfamiliar planet, yet so boldly colorful they could still catch the eye of an amorous alien empress.

Kirk's 23rd-century wardrobe surely helped him score the best otherworldly females (assuming they were all females; who but Kirk knew for certain?). Yet his slacks-and-V-neck ensembles pale in comparison to some of the space-age clothes we and our kids will likely be wearing in the not-too-distant future. Sooner than you might think, in fact, we may be outfitting ourselves and our babies in high-tech, high-comfort garb that today seems pretty far-out but in reality isn't too far from entering the fashion mainstream. Already, some of the world's preeminent clothing visionaries are providing intriguing glimpses into the future of fashion, as well as insight into what a baby's wardrobe might look like later in the 21st century.

At the Smart Clothes and Wearable Technology Research Unit in Wales, they're talking about children's clothing that comes equipped with a global positioning system, certainly a useful technology for parents to locate wayward kids. That's just one example of the wear-

## Grow with Gronk

What the caveman stands to gain from reading Chapter 5:

- Familiarity with basic baby fashion fundamentals

- A perspective on how clothing has evolved and what the future holds for human attire

- The aptitude to avoid subjecting his baby to certain fashion *faux papas*

- The ability to distinguish between natural and synthetic clothing materials

- A working knowledge of the components that comprise an infant wardrobe

- A grasp of the measures parents must take to protect baby's skin from the sun, elements

- An awareness of the distinctions between, and merits of, cloth and disposable diapers

- A clear understanding of sound diapering techniques

- Keen insight into diaper rash: causes, cures, and preventive measures

- The skill to handle every facet of household laundry duty

- An appreciation for one of mankind's greatest inventions: the clothesline

able technology movement, which could soon produce such items as shirts with MP3 players or mobile phones built into their collars, powered by tiny solar cells integrated into the garment.

As you read this, researchers are working feverishly to develop super-strong natural silk that can be factory-manufactured, as well as electric-conducting polymers that can be woven into clothing to sense what's going on with a wearer's body. It won't be long before we also have access to new kinds of disposable garments, including underwear, handkerchiefs, even sportswear. Using advanced textiles, micro-technologies, and new manufacturing techniques, they're also developing "smart" garments that adjust to ambient environmental conditions and the wearer's body temperature, warming or cooling as conditions dictate. Sometime during your baby's lifetime he or she might also be able to buy items that change color according to surroundings. This customizable clothing could be made from conductive fabric that allows consumers to download different patterns or colors to be displayed on the garment as if it were a computer screen.

Here's a biggie for babies and cavemen for whom bodily bouquet is an issue: Soon we are likely to see clothing with micro-encapsulation technology that releases substances such as essential oils or deodorants from its fabric. Also in the offing is clothing that monitors a wearer's health by tracking such indicators as heart rate, blood pressure, and blood sugar. If the garment senses a problem, it sounds an alarm. Tiny sensors embedded in the fabric would allow doctors to monitor patients remotely.

These aren't pie-in-the-sky technologies either. Some experts predict that within 10 years, as much as 20 percent of our garments will come with electronic components in them. The matrix at right offers a look at what's afoot on the clothing cutting edge and what it might bode for babies and adults alike.

This is exciting stuff, particularly for you fashionistas in the crowd. But as a parent entrusted with the task of fulfilling a baby's need for clothing, there's no time to wait around for the next high-tech fashion wave. Your little one will not be permitted to leave the birthing facility naked.

So what to wear? Now you must answer the question not just for yourself but also for your little offspring, who knows nothing of color coordination, fashion *faux pas*, layering or even textiles in general. Nor, for that matter, might some new dads. This chapter

| Technology | Kiddie Application | Adult Application |
|---|---|---|
| **Olfactory-oriented clothing** | Diapers and clothing made of material that masks odors and provides a warning signal to indicate a child is in need of a change | Clothing that emits subtle smells and/or pheromones to say "I'm here, I'm available, get yourself some." |
| **Stretchable garments** | Clothing that accommodates a child's growth spurts, thus limiting costly wardrobe turnover | Clothing that accommodates adult "growth spurts," limiting costly wardrobe upsizing |
| **GPS-equipped garments** | Wardrobe items that track baby's whereabouts, signaling to warn caregiver of potential security breach or danger | It's 10 p.m. Do you know where your spouse is? |
| **Ultra-strong fabrics** | Extra-durable pants to combat wear and tear from crawling | You'll need reinforced pant legs as well, for those moments when parenting brings you to your knees |
| **Disposable clothing** | Why put a freshly laundered outfit on a baby who's been vomiting or having diarrhea when you can use a disposable one? | Every person with whom the caveman has ever cohabitated would have been ecstatic had his wardrobe included disposable socks and underwear |
| **Clothing made from wash-and-go fabric** | Babies burn through outfits because they can't keep clean; not so, however, if stains come off with the wipe of a sponge | Babies don't just soil themselves, they mar the clothing of anyone within reach; this wouldn't be an issue for caregivers wearing quick-wash garb |
| **Garments with sound transmission, motion-sensing capability** | A "Big Brother" baby onesie equipped with a small microphone and/or motion sensor that parents can monitor to detect distress, signs of stirring when baby is in bed | It's midnight. Do you know where your spouse is yet? |
| **Clothing with extra padding** | Babies learning to stand and walk tend to topple as often as a beginning snowboarder; clothing with integrated padding that isn't too bulky would provide much-needed protection | Wearing padded clothing could be like having a built-in bed, ideal for sleep-deprived parents looking to steal a few moments of horizontal shut-eye |
| **Garments with built-in MP3/audio playback capability** | Find a baby onesie you can program to play soothing classical music or lullabies and you have a new sleep and relaxation tool in your arsenal | Now you really can dance to your own drummer |

is written especially for those who want to learn what it takes to clothe a child appropriately for his or her surroundings, without subjecting parent or offspring to ridicule.

Captain Kirk said space is the final frontier. However, the voyage charted in this chapter will take you farther, to the realm of baby clothing—and specifically to the basics of selecting it, coordinating it, getting a child in and out of it, and laundering it. Your mission there is the same as that of the Starship Enterprise: *to explore strange new worlds, to seek out new life and new civilizations, to boldly go where no man has gone before.*

Best wishes for the journey. Live long and prosper.

## DRESSED TO CRAWL: AVOIDING FASHION FAUX PAPAS

An early morning fog hangs over the goat path that passes for a golf course, where at the first tee mills a foursome that includes Gronk and a few of his buddies. They are performing what looks to be a series of awkward, halted movements vaguely resembling calisthenics as they prepare to tee off for their regular weekend golf outing.

While his counterparts limber up using the latest high-tech clubs featuring monstrous composite-carbon clubheads, everything about Gronk's equipment and garb says, "Old school." His weapons of choice are the wooden-shaft clubs he inherited from his granddaddy. No electric cart for Gronk, who prefers to walk the course caddyless, carrying his tattered bag of clubs instead of riding in one of those newfangled electric chariots.

Gronk often plays in plaids, but today he's in flares fashioned from a kelly green synthetic fabric, a la vintage mid-1970s Jack Nicklaus. Beneath the gaping openings of his pant legs peaks a pair of black Converse canvas sneakers. No turf spikes for this guy. The only sign he's living in the 21st century is his Izod shirt, which could suggest that Gronk is at least aware of, if not in tune with, modern golf fashion. The shirt wasn't purchased anytime recently, however. It has had a place in Gronk's closet since the early 1980s, when the fabled alligator shirt was reaching its first fashion zenith. Today, it is frayed and stained in spots, a tad snug in others, but still functional.

Functionality also happens to be a key consideration in meeting a baby's wardrobe needs. Baby clothing must not only be comfort-

It must have been with great longing that people of the Paleolithic period eyed animals like the woolly mammoth, blessed as it was with a thick coat for protection against the cruel Ice Age climate that 20,000 years ago locked much of Northern Europe in permafrost.

Rather than cower from the elements in their caves, however, our ever-adaptive and resourceful ancestors eventually figured out how to cope with the climate by wearing what the mammoths wore. Once able to slaughter animals, they taught themselves how to skin them, tan the hides, and use the leather and furs for clothing.

Then they developed tools like needle and thread, which empowered them to sew. During the Neolithic period mankind invented weaving tools such as the drop spindle and loom, and began to master dyes to color their clothing. Back then, clothing, from headgear to footwear, was meant to be functional and durable but hardly fashionable. We owe much of our understanding of Neolithic garb to Otzi (rhymes with "tootsie") the Iceman whose remains were discovered in 1991 by two hikers in the Tyrolean Alps, a mountain range straddling Austria and Italy. Encased in a glacial tomb at 10,000 feet, Otzi and his outfit were incredibly well preserved, even after more than 4,000 years.

Otzi, all 62 inches of him, was clothed mostly in animal hides. He wore a cap, an upper garment, leggings, a loincloth, a pair of shoes, and a cloak. The cap was made from individually cut pieces of fur sewn together. Attached to it were two pieces of leather that probably served as a chinstrap. Otzi's fur-lined, cape-like upper garment was made from deer hide. His leggings were also made of fur and hide. And since he wore no pants, a leather loincloth provided the necessary genital coverage. It dangled to his knees, so presumably coverage was ample. The shoes worn by the Iceman were made of cowhide held together by leather straps and plant fiber, insulated on the inside with grass. Evidently Otzi understood the value of layering his garments, for he was discovered wearing a knee-length overcoat made of grass.

Clothing for people of Otzi's era was all about protection from the elements. But as mankind advanced into the upper levels of Maslow's Hierarchy of Needs, developing traits such as vanity, modesty, and flamboyance, the garments people wore took on a different meaning. Besides offering functionality, clothing became a means of expression and of hiding body parts that were no longer culturally acceptable to bare publicly.

The recent popularity of mesh clothing, midriff shirts and low-slung, plumber's-crack pants suggests, for better or worse, that we may be returning to our immodest ways. Perhaps it's time to bring back the loincloth, updated for contemporary times with spandex or a fleece lining.

able and durable, it must also provide adequate protection from the elements: heat, cold, wind, sun, moisture. Otzi the Iceman and his contemporaries apparently understood that principle. But if Otzi were alive today, he, like Gronk and many other modern-day new dads who must find their way in the confusing wilderness of baby fashion, might not even consider some of the other factors that go into choosing what's appropriate for a child to wear on a given day. To avoid flagrant fashion violations, here are some simple guidelines to follow:

- **Clothe your baby.** This is the norm in Western cultures such as ours, at least when out in public. At home, nudity's not necessarily a bad thing.

- **Dress baby in clothes made from soft, lightweight, breathable fabrics such as cotton.** Items made of rough-hewn materials or synthetics can wreak havoc on sensitive baby skin. Also be aware that some babies might be allergic to a material, whether it's natural like wool or synthetic like polyester.

- **Be sure the outfit you put on the baby is appropriate for prevailing weather conditions.** Turtleneck at the beach—not advisable; water-resistant outer layer on a damp day—good choice.

- **Use layers.** When a day that started out cool suddenly turns warm, you can peel away layers of the baby's clothing to maintain maximum comfort.

- **Avoid clashing ensembles.** Mixing stripes, plaids, polka dots, paisley, and other patterns in any combination will get you flagged by the fashion police.

- **In extreme conditions, keep baby indoors.** Young bodies don't self-regulate as readily as ours do, making them much more vulnerable to extremes of heat, cold, wind, etc.

- **Limit public PJ displays.** Granted, many clothing items for babies resemble pajamas. But once you learn how to distinguish which is which, you lose your excuse for leaving the little one (and yourself) in PJs all day.

- **If you're going out in the sun, cover as much of the youngster's skin as possible without mummifying the child.** Pristine baby skin is especially susceptible to the sun's harmful rays. If you're taking the tykster outdoors, cover him or her up and apply sunscreen to areas that aren't protected by clothing.

- **Utilize accessories.** No, not bling or other gaudy *accoutrements*, but items like hats, mittens, blankets, and sunglasses that protect baby from overexposure to the elements.

Babies can't explicitly tell you when their extremities are frigid, when they are sweating in their booties or when they're blinded by sunshine. They'll just holler. It's your job to consider those possibilities and act accordingly.

- **Branch out from pinks and blues, the traditional gender hues.** Some parents are bothered when a stranger misidentifies a baby's gender. Others revel in causing that kind of confusion. Consider occasionally equipping your baby with gender-neutral garb that at least keeps people guessing.

- **Choose clothing that accommodates baby's prevailing mode of propulsion.** For crawlers, that means pants with durable knees. For upright types, that means shoes appropriate for beginning walkers.

- **Beware items with too many snaps, clasps, buttons, straps, and the like.** Extended grappling with baby clothing that has too many bells and whistles has been shown to cause stress in fathers of infant children, leading to bloody calluses, premature hair loss, and shorter lifespans.

- **Remember, this is a small human over whom you may exert tremendous influence from a fashion perspective.** By dressing a baby with taste and common sense, a caveman can help his offspring break the fashion-sense curse that has plagued males in his family for generations.

- **Be sure it fits.** A guy with troglodyte tendencies might prefer to dress his child in ill-fitting clothing, thinking sleeves and pant legs that are too short make the youth look bigger. He may apply the same philosophy to his own wardrobe, in fact. However, clothing for babies should be roomy but not so baggy that it's cumbersome or dangerous to the little one. Kids grow fast, so shop for clothing accordingly and brace for continuous wardrobe updates.

- **Explore and experiment.** Cool baby clothes are a great way to revel in a caveling's babyness. Eventually during the fourth stage of labor, there will come a time to pass the fashion torch from one generation to the next, to relinquish clothing selection responsibilities to the actual child. But before your kid begins asserting his or her own fashion sense, pounce on the chance to occasionally put the little one in outfits and colors so ostentatious, so cute, and so babyish that only babies themselves could get away with wearing them. And be sure to take lots of photos.

Mankind took up sewing way back in the Neolithic period, with the help of the needle, thread, spindle, and loom. But it wasn't until more contemporary inventions came along, like the sewing machine and the textile mill, that our fashion vistas really opened wide.

Now, thanks to your little one's need for clothing, you are on the brink of your own personal fashion awakening (not something you care to publicize to your buddies, understandably). One way to feed this newfound curiosity is to spend some spare time reading the tags on the items of clothing hanging in the closets of your home (another pursuit you are better off keeping to yourself). A little closet sleuthing will tell you all you need to know about the innovations occurring on the clothing front, and how they translate into a head-spinning array of choices for attiring a baby and yourself.

The clothing industry is churning out garments made of all sorts of textiles, some produced from natural sources, some from synthetic materials, and others from a blend of both. Of course, there are the old stand-bys like cotton, wool, cashmere, catgut, hemp, alpaca, and spider silk that people have been turning into wearable garments since primitive times. But what to make of some of the space-age materials you're reading about, like polyester, nylon, Lycra, spandex, and fleece? You wonder, what exactly is in this stuff and, just as importantly, is it appropriate for a baby to wear?

Generally speaking, what's best for a baby are lightweight, breathable fabrics that allow enough air in and out for moisture to evaporate, without being so porous they can be easily penetrated by the elements. They should be soft, not abrasive to the skin. Extended contact with them should leave a baby comfortable and rash-free.

With those general guidelines in mind, here's a brief primer on some of the fabrics and materials you're apt to come across as you peruse the labels of a baby's wardrobe.

**Natural materials: Cotton** is king in the realm of baby clothing, with its versatility, softness, washability, and breathability. Items made of all-cotton or a high-cotton blend are best. **Silk** is soft, but may trap more moisture than cotton does. **Hemp** clothing is durable, but typically neither as soft nor as breathable as cotton. **Wool** is a good layering material, best suited to outerwear because it can be rough on the skin. **Furs** are appropriate for troglodytes and socialites but not babies.

**Synthetics:** The revolution began with **polyester** (aka Terylene), the first manmade material to truly cross-over from the laboratory into the world of apparel. Sure, it can be combustible at high temperatures, but it's still the most widely used manufactured fiber in the United States. In woven form, it tends to be more stain- and wrinkle-resistant than cotton but usually not nearly as natural-feeling, which is why in clothing it is often blended with a natural material. Polyester blazed the way for all sorts of other manmade clothing materials to enter the fashion mainstream. Made from chemical compounds very few cavemen can pronounce, (hence their nice, simple street names), this new wave included nylon and acrylics, which made for cheaper clothing that retains its shape well, though often at the expense of softness and comfort. These were followed by materials such as synthetic **fleece**, a popular fabric for outer layers because of its softness and ability to wick moisture and provide warmth. Then along came stretchy, versatile, and resilient **spandex** (aka elastane). Devotees of this material run the gamut from serious athletes, who appreciate its elasticity and other high-performance characteristics, to serious non-athletes, for whom it functions as a casing for transforming themselves into human sausage.

You live in a material world, so here are a few do's and don'ts to help you evaluate and select the right materials with which to clothe a baby:

| Wise Material Choices | Flagrant Fashion Violations |
| --- | --- |
| Items made entirely or mostly of natural material that gets softer with repeated laundering | Clothing whose label indicates it may also be used as a sandpaper substitute |
| Items with large neck openings to accommodate baby's disproportionately large gourd, multiple chins | Items heavy on zippers, chainmail, other metallic features that for a baby may be fun to fiddle with but are potentially hazardous and without identifiable purpose |
| Items with a bottom opening that provides easy access to diaper, baby's plumbing | Items that, upon contact, cause outbreak or other form of skin irritation |
| Garments stretchy or roomy enough to accommodate rapid post-meal expansion of baby's midsection | Garments with tight seams, bulky collars, elastic neckbands, built-in belts, other features that may cut circulation, give baby a sausage-like appearance |
| Clothes made of material stout enough to withstand repeated laundering, scouring | Items too stiff to fold, even after repeated washings |
| Garments whose colors hide or at least obscure stains | Garments that bleed, dyeing baby's skin in odd hues |
| Items that accentuate cherubic features, particularly protruding belly and backside | Any all-white garments; stains have nowhere to hide |
| Cotton undergarment underneath a synthetic layer | Any items requiring dry cleaning |

## WARDROBE 101

Visits to shopping malls and clothing boutiques are necessary rites of passage in your indoctrination into the world of baby fashion. Cavemen who become overwhelmed in a retail setting will do best to try blocking out potential distractions: bright lights, swarming salespeople, and the full-contact in-store maneuvers employed by competing shoppers. Instead, focus on the specific items you are there to purchase and the labels of the individual garments you are considering. Labels not only help you evaluate the composition of various items, they also indicate the age group for which the clothing is appropriate.

Use this sizing information only as a broad guideline, however. Whether an item fits depends on the size and proportions of your baby relative to the norm. Also keep in mind that sizing differs by brand, such that one item sized for a three-to-six-month-old might fit differently from another designed for the same age group. The basic baby wardrobe might include the following items:

- **Sleepwear—PJs, sleepsacks, etc.:** The long hours babies log in the Land of Nod put a premium on wise sleepwear selection. Cotton and cotton blends are the materials of choice. Seasonal conditions also weigh heavily in the selection; sleepwear must keep the little one comfortable whatever the weather. Among the variables to weigh: built-in feet or no; one-piece or two; roomy or snug-fitting. Whatever the case, comfort and safety are overriding considerations. To gauge the appropriateness of your baby's sleepwear, look for indicators such as excessive sweating (could also indicate the caveling is running a fever) and cold, clammy extremities. In chilly climates, parents may opt to add a second layer such as a sleepsack (similar to a sleeping bag, but typically more lightweight, with holes for the baby's arms and head).

- **Blankets:** Because they can slide and migrate around a baby's sleep area with the movements of the little one, potentially hampering breathing, parents may opt not to use blankets as bedding for the first year or two. Still, they serve a critical function as a swaddling tool. Swaddling is akin to assembling an eggroll or burrito, where the baby is the filling and the blanket is the shell. Flannel, knits, terrycloth, and fleece are popular fabrics for swaddling blankets.

- **Base layer—onesies, undershirts, etc.:** The layer closest to baby's skin must offer the most comfort and breathability. Here again, you're probably picking cotton (or a blend with high cotton content).

# DR. BRIAN

## Here Comes the Sun(screen)

Catching a glimpse of himself in the reflection of a placid Paleolithic pond, a Cro-Magnon who was stout enough and fortunate enough to survive to the ripe old age of 40 likely would have seen a weathered man staring back at him, with skin like a deeply tanned hide, pitted and toughened by years of unmitigated exposure to the sun and elements. If a peat bog or a predator didn't swallow him first, exposure-related issues might get him later.

Who knows how much more comfortable the typical cavedweller would have been in the twilight of his life or how much longer he would have lived had he had access to such modern-day protective gear as sunblock and sunglasses. Today these tools are invaluable in shielding babies and big folks alike from potentially harmful ultraviolet rays, exposure to which can cause skin cancer and various forms of permanent skin damage.

Baby skin is a pristine landscape, delicate, sensitive and highly vulnerable to the strong rays of the sun. Because even a wee bit of overexposure to those rays can cause irreparable damage, it is incumbent on you to see that the caveling's skin is protected, either by clothing, shade or sunscreen. A few basic rules of thumb to keep your baby's skin pristine:

- Try to keep baby out of direct sunlight for the first six months, looking for shady places for the baby to roost when outdoors and using props such as an umbrella or stroller sunshade to block direct exposure when no shade is available.

- In the summer, provide skin coverage with lightweight clothing, preferably made of cotton. Whatever the season, equip baby with garments made of tightly woven fabrics, which allow fewer harmful rays to pass through them.

- Augment clothing with sunscreen, preferably the kind made especially for babies. First test the stuff on baby's back to see if there's a skin reaction. If there isn't, use it in light but adequate quantities, applying it at least 30 minutes before you plan to take baby outdoors. Be sure to be thorough in applying it, but avoid areas around the eyes and hands so irritation isn't an issue.

- Periodically reapply the sunscreen, especially if he or she is going to be frolicking in water.

- When shopping for sunscreen, look for stuff that promises "broad-spectrum" protection against both ultraviolet A and ultraviolet B radiation and make sure it has a high SPF—preferably in the 30s or 40s.

- Since babies don't understand the consequences of looking directly at the sun, equip them with baby-appropriate sunglasses that offer protection from UV rays. Sunglasses with straps are especially useful for babies who tend to meddle with eyewear.

- Use a hat that shades baby's face and covers the ears, with a chinstrap for secure fit, if necessary.

- If possible, limit baby's exposure to the sun during the midday hours (10 a.m. to 4 p.m.), when UV rays tend to be strongest.

- Keep in mind, UV rays can cause sunburns on overcast days and when reflected off surfaces such as snow and sand.

- If despite all your efforts your little one somehow gets a sunburn, contact the doc immediately. Keep the toasted one hydrated with fluids, provide relief by periodically bathing the baby in cool water (or applying a cool, damp and very soft cloth to the affected area) and avoid medicated lotions unless the doctor recommends them specifically.

- **Overlayer—pants, shirts, dresses, etc.:** Here is your chance to add color and flair to an ensemble and to branch out into synthetics while still staying in the realm of the practical and functional.

- **Extra layer—sweaters, vests, etc.:** Cardigan or pullover; cotton, wool, yarn, cashmere or synthetic fleece—these are just some of the choices you have for the next layer.

- **Dressy attire:** Special occasions demand special outfits—a Shirley Temple-type number for the young lady, something in the Buster Brown vein for the dapper little master.

- **Outerwear:** Here's one area where synthetics have made a major difference. The type of jacket(s) you provide the young one depends largely on the climate in which you live. Think versatile. Many jackets today provide protection from wind, moisture, and cold. Some come with removable inner linings, others with built-in hoods. Some also offer hems that can be let out to accommodate the wearer's changing bodily proportions.

- **Footwear—socks, booties, shoes, etc.:** Shoes come into play when the tykster begins taking steps. Until then, socks will suffice to start, with slip-on booties for extra warmth, protection, and traction.

- **Accessories—hats, mittens/gloves, etc.:** On sunny days, hats provide much-needed sun protection. On cold days, hats made of cotton, fleece or wool keep heat from escaping through the baby's dome. With baby's still-developing circulatory system, mittens and gloves can be crucial to keeping those hard-to-heat extremities warm.

## THE DIAPER DEBATE

By the time your baby is completely potty-trained, probably sometime in the first several years of labor's fourth stage (with occasional relapses, particularly during the college years), he or she will have gone through enough diapers to fill a small landfill—an estimated 6,000 to 12,000 in fact, assuming a consumption rate of six to 10 diapers per day and 2,000 to 3,000 per year.

One thing is for sure: You and other members of the caregiving team will be up to your elbows in bodily excretions in the years ahead. Diapers are probably your most valuable means for containing them. Whether the diapers you use are of the disposable or reusable variety is a matter of personal preference, based on your weighing of environmental factors, finances, and other practical considerations, such as ease and speed of changing.

There are two main camps in the diaper debate: those who favor disposable types and those who prefer the reusable variety. While disposable diapers are the choice for many modern households, others still prefer the cloth variety. Some choose to use both, as circumstances dictate. Since babies are prolific waste producers, you and your woman best be comfortable with your choice on the matter.

Strong preferences aside, no type of diaper is clearly superior to the other. From both a cost and an ecological standpoint, studies say it's a wash. Each kind has its advantages and its trade-offs. For example, while studies show that disposables tend to be better at keeping babies dryer and maintaining normal skin pH level, their makeup—polyethylene, polypropylene, and other materials that aren't exactly environmentally friendly—is enough to give pause to green-leaning parents. Here's a side-by-side comparison of the two main options:

| | CLOTH | DISPOSABLE |
|---|---|---|
| **PROS** | Softer on skin | Convenient: use and toss |
| | Reusable | More absorbent |
| | Less expensive to purchase | Less leaky |
| | More breathable | Keep baby's skin drier |
| | Now come in a variety of configurations, including form-fitted, pre-folded, pre-shaped, and multilayered, with waterproof covers and adjustable snaps | More acceptable in many daycare situations |
| | Can be doubled up for added absorbency | |
| **CONS** | Leakier | Rougher on baby's skin |
| | Laundering takes time | May cost more to purchase |
| | Laundering uses resources: water, energy, detergent, etc. | Landfill factor: lack of biodegradability |
| | Potentially unwieldy to change | Incidence of infrequent changing makes wearer prone to diaper rash |
| | Users sometimes meet resistance in daycare setting due to hygiene concerns | |

# DR. BRIAN

*Fire Down Below*

Deep in the folds and dark recesses of a baby's lower regions lurk conditions that, if left unaddressed, may give rise to a common and uncomfortable condition called diaper rash. If you've had jock itch, you can imagine what baby is enduring with diaper rash: chafing, burning, itching, and in particularly acute cases, oozing and bleeding.

Most babies will contract a diaper rash at some point during their first year. Skin sensitivity (which has much to do with pH level—the balance of acidity and alkalinity) makes some little ones more prone to diaper rash than others. But what causes diaper rash, how best to deal with it, and how to prevent it?

**Causes:** Rashes often arise because a baby has been marinating in its own waste for too long. Sometimes the culprit is a yeast called *candida albicans*, which makes itself known with a red, raw rash that can quickly spread. Other times the issue might be dietary or have to do with exposure to soaps and other substances that prove inhospitable to a baby's skin.

**Treatment:** When in doubt, ask a doctor. Unless the condition is especially acute, diaper rashes oftentimes can be banished in a matter of several days using homespun and over-the-counter remedies ranging from warm baths to frequent application of diaper creams and/or ointments. Gentle cleaning of the area is best; avoid baby wipes and pat the area dry or let it air-dry. Some yeast-based rashes may call for a special cream prescribed by a doctor. Conditions like large sores, pimples, blisters, bleeding, crustiness, sleeping problems due to extreme discomfort, and spreading of the rash to other areas of the body warrant a call to the doctor.

**Prevention:** Change diapers frequently—preferably immediately after elimination and right after baby awakens from a sleep session. Clean the baby well, but not to the point of scouring. Use gentle soaps. Allow the little one extra naked time to let the ambient air work its magic. If problems persist, try changing to a new brand of disposable diaper or switching from disposable to cloth or vice versa, as the issue may be related to how diapers fit baby's body. Use creams and ointments proactively instead of reactively.

Everything you need to know about changing a baby's diaper you can learn from watching a NASCAR pit crew in action. The goal is to complete the process with speed, precision, and thoroughness in order to send your little motorhead on his or her merry way with minimal disruption.

NASCAR pit crews are composed of seven or eight mechanics, each with his or her own specific responsibility. There's a crew chief, a jack man, front and rear tire men, a fuel man, and a catch can man. During diapering pit stops, however, you are a crew of one who must be capable of performing changes in unfamiliar surroundings, amid tight quarters, in a big hurry, and in some instances, with a squirming, uncooperative, and highly messy subject. You must be prepared at times to perform minus some of the necessary changing tools. And like members of a NASCAR pit crew, you must grow accustomed to working unflinchingly with toxic materials.

A task that seems daunting at first eventually should become second nature. Once you've been through the diapering drill enough, you likely will be able to freshen a baby blindfolded, with one hand tied behind your back, at least until the little one develops greater strength, mobility, and resolve, at which point you may wish a straightjacket was part of your diapering arsenal. That arsenal should include a washable surface on which to lay the caveling (a changing table at home and a plastic or vinyl mat for the road kit, aka the diaper bag), proper-fitting diapers, wipes, creams or other means to treat rashes and irritation, and anti-bacterial hand sanitizer.

NASCAR pit crews know how to handle a blow-out and so should you. For those bowel movements that are so explosive or voluminous they cannot be contained by a diaper, you will need a new outfit to change baby into once clean-up is complete. Blow-outs are bound to occur, sometimes in baldly public situations, so don't leave home without back-up attire.

To handle any one-two punch a baby might throw at you, follow the nine F's of diapering fundamentals:

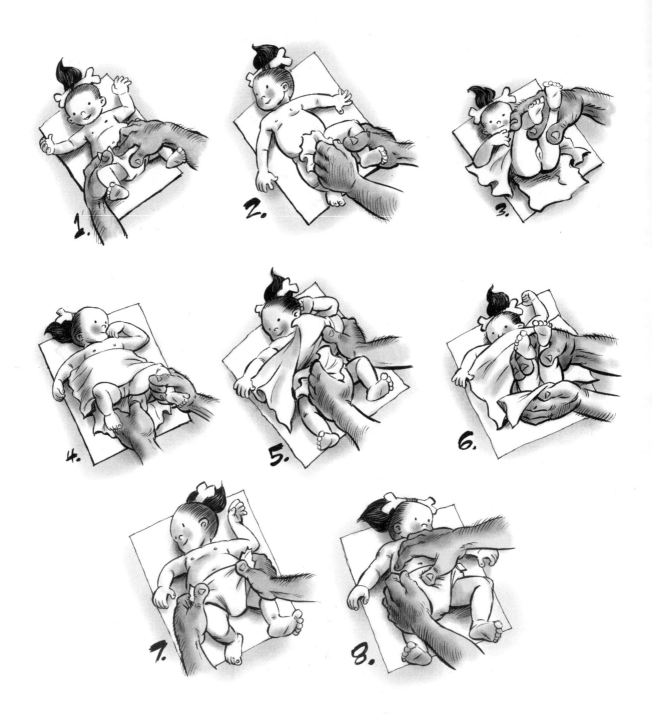

1. Locate a **flat**, relatively level and clean surface on which to perform the change, preferably one at a height that is comfortable for you.

2. **Frame** the baby on the changing surface such that you are in control of the little one and in position to react to anything from untimely urination to sudden movement.

3. **Firm** your grip on the little one, perhaps by laying a gentle, controlling hand on the chest.

4. **Furnish** a distraction to occupy the youth's attention while you work—an easy-to-hold toy or chewable item, a lightweight book, even a lullaby sung by you.

5. **Follow** protocol for dirty diaper removal and clean up: take off the offending item and, while holding baby's legs in the air, wipe soiled areas (technique will vary according to the child's gender and whether the waste you are dealing with is liquid or solid). Then fold and set soiled diaper aside, out of baby's reach before application of new garment. *Tip:* With girls in particular, always wipe frontside to backside to avoid spreading fecal matter into the frontal regions where it may cause a urinary tract infection. Also with poops, use the front of the diaper to wipe the stuff toward the back of the diaper.

6. **Find** the sweet spot, positioning the new diaper under the baby such that the alignment of the tush relative to the interior of the diaper's backside allows you to easily bring the front of the diaper around to below the navel, and to fasten the sides of the diaper around baby's waist snugly but comfortably.

7 & 8. With baby's legs in the air, **fold** the new diaper around front and **fasten** the sides using decisive and quick movements.

9. **Finish** by ensuring proper coverage, seal and fit. If you can't slip two fingers between the diaper and the baby's belly, the fit may be too snug.

## LAUNDROMATISSE

Men don't need a clothing label to understand the shrinkage phenomenon. But when it comes to less familiar subjects such as the proper care of baby clothing, the tag usually spells it all out in language even a greenhorn can comprehend.

With a baby in the house, comprehension, retention, and application of basic laundering techniques are crucial, since the caveman will be expected to handle at least some of the extra laundry burden that comes with the arrival of a new household member—and one prone to explosive incidents of soiling, staining,

## Honor Thy Ancestry and Mother Earth: Erect a Clothesline

One of the sad by-products of the inexorable march of technology has been the marginalization of the clothesline. Once a fixture in so many backyards, the rise of the clothes dryer has rendered the practice of hanging items of clothing outdoors, suspended from a cord so the elements can dry them, virtually obsolete. Time hasn't made the clothesline any less effective, however. If anything, global climate change makes it more viable than ever. The energy and money saved by hang-drying clothes versus running them through the electric or gas-powered dryer are reasons to consider equipping your home with a clothesline on which you can fly the knuckledragger flag by hanging your pelts and formless, fraying tighty-whities alongside baby's tiny onesies and Mom's teeny-weenie lingerie. Granted, items that are hang-dried are more susceptible to errant bird droppings and mischievous squirrels. But those are risks worth running for a guy who is driven to keep alive a practice that dates back to his primitive ancestors.

smearing, and smudging. Guys who believe the term "spin cycle" describes a health club workout would do well to heed the following laundry fundamentals:

**Shrinkage:** In males it's caused by exposure to cold; with clothing it's just the opposite, as certain garments are prone to shrink in the high heat of the dryer, especially during their initial laundering. Clothes made of natural fibers are more apt to shrink than items made entirely or partially of synthetic material.

**Water temperature:** Think cold for colors, warm (or hot) for whites. Confuse the two and you may have to contend with bleeding (see below).

**Bleeding:** Certain colorful garments tend to leak dye during laundering, particularly during their first washing, potentially altering the color of other items in the load. Washing those garments by themselves in cold water the first time around, and always in cold water in subsequent launderings, should prevent the problem.

**Delicates:** Some items—particularly those made from wool, cashmere, silk, and other fine fabrics—demand special handling, from handwashing to air-drying. The fewer items like this that you allow into the baby's wardrobe, the better off you'll be.

**Detergent:** Have your baby's skin in mind during detergent selection. Some products that are especially heavy on perfumes and chemicals can cause skin irritation. For babies, the milder the better.

**Bleach:** It's eminently useful for restoring the original pristineness of white items, but be sure to rewash garments exposed to bleach, even small traces of which can irritate sensitive skin.

**Stain removal:** Supermarket aisles are stocked with products made from chemicals powerful enough to take the polish off a bowling ball. Use them with discretion and be sure to relaunder the item after application.

**Soaking:** Sometimes all it takes to remove a stain is prolonged soaking in water mixed with a bit of mild detergent.

**Ironing:** Babies are generally oblivious to wrinkled clothing, unless it's causing them discomfort. Thus ironing is only for supremely fastidious parents who get irked by an unpressed baby outfit. Do so only while the garment is unoccupied.

# CHAPTER 6

# HEALTH & WELNESS

## HOW TO KEEP A BABY HEALTHY AND THRIVING, WITH YOUR NEW ALLIES, DR. PROBE & NURSE NEEDLE

DRESSED IN FORMLESS TWO-PIECE UNIFORMS, WEARING sinister accessories like masks and rubber gloves, they lurk throughout your woman's pregnancy, poking, prodding, measuring, observing. They're there during labor and delivery as well, going about their business with even greater purpose and urgency, armed with imposing instruments and strange devices. Upon the baby's arrival, these people in scrubs descend upon the little one with their charts, their high-tech monitors and their oddly shaped tools, speaking amongst themselves in a tongue unfamiliar to most troglodytes, even those who regularly watch "E.R." Some of them you may never see again after the birth—and happily so, especially in the case of that doc, the anesthesiologist, who you watched stick a huge needle in your poor woman's spine. Others will become fixtures in your lives as members of the caveling's health care team.

Caveman, meet Dr. Probe, Nurse Needle, and the other medical professionals who will provide your baby with the medical care he or she needs throughout the first year and well beyond. If you are like many contemporary Cro-Magnons, you may get uneasy around members of the medical profession. You may even have an outright aversion to modern medicine. It is time to put those irrational thoughts aside, for these are the people who will be looking out for your baby's best interests. Their methods and tools may occasionally cause your little one (and therefore, you) discomfort, but generally it's all for the greater good. These folks will be right there beside you on the health care front lines, identifying threats and providing the arsenal to banish illness, quash bacteria, and protect the little one's vulnerable bod until it becomes more capable of defending itself.

Doctors, nurses and other medical practitioners are friends, not foes. What prehistoric peoples of the Paleolithic period would have given to have such highly trained and skilled professionals at their disposal when illness or injury struck. Instead of the clan shaman

## Grow with Gronk

What the caveman stands to gain from reading Chapter 6:

- The fortitude to overcome his own medical anxieties

- An understanding of how modern medicine can benefit his kid

- Insight into the health care script for baby's first year

- Strategies for how best to deal with baby's doctor

- The tools to evaluate a baby boy's circumcision options

- A grasp of the issues that come with having a premature baby

- Topical insight into neonatal dermatology

- An injection of common sense about vaccinations

- The smarts to distinguish between wives' tales and valid health remedies

- An ability to assess the threat bacteria and viruses pose to a baby

- A dose of reality about medications suitable for infants

- The know-how to troubleshoot common illnesses and injuries

- The skill to construct a first aid kit fit for a caveling

- A clue about what life might be like with a colicky baby

- Tasty tidbits about infant dental care

- Hands-on grooming skills

performing a trepanning procedure—grinding a hole in the skull with a stone or metal tool—to relieve a tribesman's troublesome migraine, a medical practitioner with more modern training might have recommended a slightly less invasive remedy, such as swallowing a pill or two.

Unfortunately the shaman, as well-intentioned and diligent as he or she may have been, was all our Cro-Magnon ancestors had. Five troglodyte skeletons found at the Les Eyzies cave site near Dordogne, France, tell a revealing story about the kind of bodily conditions people endured back then and the limits of the shaman's powers, at least in the material world. Pathological analysis of those remains showed that several of the cavedwellers had fused vertebrae in their necks, evidence of traumatic injury. One seemed to have survived for some time with a skull fracture.

Let's all raise our hands to the sky and give thanks that we live in the 21st century, where we have access to modern medicine and the people who practice it. Instead of blaming the spirits when your baby is afflicted with some unidentifiable malady and hoping the medicine man has a potion to treat it, you can call or visit the doctor for prompt and much less haphazard evaluation, diagnosis, and treatment.

Chances are you won't need to go to those lengths too often during baby's first year. Most babies make it through the first 12 months relatively problem-free, save for the occasional bump, bruise, cold, and infection. This chapter is here to help equip you to be a protector of your offspring's health and wellness. The keys to fulfilling that crucial role are:

- observing your baby closely enough to know what's normal about his or her condition and behavior and what's not;

- trusting your own instincts and judgment as well as those of the medical pros you select to care for your baby;

- arming yourself with enough sound medical and health insight and information to be able to act in your little one's best interests.

Now let's meet the health care providers who you (and, perhaps, the insurance company) will be paying big bucks to help protect those interests.

Medical terminology can be befuddling. So let's put things in terms any dyed-in-the-wool troglodyte can understand. Think of your baby's doctor—a pediatrician or family physician—as the quarterback of the caveling's health care team. You own the team, so the quarterback and other professionals who work alongside him or her will be working for you—and with you—toward your baby's best interests. Pediatric nurse practitioners and other nurses may be part of the team, as may specialists (doctors with expertise in an individual area of medicine), dentists (we'll address dental health later in the chapter), and perhaps even naturopathic doctors.

Hopefully in the pre-birth draft you will have chosen a primary-care doctor to quarterback your dream team, so you don't have to scramble to find one right after the birth. If you procrastinated and now must find one in a pinch, look for a doctor whose practice accepts your insurance. Ideally, you want a provider who is convenient (location and hours), qualified (board certification and reputation are helpful), and with whom you feel comfortable. References from friends, family, etc., can help in the search. Look to the American Board of Pediatrics (www.abp.org) for a list of board-certified pediatricians and to the American Board of Family Medicine (www.theabfm.org) for board-certified family physicians. Other potential sources of information include your local hospital's "referral line" and local medical society offices.

- A **pediatrician** practices pediatrics, a medical specialty focused on the physical, mental, emotional, and social health of children from birth through adolescence. Pediatricians must complete four years of medical school plus a three-year pediatric residency. To gain board certification, they must pass a written examination administered by the American Board of Pediatrics. Some pediatricians have additional training in a subspecialty area, such as cardiology, critical care or emergency medicine, or hematology. These specialists usually have three years of additional training after their residency to earn board certification in their subspecialty.

- A **family physician** (like Dr. Brian) also must spend four years in medical school, then complete a three-year residency program. But while pediatricians focus on children, family docs train in many areas so they are qualified to treat patients of all ages. That means a person could see the same doctor from birth through adulthood, and that all members of a family might receive primary care from the same doctor. Family medicine residents train in pediatrics and several other areas, including internal medicine and obstetrics and gynecology. They may become board-certified by the American Board of Family Medicine.

- A **pediatric nurse practitioner** usually works closely with doctors in hospitals and doctors' offices. They have a master's degree in nursing and special training to perform medical histories and physical exams, make diagnoses, and treat patients. A nurse practitioner can be a valuable addition to the caveling's health care team because he or she may have more time than the doctor to spend with patients and families. If a nurse practitioner wants help with a complex medical case or question, he or she can easily consult with a physician.

If you like to dress up for medical visits, keep your surgical scrubs pressed and handy, caveman, because you, your woman, and your baby will be seeing lots of the doctor in year one, regardless of how healthy the little one is. The schedule of routine check-ups during baby's first year typically includes no fewer than seven "well baby" visits, starting with one within a few days of birth, followed by others at two weeks to one month, then again at two months, four months, six months, nine months, and one year. These visits are vital for getting recommended vaccines and to monitor growth and development. They also offer an opportunity to pose health-related questions to, and bounce ideas off, people more medically qualified than your bowling buddies.

What might unfold for the average baby over the course of these first-year doctor visits?

- Baby likely will get initial **vaccines** just after birth, with additional vaccinations performed at the two-, four-, six- and 12-month visits. For the U.S. government's current recommended vaccine schedule, visit: www.cdc.gov/vaccines/recs/schedules. The Dr. Brian box on pages 150–151 provides more details on specific vaccinations.

- **Growth measurements.** To see how a baby is growing and developing, a nurse or medical assistant typically will record three measurements at each visit: height/length, weight, and head circumference. This info then can be compared to growth chart averages (one for boys and another for girls) to

# DR. BRIAN

*Do's and Don'ts When Dealing with the Baby Doc*

You and your woman have questions. The family physician or pediatrician who treats your baby should certainly have answers. Here are some tips for getting the most out of the time and money you spend with your child's medical providers:

- **DO** bring specific questions to the baby's doctor visits and have them ready to pose to the doctor.

- **DON'T** inundate the doc with so many questions that they divert time and attention from more essential health matters. While it's important to get your questions answered, some parents feel that the more questions they ask, the more value they can squeeze out of a doctor visit. But answering so many questions may take a doctor's focus away from key issues.

- **DO** own and use a thermometer. Fever is defined by a number (*data*), not a *feeling*. Just because a baby feels warmer than usual to the touch doesn't mean he or she has a fever. If you suspect the little one is running a fever, take his or temperature before you call the doc.

- **DO** bring your child's shot records to any "well baby" exam (general check-up) and to any visit to a new doctor. It is also a good idea to keep a medical file for each family member, including children, in case you need to see a new doctor or if your doctor's office has misplaced your child's records.

- **DON'T** let melodrama get in the way of accuracy in the info you're providing a doctor about your baby's condition. Doctors rely upon facts and unembellished observations to make accurate diagnoses and recommendations. For example, if you say something like, "She hasn't eaten or drunk anything in a week!" a doctor will know that's not completely true, since humans can't live more than a few days without fluids. Parents might be tempted to use hyperbole to get a doctor's attention and convey how serious they believe a baby's condition to be, but such exaggeration can make a doctor question a parent's credibility.

- **DON'T** be repetitive. That is, try not to repeat info you're trying to convey to a doctor. In other words, don't say something multiple times when discussing a child's condition. To reiterate: Avoid repetitiveness. Odds are the doctor registered the relevant details the first time around.

- **DO** bring any prescription medication, over-the-counter medication, and "herbal" product you're giving your child to an appointment so the doctor can confirm the medication and the dose. You may think you know what it is, but there are differing strengths, combination medicines, and other potentially confusing issues.

- In paging a doctor after office hours, **DO** remember to take the baby's temperature before you call; have the packages of any medicine you've given the baby handy by the phone so you can provide the doc with the name and ingredients if necessary; have a pharmacy number ready to provide so the doc can phone in a prescription.

determine how a baby compares with like-aged peers for each measurement. For example, if a caveling is found to be in the 30th percentile for weight at his or her age, it means that in a group of 100 children with the same birth date, about 70 children would be heavier and 30 would be lighter.

The "size matters" thing has been so ingrained into our culture that many parents place great emphasis on a kid's percentile numbers. But beyond abnormal measurements that might indicate to the doctor or nurse practitioner the presence of a health or developmental issue, there is little meaning or prestige attached to higher or lower percentile rank. For

example, if a child's weight percentage is decreasing, even though he or she is gaining some weight, the baby may be said to be "falling off the curve," which could be attributable to illness or inadequate nutrition. Interestingly, when babies are sick even for a relatively short period, they may drop enough weight to affect their standing on the growth chart, then quickly find their way back to the previous percentile after the illness resolves.

Of all the factors that affect a baby's development, genetics is the biggest predictor. Nutrition, health problems and activity are other key determinants. Head circumference measures the distance around the largest part of a baby's head. A very large or very small head could indicate a medical problem or it could merely be a trait connecting the little one to his or her cavedwelling lineage.

- **Developmental milestones.** During visits, the doc or nurse will likely ask parents a series of questions, and make their own observations, to ascertain whether a baby is meeting certain developmental milestones related to language, gross motor and fine motor skills. (See the timeline in Chapter 2 for an idea of when some of these milestones tend to occur).

- **Physical exam.** The caveling will get a thorough, head-to-toe exam at most or all scheduled visits.

- **Screening blood tests.** It's typical for the doc to have a baby tested (screened) for lead and anemia sometime within the first year.

- Other **health questions** a doc will want to cover with parents during the exam include habits related to feeding, bowel movements, urination, and sleep.

## PREEMIES: EARLY TO THE PARTY

There are some things never to call a guy in his prime. One of them is "premature," particularly in a context relating to hair loss or sexual performance. Using the term with newborns is another matter, however, because a significant share of them—8–10 percent in the United States—are born prematurely, and because they have yet to attach any negative connotations to the word.

By definition, a baby born before the 37th week of pregnancy (full term is considered between 38 to 42 weeks of gestation) is dubbed "premature." Early-arriving babies—in the neonatal ward they're nicknamed "preemies"—bring with them a unique set of circumstances, issues, and parental responsibilities. For example, because their organs haven't had enough time to develop *in utero*, preemies may need supportive care after birth. That care can range from being treated with IV (intravenous) fluids and oxygen in the newborn nursery in more mild cases to more severe cases in which a little one is treated with intensive support in a NICU (neonatal intensive care unit), where he or she may stay until all organ systems are functioning on their own.

Just because a baby is born prematurely doesn't necessarily mean he or she will have problems right out of the womb. However, the severity of a premature baby's health problems usually is closely related to how premature the caveling was. Even after receiving initial additional care at a hospital right after birth, some preemies may continue to require treatment for special health needs. Let's look at some of the most common health issues with premature neonates:

**Respiratory.** A baby whose lungs aren't fully developed may need supplemental oxygen for a time, possibly even via a ventilator. A condition called **Respiratory Distress Syndrome** (RDS), where the lungs don't have enough "surfactant" to properly expand, can be an issue, as can apnea—periods when breathing actually stops temporarily. Either may require special monitoring after baby leaves the hospital.

# DR. BRIAN

*It's a Boy!*
*Which Helmet*
*Will He Wear?*

As the proud parents of a boy, one choice you'll be confronted with soon after birth could reverberate throughout the lad's lifetime. We are, of course, talking about the decision whether to **circumcise**—that is, what to do with the foreskin of his penis. The thought of a masked medical marauder using an instrument called a **Mogen, Gomco** or **Plastibell** to permanently alter the topography of your offspring's genitalia is enough to make many male troglodytes mighty fidgety.

Let's cut to the meat of the issue: Boys are born with a hood of skin called the foreskin that covers the head (glans) of the penis. Circumcision is the surgical procedure to remove all or part of the foreskin and thus expose the head of the penis. It's usually performed in the first few days of life, though prematurely born boys may not be circumcised until they're ready to leave the hospital.

The choice whether to circumcise is hardly cut and dried. It is one for which you must use your head, so the lad doesn't feel shafted later in life by your rash decision. There's even debate in some circles about whether circumcision is medically unjustified and an infringement upon individual bodily rights.

While the circumdecision often comes down to the parents' cultural and religious beliefs and personal preferences, matters of health and hygiene also should be part of the discussion. These days about 60 percent of all boys in the U.S. are circumcised. A practice that dates back to prehistoric times, circumcision is also common in parts of Africa, Asia, the Middle East, and Canada (it's especially prevalent in Jewish and Islamic cultures), and less so in Europe, Central and South America, and Asia.

As far as the nuts and bolts of the operation, the doctor who performs it essentially has a choice among three circumcision tools. The best tool is the one the operator is most comfortable using. Each is basically safe when used correctly, as is the procedure when performed properly.

Dr. Brian's weapon of choice is the **Gomco**, which stands for the **Go**ldstein **M**edical **Co**mpany, its manufacturer. It looks something like an opener you'd use in the kitchen, with parts that include a "rocker arm," a "bell," and a "yoke," names that conjure awful thoughts in the uninitiated caveman's imagination. It is known for the ability to minimize bleeding. Leave it lying around and someone might be tempted to use it to open a bottle of wine.

Now a joke to take your mind off what you just read:

### DID YOU HEAR ABOUT THE MOHEL WHO MADE A WALLET OUT OF OLD FORESKINS?

WHEN HE RUBS IT, IT TURNS INTO A BRIEFCASE.

There is also a device called the **Plastibell.** It is placed over the glans and the foreskin is tied tightly with a string (a ligature). The handle is broken off, but the tip is left on and falls off with the foreskin a few days after the procedure. Practical folks might envision also using it to clean golf cleats.

The **Mogen** clamp was designed by a Jewish mohel (rhymes with "foil"), a rabbi who performs circumcision in the ritual "bris," for which it is still commonly used. By its looks, its designer must have been a cigar afficionado, for it looks much like a cigar cutter. It is similarly quick and easy to use, functioning as a true clamp by pinching the foreskin, while the Mogen crushes the foreskin. Although the Mogen looks like it might cut off more than it should, it is very safe when used correctly.

Another joke to lighten the mood:

**TWO LITTLE BOYS ARE LYING ON STRETCHERS NEXT TO EACH OTHER OUTSIDE THE HOSPITAL OPERATING ROOM.**

**"WHAT ARE YOU IN FOR?" THE FIRST BOY ASKS.**

**"I'M HERE TO GET MY TONSILS OUT," SAYS THE SECOND. "HOW ABOUT YOU?"**

**"CIRCUMCISION."**

**"OH, NO," SAYS THE SECOND BOY. "I HAD THAT DONE RIGHT AFTER I WAS BORN AND I COULDN'T WALK FOR A YEAR!"**

The previous descriptions alone might put you squarely in the anti-circumcision camp. But rather than making a knee-jerk decision, talk it over with your woman. Since you own one yourself and likely have seen both versions of the willy, your woman may defer to you, not only to make the final call, but also to provide the bulk of the post-operative care for the wound if you ultimately decide to go the surgical route.

However you choose to proceed, you and your woman should be cocksure about your decision. Here are some factors to consider:

## Pros of circumcision

- Tenfold lower risk of contracting urinary tract infections (the risk decreases from 1 in 100 for uncircumcised boys to 1 in 1,000 for circumcised boys);

- A lower risk of contracting the HIV virus, based on convincing research from Africa;

- Probably a lower risk of getting penile cancer, although this is not a common problem to begin with;

- Easier to keep clean. Uncircumcised boys can develop infections under the foreskin. After the foreskin becomes "retractable" (able to pull back over the head) it becomes easier to keep clean, but this may not occur until the kid is five years old, or older.

## Cons of circumcision

- As with any surgical procedure, there is a small but present risk. For circumcision, the complication rate is between 0.2 percent to 3 percent. The most frequent problems are minor bleeding and local infection, both of which are easily treatable.

- Pain from the procedure. It has become more common to use local anesthesia on baby boys during circumcision, a practice that is endorsed by the American Academy of Pediatrics. Either an injectable or topical cream (or sometimes both) is used. If you are concerned about the pain, ask if the doctor plans to use anesthesia.

For you dads who are concerned about any down-the-road ramifications of the circum-decision you and your woman will make for your male caveling, it's worth pointing out that sexual function and pleasure has not been shown to differ according to whether a guy is circumcised or uncircumcised.

If you opt to go forward with the procedure, here's how to care for the site of the slice, which should take about a week to heal:

- Cleanse with soap and water. No need for special products.

- Dressing may need to be changed during the first two days after the surgery. Put petroleum jelly (Vaseline) on the site before you apply any gauze to prevent sticking (wince) and decrease friction against the diaper.

- Seek medical care if there is persistent bleeding, pus-like discharge, increasing redness, fever or an inability to urinate.

If you decide not to circumcise, follow these penis care instructions:

- Don't forcibly pull back the foreskin (wince!). This could lead to an inability to pull the foreskin back over the tip, strangulating the penis in a potentially dangerous condition called paraphimosis (big bleeping wince!).

- Smegma is the whitish, cheesy material that collects under the foreskin. It is made of oils from the body and old skin cells. It is not evidence of any infection. As a boy gets older he can be taught how to clean under the foreskin. Now there's a mentorship opportunity a cavedad can relish.

**TTN**, or transient tachypnea of the newborn, is a fancy way to describe a rapid breathing condition that commonly occurs during the first hours after birth. A baby with TTN may need close observation; if it persists, other causes for the condition may be sought.

**Bronchopulmonary dysplasia** is a chronic lung condition that may arise from a combination of the premature baby's immature lungs, problems such as a lung infection, and the treatments used to help the baby (ventilator machine and oxygen).

**Gastrointestinal.** Trouble with digestion is also common among preemies. A lack of development can lead to difficulty swallowing, in which case the newborn may need nutritional support until the condition subsides.

**Brain and nervous system.** Issues such as intraventricular hemorrhages (bleeding in the brain), seizures, and learning disabilities are of particular concern.

**Blood.** Anemia is a problem for some preemies, as is jaundice, a condition in which the baby's skin acquires a yellow color due to elevated bilirubin in the blood. Bilirubin is a normal by-product of the natural breakdown of blood cells. While elevated bilirubin is common even in healthy newborns, it is more common in premature infants. It may be treated with lights that help to break down the bilirubin.

**Cardiac (heart). Patent ductus arteriosus** (PDA) is a condition in which a part of the baby's heart called the ductus arteriosus stays open following birth. Since a fetus *in utero* is not yet breathing air, the fetal heart has a clever way of bypassing the fluid-filled lungs to get oxygen to the rest of the fetus' body. The ductus arteriosus acts somewhat like a bypass road when the main freeway is still being constructed. In full-term babies, the ductus arteriosus closes shortly after birth, but it frequently stays open (or "patent") in premature babies. Sometimes a PDA causes symptoms, such as heavier breathing, a fast heart rate and poor weight gain, due to less efficient use of oxygen. Medicines, and sometimes minor surgery, may be needed to close the ductus.

**Low blood pressure** is more common in premature infants. Issues with the brain or other organs may result from lower blood flow and reduced oxygen supply. Treatments may include giving IV fluids, medications to raise blood pressure, and steroids.

**Infections. Sepsis** is an infection in the blood. If it is a concern (and it often is in preemies), the doctor may start the baby on antibiotics until blood cultures are completed (it takes about 48 hours for the final culture result). Pneumonia is also more common in preemies than in full-term infants.

**Eyes.** Preemies are more susceptible to retinopathy, where there is abnormal growth of blood vessels in the eyes, a condition that may lead to severe visual impairment.

The list of potential problems is indeed daunting. But don't despair. Preemies may struggle more than other babies early on but most go on to live normally and healthily, with no ill effects from their early arrival. Even without the benefits of modern neonatal care, the likes of Winston Churchill, Albert Einstein, Mark Twain, Renoir, Isaac Newton, Charles Darwin, Jean Jacques Rousseau, John Keats, Victor Hugo, and Daniel Webster somehow managed to overcome being born prematurely.

Any of the following websites provide a good starting point for people seeking additional information on premature birth and babies:

**American Academy of Pediatrics,** www.aap.org

**The National Institute of Child Health and Human Development,** www.nichd.nih.gov

**Medline Plus** (from the National Library of Medicine and the National Institutes of Health), www.nlm.nih.gov/medlineplus/

**KidsHealth,** www.kidshealth.org

There are steps potential parents can take to lessen the chances of premature birth. Good prenatal care from a qualified health care provider is one; avoiding tobacco, alcohol, and illicit drugs when pregnant is another; getting good care for chronic illnesses (such as diabetes) is a third. Keep those in mind the next time you and your woman start talking about making another caveling.

# DR. BRIAN

## Who Needs Vaccinations? Your Baby Does

There's been a backlash of late against childhood vaccines among people who suggest immunizations might do more harm than good. Theirs is a difficult viewpoint to defend, given that pediatric vaccinations are responsible for the greatest improvement in serious preventable diseases in infants and children that history has ever seen.

Just a few decades ago, thousands of children (and adults) in the U.S. developed diseases such as measles, polio, smallpox, and diphtheria every year. Today, due largely to advances in immunizations, smallpox has been eradicated, polio has been mostly eliminated, and many other diseases are either controlled or declining in incidence, including measles, mumps, rubella, tetanus, diphtheria, varicella (chicken pox and shingles), and potentially life-threatening infections with bacteria that cause meningitis and pneumonia.

As time goes by, it becomes easier to forget the impact these diseases had on children, their families, and society. As the need for hospitalization has decreased, hospital pediatric wards have been converted to care for other patients. Countless children have been spared suffering and the economy has benefited from lower costs to care for their illnesses. Pediatric vaccines have, by all measures, been an unmitigated success.

So why the resistance to them? One reason is the Internet, which affords people access to the misinformation superhighway. Another is the public's collective short memory. Now that so many childhood diseases have been kept at bay, some wonder if all the shots are actually necessary. Furthermore, childhood conditions such as autism are recognized at an age when vaccines are typically administered, giving rise to a perceived causal relationship. A word of caution to gullible Paleolithic papas: Don't believe everything you read or hear about vaccines. The following Q&A might help set the record straight.

**Q. Could being given many vaccines overwhelm a child's immune system?**

A. No. While it's true that ever more vaccines are being introduced, they don't overload a baby's system. Even though a child may get as many as 23 shots before age 2, their immune systems, if healthy, are well equipped to handle new challenges such as vaccines. Indeed, studies have shown that in theory, a child could safely receive *thousands* of vaccines at once.

**Q. Do vaccines cause autism?**

A. No. There have been multiple well-designed research studies that show no causal relationship between vaccines and autism. The MMR vaccine has been targeted as a potential cause, partly because it is usually given at one year of age, a time when many children with autism begin developing autistic symptoms. Considerable controversy also surrounds a substance called thimerosal, a vaccine preservative that contains ethylmercury. Although studies show no link between thimerosal and autism, it is no longer used in vaccines. It was a case of "better safe than sorry."

**Q. Wouldn't it be better for babies to contract some diseases, like chicken pox, so they develop a "natural" immunity?**

A. It's not a birthright to get a disease like chicken pox. For most children, the disease is benign, but for some it can be dangerous, even fatal. Before the varicella vaccine was introduced, many children were hospitalized with complications from the disease, such as pneumonia and serious secondary skin infections. Also, it's a fallacy to believe that getting chicken pox makes a person immune to the virus. On the contrary, after the primary chicken pox virus affects someone, it then lives in a dormant state inside the body and can recur later in life as shingles (herpes zoster). Vaccination against varicella protects against both incarnations.

**Q.** **Since many of these diseases have been eradicated or close to it, why should I put my child through the extra pain of vaccinations?**

**A.** Excellent question, the answer to which lies in parents viewing their children as part of a larger community. Vaccines protect a child not only because of the immune protection they offer that individual but also because of "herd immunity," where if enough members of society are vaccinated against a disease, then that disease will generally disappear. So by vaccinating your child, you are protecting your neighbor's children as well.

**Q.** **Should I worry about serious side effects from vaccines?**

**A.** In very rare circumstances, vaccines can produce serious side effects. But children are much more likely to experience a minor side effect, such as a slight fever, rash or pain at the injection site. Bottom line: The benefits of vaccinating against preventable diseases far outweigh the risks.

# YOUR NEXT-OF-KIN'S SKIN: NEONATAL DERMATOLOGY

Scan the delivery rooms of most hospitals and birthing facilities and you will likely see lots of high-tech devices, machines, and medical equipment, intermingling with institutional-looking furniture with laminated upholstery (moisture-repellent furnishings your beer-spilling college roommate really could have used back in the day). There might be a TV, windows, and perhaps some doughty wall adornments. But something is conspicuously absent: mirrors.

Why no mirrors? Members of the caveling's medical team appear to you in daylight and show no aversion to garlic or a crucifix, so you can rule out vampires. Perhaps it is a vanity issue. The last thing expectant and new moms and dads want to see are reflections of their exhausted, drained, and disheveled selves while in the throes of, or in the immediate aftermath of, labor and delivery. There's also the matter of the newborn's appearance. Somewhere there lurks a baby with pristine, smooth skin, but oftentimes it takes time for those qualities to surface. Initially, at least, many newborns arrive looking like adolescent kids, riddled with blotches and blemishes.

In most cases newborn skin conditions are treatable and temporary. The caveman's perma-tanned, heavily Botoxed mother-in-law wonders if a chemical peel or dermabrasion might be in order. The caveman's own first urge might be to over-wash rashes or use soaps that are too strong for a newborn's skin. But often that only makes matters worse. Here's a rundown of things you may see and what to do about them.

......................................................................

**Baby acne** (acne neonatorum): small red bumps on the face that look like little pimples; appears in first one or two weeks; caused by mother's hormones stimulating baby's facial oil glands.

- *Treatment:* not necessary, since it usually disappears within about three months and won't scar or cause lasting effects; use of stronger soaps may worsen condition; in more severe cases, a doctor may prescribe benzoyl peroxide or low-dose hydrocortisone.

......................................................................

**Milia:** small white bumps present right after birth, mostly around the nose and eyes.

- *Treatment:* none; condition disappears in two to four weeks.

**Stork bite/salmon patch:** common pink-orange patch usually appearing at the back of the scalp or neck, forehead or upper lip; found in almost half of all newborns; often fades by one year, but seen in some adults; more obvious with crying.

*Treatment:* none; it poses no danger.

**Mongolian spot:** blue patch, usually appearing on the low back or buttocks; may look like a bruise (consider this before accusing hospital staff of dropping precious caveling); very common in darker-skinned babies (African, Native American, Hispanic); usually fades by about two years, most disappear by age 5.

*Treatment:* none; poses no risk of future cancer or skin problem.

**Strawberry mark/patch** (capillary hemangioma): a bright red, sometimes raised patch that varies in size and location; caused by a massed collection of blood vessels under the skin; slow to go away— may grow before gradually shrinking; on average, tends to fade by 50 percent by five years of age and by 90 percent by age 10.

*Treatment:* none needed in most cases; it's usually a cosmetic issue.

**Port wine stain:** variably sized and sometimes large splotch, often found on the face; initially pink in color but likely will turn red; think Gorbachev; may be a significant cosmetic issue if it doesn't go away.

*Treatment:* by a specialist, with a laser, if it doesn't disappear.

**Cradle cap** (seborrheic dermatitis): yellow, crusty, scaly rash on scalp, around ears or eyes; doesn't hurt or bother baby; possible causes include overactive oil glands due to hormones and certain types of yeast organisms (the fungus is among us!); usually goes away over time, though may morph into seborrhea in some kids.

*Treatment:* ask your doctor; to remove scale, apply mineral oil or petroleum jelly overnight, then softly brush off scale in the morning; baking powder paste left on for several minutes can also loosen scale; to treat eyelids, gently wash the area with diluted baby shampoo using a cotton swab.

# DR. BRIAN

*Second Opinions*

The good doctor swings his caduceus-shaped club to shatter 10 of the most commonly held medical **myths** and **misconceptions** about babies. Let's count them down:

**10. Colds and ear infections are caused by going outdoors with wet hair or without a hat.** Brief exposure to cold has not been shown to cause infections. Wintertime is more likely the season for more frequent colds and ear infections because we spend more time indoors, where germs are passed more easily. Viruses, not wet or hatless heads, are the cause of colds and ear infections. Still, it's important to keep baby's head covered when outside in cold weather.

**9. Babies who are sick shouldn't drink milk.** It is a myth that milk can make mucus thicker and harder to bring up if a child has a cold. It is also untrue that milk exacerbates diarrhea in a baby who has an intestinal bug. Babies should be able to stick to their usual diet unless they are vomiting. Sick babies tend to lose their appetites, so the more important issue is to make sure they consume enough fluids to avoid dehydration.

**8. You should/shouldn't let a baby sleep in your bed.** There are no definite right or wrong ways to put your child to sleep. If your current routine works—that is, it provides everyone involved with adequate sleep—then stick to it. Chapter 7 explains the various sleep strategies open to cavelings and their parents.

**7. A mobile infant walker teaches a child to walk earlier.** Not only won't a mobile baby walker turn your child into a walker sooner, it can expose a wobbly baby to peril. Stationary walkers are much safer.

**6. Babies need to take multivitamins.** Vitamins generally are unnecessary for healthy cavelings with an average diet. However, preterm (premature) infants and those with a chronic illness may require supplemental vitamins and minerals. Also, children may need fluoride supplements if they do not drink fluoridated water.

**5. Eating cereal will help your baby sleep through the night.** Some parents want to start feeding their baby cereal as early as possible with the hope of catching more Zs. But there is no medical evidence that cereal helps babies sleep better or longer. Rather, their sleep habits depend more on development.

**4. Teething causes fever (and in some cases diarrhea, vomiting, and rashes too).** Teething causes many things in a baby—discomfort and fussiness along with drooling—but high fever isn't among them. So if your baby has a fever, look for another cause. To help with teething symptoms, you can massage the gums or let your baby chew on a teething ring. Treating teething with acetaminophen, ibuprofen or teething gels is OK but not necessary.

**3. Production of green or yellow snot means your child needs antibiotics.** This is *usually* false. Most upper respiratory infections, including sinusitis and the common cold, are caused by *viruses*, and these infections often cause a green or yellow nasal discharge. Antibiotics will do nothing to help cure these infections. The body's own natural immune system generally fights them off. If your child continues producing colorful snot for periods of more than 10–14 days, he or she may have a *bacterial* infection, which could respond to antibiotics.

**2. Alternating acetaminophen (e.g., Tylenol for babies) with ibuprofen (e.g., Motrin or Advil for infants) is more effective than giving baby either one alone.** There is no evidence that this is true, although it is so ingrained in medical culture that many doctors and emergency rooms still recommend alternating them. However, it may be more dangerous to alternate these drugs since that poses a higher risk of giving the wrong dosage amount or administering the wrong medication. It's less risky to stick with one medication or the other.

**1. Fever is inherently harmful.** Unless a baby's temperature hits 106°F or higher (which is rare), fever itself should not hurt the child. It is a *symptom*, like cough or diarrhea. Even febrile seizures usually are not harmful (unless they cause parents to drive so recklessly that they get into an accident on their way to the emergency room).

What does fever tell us? In most cases, that there is some type of infection. Sometimes infections can be dangerous, but not *because* the baby has spiked a temperature. Also, higher temperatures do not necessarily indicate a more serious illness. Other symptoms, such as decreased responsiveness, confusion, irritability, difficulty breathing, and recurrent vomiting, are far more worrisome.

However, the younger the baby, the more concerning a fever may be. In general, if an infant younger than three months has a temperature above 100.4°F (measured rectally), contact the doctor promptly. For infants older than three months, recommendations vary depending on other symptoms. If you are unsure of how to handle matters, call the doc.

Treating fever does not make an infection go away any quicker. It's simply a symptom-reliever. If your child has a fever but doesn't show outward signs of discomfort, then you needn't provide medication to reduce the fever.

An ability to separate fact from fiction, myth from reality, legitimate info from pure BS, is a valuable attribute for parents when it comes to their own health and that of their youngster. You and your woman need to be able to distinguish bona fide remedies and legitimate tactics from the many wives' tales and urban legends that continue to circulate despite having zero basis in fact. Here's an objective look at some strong and flimsy claims you may confront during the course of caveling's first year.

| You've heard that... | The verdict |
|---|---|
| **Everyday exposure to pets can help a baby build resistance to allergies.** | **Probably true:** Recent studies from respected sources have shown that kids who are raised in a household with two or more dogs or cats during the first year of life may be less likely to develop common allergies to pets, dust mites, ragweed, and grass than children raised without pets. One study found that babies raised in a home with two or more dogs or cats were up to 77 percent less likely to develop those allergies at age 6 than kids raised without pets. Another found that the longer children had pets when they were young, the lower their incidence of developing allergies to pets later. |
| **Rubbing a bit of liquor on baby's gums is a good way to ease teething pain.** | **Wives' tale:** Liquor may have served as a stand-in anesthetic back in the day for a cowboy who needed a hatchet wound stitched, but today there are many more proven (and less toxic) alternatives to help ease a baby's teething pain. No doctor we know endorses providing liquor to a minor, let alone a baby. So save the hard stuff for your own lips. |
| **Applying cabbage to a woman's breasts can ease the pain of breastfeeding.** | **Maybe so:** Women whose breasts hurt from suckling who have tried this technique say it really does soothe their overworked milk sources, though no medical studies have confirmed that to be the case. Use whole cabbage leaves cooled in the fridge—coleslaw won't work. |
| **Fatter babies are generally better-sleeping and happier than skinnier ones.** | **Not necessarily so:** A child's physical development, not body fat, is a major factor in how a baby sleeps. For example, a full-term infant might sleep better than a premature infant whose systems aren't as well developed and thus aren't working as efficiently. |
| **Consuming the placenta (afterbirth) expelled by a woman during the third stage of labor provides the eater with all sorts of benefits.** | **It's a free country:** Strange (and to some, barbaric) but true: People in some cultures (including ours) store the placenta for consumption at a later date. It's called placentophagia and it's practiced by people who generally believe eating this nutrient-rich organ helps the diner (usually the mom) bounce back more readily from childbirth. While the Internet is rife with recipes for cooking placenta, there is little medical evidence documenting the benefits of this practice. |
| **Delaying clamping of the umbilical cord for a couple minutes after birth benefits the newborn.** | **Probably true:** Medical studies have found that delaying clamping of the umbilical cord reduces the rate of neonatal anemia. A two-minute delay in clamping the cord can boost a child's iron reserves and prevent anemia for months, nutritionists at the University of California, Davis, concluded in 2006. |

## A First Aid Kit for Treating Cavelings

Here's what to keep in the cabinet (and have at hand) to treat what ills or ails a baby. Note to Cro-Magnon paramedics: While the first aid you administer at home is very necessary, it should not be a substitute for prompt, professional medical treatment when the situation warrants.

**Adhesive bandages** (like Band-aids) to cover small cuts, scrapes, etc.

**Antibacterial/antibiotic ointment** to apply to open wounds large and small to prevent infection.

**Aspirating bulb**, a rubber, bulb-shaped implement used to suck mucus and other material from a baby's nose or mouth. Since nose-blowing and decongestant medication aren't options for infants, you need some way to help them breathe better amid allergies, colds, and other congestion-causing afflictions.

**Baby acetaminophen** and/or **baby ibuprofen** to ease pain and reduce fever.

**Cold pack** to apply to bumps and bruises to reduce swelling.

**Hydrocortisone cream** to relieve pain and itchiness from insect bites, rashes, etc.

**Nonstick sterile gauze** to protect larger cuts and scrapes, plus **adhesive tape** to use with the sterile gauze.

## THE PEDIATRIC PETRI DISH

One of the overarching goals of parenthood is to eventually bring the fourth stage of labor to a close—to equip one's kids to handle life's challenges and prepare them to stand tall in the world. Nobody wants a two-year-old who can't stand on his own, an eight-year-old who can't tie his shoes, a 20-year-old who never bothered learning to drive or a 30-year-old who still lives with his parents.

Part of that preparatory process here in baby's first year is helping the little one build an immune system strong enough to fend off illness. While genetics and *in utero* nourishment certainly play a role in building immunities, so, too, do factors that are within parental control: seeing that a baby gets enough sleep; practicing good hygiene, including lots of handwashing; breastfeeding, if possible; keeping baby current with vaccinations and clear of very harmful secondhand smoke (and even more harmful firsthand smoke—no Marlboro babies).

Babies receive immune cells from their mothers *in utero* via the placenta and once born, they get a major additional immune system boost from breast milk, as discussed in detail in Chapter 3. Milk from Mom's breast contains stuff called "bioactive" factors—among them hormones, growth factors, and colony stimulating factors—that strengthen the immune system. Breast milk also performs good deeds in a baby's intestines, where it stimulates maturation of the gut lining, alters gut microflora, functions as an anti-inflammatory, and decreases the risk of infection (intestinal, ear, and respiratory). For all these reasons, doctors recommend that new moms breastfeed their babies for at least six months.

As powerful a nectar as breast milk is, it cannot singlehandedly protect a little one from bombardment by the many viruses, bacteria, and potential allergens that inhabit our environment. To what extent should you try to protect the caveling from this stuff? To what extent will a baby benefit from exposure to it? Good questions—and ones to which medical research is seeking clear-cut answers. Some theorize that our increased effort to prevent infections in childhood has actually weakened the immune systems of babies and children. This is what's called the "hygiene hypothesis." Supporters of the theory point to the recent marked increase in the incidence of asthma and allergies as evidence of its validity. Several research studies have demonstrated that children who attend day care at a younger age have a lower incidence of allergic disease and asthma later in life. It's not clear if the cause is more exposure to allergens or if it's due to more frequent illness in day care attendees.

What's a conscientious parent to do? By no means should you *intentionally* expose a child to other children who are sick in the name of building immunity. However, such study findings might reassure parents who send their kids to day care that even if the risk for common childhood infections is higher in that setting, in the end it may not be such a bad thing. It may be a case of, "Pay now or pay later."

## MEDICINES: A DOSE OF COMMON SENSE

Parents will go to great lengths to spare an infant from pain, discomfort and distress. Modern medicine gives us access to a huge variety of over-the-counter and prescription medications and remedies to treat illnesses and ailments. But not all this stuff is fit for baby to ingest. Some of it won't work on a little one and some might be downright harmful to someone so young. Here's a look at what medications are and are not suitable to give babies in the first year:

**Believed to be safe medicines for treating fever discomfort, pain and/or inflammation:** acetaminophen, ibuprofen; remember, if a baby under three months has a fever, take him or her to see a doctor.

**Steer clear of cough and cold preparations:** A U.S. Food & Drug Administration (FDA) advisory committee for non-prescription drugs and pediatric medicine in 2007 recommended banning over-the-counter cold and cough medicines for kids. The vote was nearly unanimous for children under age 2, and a majority also recommended the ban apply to kids up to age 6. Their reasoning? Not only have such medications been shown not to work on kids that age, dosing errors can cause more harm than good. For example, some "infant" drops are more concentrated than other "children's" medicine, and parents might mistakenly give a higher than recommended dose. There have even been deaths attributed to improper dosing with infant and children's cough and cold medications. You've heard the adage, "If it ain't broke, don't fix it." This is a case of, "If it don't work, let's nix it."

 Concurrent to issuance of the FDA panel's recommendations, the Consumer Healthcare Products Association (CHPA), on

**Rectal thermometer** (preferably digital), to take the little one's temperature. Be sure not to confuse it with the household oral thermometer.

**Tweezers** to extract a splinter, a super-sized booger, earfluff, and the like.

**Warm water**, **soft cloth**, and **mild liquid soap,** not hydrogen peroxide, to cleanse cuts, scrapes, and the like.

behalf of the leading makers of over-the-counter cough and cold medicines for kids, announced a voluntary withdrawal of oral cough and cold medicines that refer to "infants" and those touted for children under age 2.

- How to treat cold symptoms, then? Have baby breathe humid air, such as that provided by a humidifier or in a steamy bathroom. Provide plenty of fluids to keep mucus thin and use acetaminophen or ibuprofen (infant formulations) as directed for fever and discomfort.

**Wait on other over-the-counter medications:** In general, using OTC medicines with kids one year and under isn't recommended.

**What about antibiotics?** The vast majority of infectious diseases in childhood are caused by viruses. Antibiotics attack bacteria, not viruses, so doctors generally don't prescribe antibiotics to rid a kid of a virus. Colds and diarrhea are among the most common viral infections to afflict kids.

- If viruses don't get them, bacteria might. One reason so many resistant bacteria have emerged in the world is the overuse and misuse of antibiotics, much of it with infants and children. Now, with the appearance of hearty new bacterial strains, we're feeling the consequences of those misguided ways. If a child is found to need antibiotics, his or her doctor should prescribe an appropriate drug and dose. Not all antibiotics are safe and approved for children, but many good, effective ones are.

As for **other prescription drugs**, in rare cases an infant's condition may prompt a doctor to prescribe other drugs, such as antacids to treat acid reflux.

## TROGLODYTE HEALTH TROUBLESHOOTER

From "House" to the Surgery Channel, watch enough medical programming on television and you might become delusional enough to believe that, having done your medical residency on the couch, you now have what it takes to diagnose and treat some of the most common illnesses, maladies, and conditions that affect babies.

Put those wild ideas to rest, caveman. It's fine to play doctor (amateur OB-GYN) with the woman in your life, but when what's at stake is nothing less than the health of your offspring, avoid the temptation to substitute layman's judgment for sound medical diagnosis and treatment from real doctors and nurses. What you and your woman can do, though, is make the most of your proximity to the little one by being vigilant in observing his or her condition, reporting any signs of trouble or abnormality to the pros—your baby's medical providers—as soon as possible, and when the situation warrants, taking immediate action (first aid) yourself. In doing so, you'll be filling a critical supporting role in your kid's medical team. To immerse yourself in the role, feel free to walk with a limp and a cane, like Dr. House.

You may never be a medical big shot like he is, but armed with the following information about how to identify and handle some of the most common health issues you're likely to confront during baby's first year, you'll be doing your baby a world of good.

.......................................................

**Allergic reaction** (also see *Stings* later in this section)

- *Causes:* contact, foods, medication, inhaled allergens, bites/stings.

- *Symptoms:* vary depending on the allergen and individual reaction, but may include rash (general, such as hives, a blotchy rash that may come and go or local, similar to poison ivy), respiratory issues (wheezing, cough, shortness of breath), swelling of lips and/or tongue, vomiting or diarrhea.

- *Treatment:* depends on the cause and symptom; rash may be soothed with cool washcloth.

- *See a doctor:* if there are respiratory symptoms.

- *Caution:* Diphenhydramine (an over-the-counter medication included in products such a Benadryl) is often used in older children and adults, but is *not* recommended for infants.

## Colic: It'll Make You Cry, Too

Nothing strikes fear into the hearts and minds of cavemen as much as the unknown. And nothing about the unknown inspires more dread in new parents than the possibility of their child having a condition known as colic. To call it a condition is a euphemism; parents who have come face to face with the beast and lived to tell the tale view colic as a disruptive, ruthless, persistent, and unpredictable monster to be shunned at virtually any cost. Think Linda Blair in *The Exorcist,* minus the revolving head and pea soup projectiles.

Describing colic is easy. Successfully treating it is a different matter entirely, in large part because no one has been able to pinpoint exactly what causes it. Colic is, plain and simple, frequent episodes of excessive, uncontrollable crying with no apparent cause. In medical circles it is more specifically defined as when an otherwise healthy, well-fed baby cries more than three hours a day, at least three days a week for more than three weeks. Colic usually rears its ugly bald head a few weeks after birth. And when it does, its turns babies who otherwise seem healthy into inconsolable crying machines with red, contorted faces, clenched fists, and tensed muscles. If your baby meets these criteria and tends to unleash the fury without warning at about the same time each day, he or she may have colic.

Confronted with colic, parents themselves may become inconsolable as well. It has the power to shatter composure, disrupt sleep routines, and generally wreak havoc on the lives of everyone who shares a household with a colicky baby. The only saving grace: Colic doesn't last forever. It usually improves once baby reaches three months of age. Also take heart in knowing that you're not in this alone, for as many as 25 percent of babies may have colic.

Since the odds of having a colicky baby are relatively high at one in four, wouldn't it be nice to have access to a test, administered during pregnancy, to indicate a fetal predisposition to colic? They've come up with tests to tell whether a woman is pregnant, tests to determine the gender of a fetus, and tests to identify fetal defects and genetic abnormalities. How about a colic test, the positive result from which would at least allow expectant parents to prepare themselves for the coming assault?

One reason no one has come up with such a test is because we have yet to identify colic's cause. Gas, developmental issues, overstimulation, iron in formula, allergies—fingers have been pointed at all sorts of potential causes, both internal and external. It has been shown that babies whose mothers smoke during pregnancy or after delivery have twice the chance of developing colic. Difficult as it is to identify what causes colic, effective treatment is equally elusive. While recent study findings suggest treating it with probiotics may provide relief, further study is needed to solidify that connection.

Until then, the only words to offer to parents with a colicky baby is to stay strong and lean on one another for support (they'll need to lean on something to keep from collapsing from exhaustion), keeping in mind that your baby obviously isn't happy about having the condition either, and that colic will

## Conjunctivitis (pinkeye)

- *Causes:* infection, viral or bacterial (viral is most common); trauma; irritant getting into the eye; allergy.

- *Symptoms:* eye(s) red, swollen, watery, crusty, pus-y, itchy.

- *Special note:* A common condition often mistaken for conjunctivitis occurs when tears fail to drain normally through a duct (the nasolacrimal duct) that goes from the inner eye to the nose (thus the sniffling we get when crying). Symptoms include lots of tearing, without redness. This typically resolves with time, but occasionally the duct needs to be enlarged by a specialist.

- *Treatment:* At home, cleanse eye(s) with moist cotton ball to get rid of crusting; also use saline (lubricating) drops to clean; keep hands of household members clean; avoid excessive contact with other children until clear; antibiotic drops usually don't help, though doctors may prescribe them.

- *See a doctor:* if the skin around the eye is warm and red (indicating potential skin infection called periorbital cellulites) or if baby seems to be in pain (indicating possible trauma or foreign object in the eye).

## Constipation

- *Causes:* in some cases, an intestinal obstruction, stool impaction (too large to pass) or inadequate breast milk intake; constipation more common in bottle-fed infants.

- *Symptoms:* infrequent bowel movements (normal for a baby varies from up to about five per day to one every three days); condition is not usually dangerous.

- *Special note:* Don't confuse a baby's straining or grunting when moving his or her bowels with constipation; these are normal histrionics for cavemen and babies alike.

- *Treatment (short-term):* Soy formulas are less constipating; a warm bath may relax the anus; a glycerin suppository inserted into the anus (use half a baby suppository for babies up to one year); glycerin enema (e.g., Babylax), a little pre-lubricated tube with a squeeze bulb of pre-melted glycerin; if you don't have a suppository, a rectal thermometer or lubricated finger may be used (cover with plastic or finger condom to keep clean and avoid scratching with nail); stool softeners and laxatives generally aren't used for kids under one year old.

- *Treatment (long-term):* Adjust baby's diet; for babies older than four months, provide more fruit juices and foods high in fiber (cereals, prunes, apricots, beans, peas, peaches, applesauce, bananas); cut back on constipating foods, such as dairy (milk, cheese, yogurt); add 1–2 teaspoons of corn syrup (e.g. Karo Syrup, Malt Supex) to a bottle of formula; more water also may help.

- *See a doctor:* if there appears to be severe or persistent pain, there's still no BM after three days and home remedies haven't worked and/or if there's bleeding from baby's rectum.

- *Treatment myths:* Iron in formula causes constipation. Because the amount of iron in formula is so small, the cause of a formula-fed baby's constipation is probably the formula itself.

## Cuts, scrapes, blisters & miscellaneous wounds

- *Seek immediate medical treatment:* for dirty wounds that are hard to get clean; deep cuts to the hand; most cuts on the face; crushed tissue; puncture wounds that are deep, with the tip missing from the object that punctured the skin (presumably it's still lodged inside the baby) or if the offending object was dirty; if bleeding won't stop after applying pressure for several minutes; for any amputation (wrap the part in a clean, moist cloth and bring it to the hospital).

- *Treatment at home:* for bruises, ice for 15 minutes, provide baby ibuprofen or baby acetaminophen for pain; for blisters, don't open them but cover as needed to protect, as they should open naturally; for cuts, stop bleeding with direct pressure, then wash thoroughly with soap and water, apply antibiotic ointment and cover with clean gauze or adhesive bandage, changing the bandage at least daily—and more often if it gets wet or soiled; for scrapes, wash thoroughly with soap and water and if dirt is still present, scrub gently with wet gauze, then apply antibiotic ointment and cover with clean gauze or an adhesive bandage, changing bandage at least daily—and more often if it gets wet or soiled. Wash with warm water and apply antibiotic ointment before applying fresh dressing.

## Diarrhea

- *Causes:* most commonly a viral intestinal infection that generally runs its own course over one to two weeks.

- *Symptoms:* increased frequency and looseness of stool.

disappear by nine months in the vast majority of babies. Your doctor might be able to suggest practical steps you can take at home to soothe a colicky baby, things like infant massage, holding the baby more, offering a pacifier or providing a bit of breast milk.

Adults in the house might require something considerably stronger.

- *See a doctor:* if there are signs of dehydration—baby lacks tears, has a dry mouth, has not urinated for at least eight hours, has a sunken soft spot on top-front of the head, is lethargic or hard to arouse, has had more than eight diarrhea stools in eight hours, has blood in the stool, the baby appears to be in pain or the condition hasn't resolved within two weeks.

- *Treatment at home:* Be sure baby consumes plenty of fluids (milk is fine). If baby is breastfed, mother should continue doing so, but with increased frequency. May add Pedialyte or similar "oral electrolyte solution" in between feedings to maintain hydration; if baby is already eating food and not vomiting, it's okay to give solid food; keep your hands clean because diarrhea is contagious (transmitted fecal to oral); keep skin in diaper area healthy with frequent diaper changes, gentle cleansing, and application of protective ointment like petroleum jelly (Vaseline), Desitin.

- *Avoid:* anti-diarrhea medication and antibiotics.

## Fever

- *Symptoms:* above-normal body temperature, as measured by a thermometer; the definition of a fever varies depending on thermometer placement; when measured rectally or in the ear, it's anything greater than 100.4°F (38°C); orally, any reading greater than 99.5°F (37.5°C); under the arm, any reading greater than 99°F (37.2°C). Look for other symptoms that might suggest a cause (like a runny nose, cough or diarrhea). Severity of symptoms may dictate whether baby needs to be seen by a doctor immediately.

- *Special note:* Temperatures measured in the ear are not very reliable with babies under six months of age; it's best to use a rectal thermometer for children in their first year.

- *See a doctor:* anytime a child under three months of age has a fever (according to the above temperature guidelines). Generally, the younger the baby, the more concerning a fever may be. For infants older than three months, recommendations vary depending on symptoms. Call the doctor if you're unsure how to proceed.

- *Treatment at home:* infant ibuprofen, 5 to 10 mg/kg (about 2.5 to 5 mg/lb) every six hours; or infant acetaminophen, 10 to 15 mg/kg (about 5 to 7 mg/lb) every four hours.

## Head injury

- *Seek immediate medical attention:* if baby is unconscious or hard to arouse; for any significant trauma if the baby is younger than six months; if baby has a seizure, recurrent vomiting (more than three times), neck pain, vision problems, deep or gaping wound(s) or bleeding that won't stop after 10 minutes; if injury was the result of a high-speed incident (car accident, fall from height at least twice child's height); if baby is crying for more than 30 minutes after the incident.

- *Treatment at home:* with head cuts and scrapes, clean with soap and water, cover with clean gauze or adhesive bandage; for swelling, ice for up to 20 minutes; stick to a clear liquid diet for the first couple of hours to ensure there won't be vomiting; awaken the baby twice the first night following the incident to make sure he or she is arousable (possible concussion).

- *Prevention:* don't leave baby unattended on surfaces above the floor; use car seat properly; keep crib side rails up; don't let baby use a baby walker; use gates at the top of stairways.

## Respiratory problems

- *Causes:* multiple, including infections, inhaling a foreign object, allergic reactions.

- *Symptoms:* fast breathing (more than 50 breaths per minute for babies up to one year old); nasal flaring (nostrils get wider with inspiration); retractions (skin above collarbone and/or below edge of ribs seems to suck inward on inspiration); in severe cases, baby's skin may turn blue, first around the lips, then in the mouth and around the nails.

- *Treatment:* Baby usually should be seen immediately at a hospital. If symptoms are on the mild side, call your baby's doctor for advice.

## Cough

- *Causes:* many possibilities; sometimes type of cough suggests a cause (like croup, an infection that causes a barking cough).

- *Treatment at home:* humid air may help; try bringing baby into a steamy bathroom for a few minutes, making sure it's not too hot in there; keep caveling well-hydrated; providing warm, clear liquids may loosen phlegm; no need to stop giving milk; avoid passive cigarette or cigar smoke exposure.

- *Special note:* Avoid cough suppressants—they don't work for babies.

- *See a doctor:* if the cough has not improved after several days, if it's severe or there's any respiratory distress.

................................................................

## Seizure/loss of consciousness

- *Causes:* possibilities too numerous to name here.

- *Treatment at home:* During any seizure, make sure the airway isn't blocked. You may "sweep" the mouth with your finger to clear any debris or food. You can also do a jaw thrust by pushing the lower jaw forward from the back of the mandible (below the ears). If there is vomiting, place the baby on his or her side and clear the vomit with a suction bulb or your finger. Don't try to restrain the baby or keep the little one from shaking during convulsions.

- *See a doctor immediately:* if it's baby's first seizure—call 911 or bring the baby to the hospital. **Be careful** driving! The risk of an accident from speeding may be greater than the risk posed by the seizure itself.

- *Special notes:* It's important to make the distinction between febrile and non-febrile seizures. Febrile seizures are generally not dangerous, although very frightening. They generally may occur during early in an illness, at the first fever spike.

................................................................

## Splinter

- *Treatment at home:* Have a good quality set of tweezers; if the splinter tip is visible, try to pull it out along the same angle of entry; wash with soap and water if unable to remove completely.

- *See a doctor:* if the area is painful or its shows signs/symptoms of infection, including redness, swelling, discharge of pus (thick yellow/opaque fluid).

................................................................

## Stings (bee or wasp)

- *Symptoms:* first try to identify the type of insect that caused the sting (about 95 percent come from yellow jackets); if unable to do so, keep in mind that bee/wasp stings typically cause an almost immediate painful red bump.

- *Treatment at home:* If you see a black dot in the middle of the site, that indicates the sting came from a honeybee. If you get the stinger out within one minute, you may reduce the venom exposure. Scrape it off with a fingernail or credit card. Medications that may help include pain medicine (acetaminophen or ibuprofen, infant formulas) and Benadryl (diphenhydramine) for itching. A paste made from meat tenderizer and water (or a paste of baking soda) can help lessen the pain, too. Rubbing with an ice cube may also provide temporary relief.

- *Seek medical treatment immediately:* if there are signs of anaphylaxis (systemic allergic reaction), call 911 or take the child immediately to the hospital. It is potentially fatal. Difficulty breathing, tightness in the throat or chest, difficulty swallowing or speaking, passing out, and a past history of serious reaction to stings are signs/symptoms of anaphylaxis. If you see those signs and an Epi-Pen is available, administer it promptly (the upper, outer thigh is a good spot). Epi-Pen Jr. is designed for children weighing 20 to 50 pounds.

- Also seek immediate medical treatment if the child is stung in the mouth or tongue (may swell), if there are multiple stings (more than 10) or if the area looks infected.

## Sunburn

- *Cause:* overexposure to harmful rays of the sun

- *Symptoms:* most sunburns are first-degree; second-degree sunburns are indicated by blistering; most sunburns won't scar but do hurt.

- *Treatment at home:* infant ibuprofen, cool baths, antibiotic ointment for any open blisters, 1% hydrocortisone cream to the affected area three times per day; provide lots of fluids to drink.

- *See a doctor immediately:* if second-degree sunburn (manifested by blisters) covers 10 percent or more of baby's body surface; if the child is very weak or has passed out; if there are signs of infection.

## Vomiting (aka booting, ralphing, yiffing, chundering, upchucking, heaving, yakking, kakking, throwing up, busting a vessel, praying to the porcelain god)

- *Special note:* Don't confuse a true vomit—emptying a large amount of one's stomach contents—with spitting up or reflux, where a baby expels one or two mouthfuls of stomach content.

- *Cause:* most commonly, a viral intestinal illness called gastroenteritis.

- *See a doctor:* if there are signs or symptoms of dehydration (see diarrhea info); if there is blood in baby's vomit; if an infant less than three months old vomits more than once (could be a symptom of sepsis or other more severe illness); if baby appears to be in significant pain; if you suspect that baby swallowed a foreign object or other non-food item (chemical, plant material, etc.); if baby is lethargic or hard to arouse; if baby recently sustained an injury (such as to the head or abdomen).

- *Treatment at home:* Provide clear liquids, such as Pedialyte or similar oral electrolyte solution, or diluted sport drink (like Gatorade). Give liquids in small amounts, since too much at once can itself trigger vomiting. Start with 1 to 2 teaspoons every five minutes and increase as tolerated, continuing that course until baby goes several hours without vomiting.

- Breastfeeding can generally be continued, but first try giving less milk per feeding, with more frequent feedings. Increase feeding volume gradually as tolerated. Begin reintroducing solids (if baby has been eating solid food) gradually after eight hours without vomiting. Foods such as bread, crackers, rice, cereals, and bananas are good starting points.

- *Special note:* Medicines to treat vomiting are not recommended for infants less than one year old.

## DENTAL ADVICE TO SINK YOUR TEETH INTO

Asked to explain the sorry state of his choppers, the late Joe Strummer, frontman for The Clash, one of the best rock-and-roll bands to ever smash a guitar onstage, acknowledged *never* having brushed his teeth. Though Strummer's premature passing at age 50 was the result of a congenital heart issue, there are compelling reasons, both health and aesthetic, to start your baby on a regular dental care routine as soon as he or she sprouts teeth.

Both the American Academy of Pediatric Dentistry (www.aapd.org) and the American Dental Association (www.ada.org) recommend a "first dental visit by first birthday" policy for babies. The main reason they say a child should visit a pediatric dentist within six months of the first tooth coming is prevention. Dental problems, such as early childhood caries (aka baby bottle tooth decay) can come early. But with the help of a dentist, they can be identified and treated early, too. Early dental visits are similar to "well baby check-ups" your baby has with the doctor. They give the dentist a chance to check for tooth decay and other problems, and to show parents proper teeth-cleaning techniques to use with a baby.

In rare cases, infants and toddlers whose teeth have been neglected experience tooth decay so severe it requires dental restorations or extractions. Usually decay occurs when the remnants of liquids like milk (cow or breast), juice or formula are left clinging to an infant's teeth for an extended period, such as during a nap. While baby slumbers, bacteria present in his or her mouth feeds on the sugars in those liquids, producing acids that can attack teeth. However, with proactive parents, all that is preventable. Here, courtesy of the ADA and AAPD, are some steps to take to spare your caveling from British Rock & Roll Bad Teeth Syndrome (co-poster boys: Strummer, Shane MacGowan, and pre-1980 Keith Richards):

- To prevent tooth decay from a bottle or nursing, **encourage your child to drink from a cup.**

- **Don't allow the little one to fall asleep with a bottle.** If he or she craves something to suck at bedtime, provide a pacifier instead.

- **Avoid providing milk (or juice)** just before bed, unless the baby's teeth will be brushed right afterwards.

- **Begin weaning the baby off the bottle** around his or her first birthday or soon thereafter.

- **Start the dental regimen early**—before the first tooth arrives—by cleaning your child's gums with a soft infant toothbrush or gauze pad and water after each feeding. Once teeth arrive, brush them before naptime and bedtime (fluoridated toothpaste isn't recommended until age 2 to 3 but there are non-fluoride toothpaste products for babies).

- If the drinking water in your home doesn't contain **fluoride** (which helps prevent tooth decay), ask a dentist to recommend an alternative fluoride source.

## GROOMING YOUR SUCCESSOR

Chimpanzees do it and so should you. Grooming is an essential part of any person's good personal hygiene. And since babies generally can't do it themselves, they rely on their caregivers to do it for them.

View grooming not as a chore but as an opportunity to better familiarize yourself with your offspring's little bod and its condition. That familiarity will also allow you to spot signs of trouble. Make it a family activity and grooming becomes both a bonding session and a laugh-a-thon that will provide you and your woman with lots of fond memories. No need for the caveman to attend beauty school to perform basic grooming responsibilities, which include:

**Clipping nails:** This is a delicate but necessary activity, since flailing babies have been known to scratch themselves with long fingernails. It's best performed by a steady-handed person armed with clippers made for use on baby nails.

**Skincare:** Odd dermatological phenomena are common to infants (see the section earlier this chapter); your job is to help the baby ward off conditions such as dry skin and diaper rash. Do so by changing diapers frequently and using very mild creams when conditions warrant. Not all store-bought products touted for use with babies are actually suitable for such sensitive skin. Talk to your doctor about the skincare products and treatment options that are best for your baby.

**Ears, eyes, and nose:** Keeping babies breathing, hearing, and seeing things clearly can be a formidable challenge given their prolific production of potentially blockage-forming bodily substances. Removing those blockages may require very careful use of cotton swabs, tweezers, etc.

**Bathing:** Few experiences for new parents are as memorable as the first bath they give a newborn. Use a special infant bathtub, warm water, and a soft cloth—and have a camera and a soft swaddling towel ready.

**Hair care:** If your little one has hair on his or her head, all it needs is gentle washing and perhaps combing or brushing. Use very mild soap/shampoo, or just water. After the bath, if there's enough hair to devise a "style," try a few different looks.

There's nothing like a nice, warm bath to prime a baby for a night of strong, uninterrupted shut-eye. Indeed, sleep is one of the most prized commodities for babies and new parents alike. Keep reading to gain insight on what it takes to groom your caveling into a champion sleeper.

# CHAPTER 7

## SLEEP

THE ESSENTIALS
TO TURN YOUR LITTLE TROG
INTO AN OVERNIGHT SENSATION

In a windowless room starkly illuminated by a single, bald light bulb, six men sit tightly packed around a wobbly vinyl-topped card table. Here in this mildewed basement turned makeshift poker parlor, Gronk and a handful of friends have gathered for some subterranean, low-stakes Texas hold 'em.

This isn't your typical boisterous, testosterone-fueled poker gathering. The music is muted, as are the interactions among players. The combatants themselves seem guarded, on edge, almost timid. But that's not a result of the action at the table so much as the edict that has come down from on high: Gronk may host poker night, but only on the condition that the festivities be conducted belowground in the remote reaches of the basement, that noise be kept to an absolute minimum, and that there be no smoking or histrionics of any kind. A strict 11 p.m. curfew applies. Gronk largely agrees with the policy, knowing full well that if anything wakes the Peanut, six troglodyte heads will roll, starting with his.

While the childless cretins who are at the table this night raise their eyebrows at Gronk as if to question his sanity and manhood, the dads who are there know what's going on: They are visitors in a household where a baby resides. And when it's time for the little one to sleep, there can be no disruptions. House rules in this case have nothing to do with poker. They are designed to protect the infant sleeper at any cost. In Gronk's household, "Silence is Golden" is the only rule that matters, even on poker night. Other rules, like no peeking at an opponent's cards, no splitting a blind, and no farting upwind, are secondary. Before the cards are dealt, the players have been warned that any actions that cause even a slight stirring from Baby Peanut will result in immediate banishment. The house has authority to close the game at any time.

Such policies may seem a bit over-the-top to the average outsider, especially when they infringe on honorable pursuits like poker, but to the parents of an infant they make perfect sense. Sleep in a household with a baby is indeed a precious commodity to be

*Grow with Gronk*

What the caveman stands to gain from reading Chapter 7:

- A deep appreciation for the value of sleep—to babies and parents alike
- A working knowledge of the lengths to which parents will go to keep a baby asleep
- A clear understanding of infant sleep requirements and habits
- The know-how to develop and execute a solid sleep strategy
- Familiarity with co-sleeping, where parents and baby share a bed
- An arsenal of proven pointers to send a baby into la-la land
- Insight into SIDS and how to keep a sleeping baby safe
- The skills to create a sleep-conducive atmosphere
- A hands-on grasp of how to swaddle a baby
- The wisdom to seek the help of a sleep consultant if necessary
- Entrée into the wonderful world of infant massage
- An understanding of the bond-building benefits of baby massage
- Techniques to give the troglodyte a deft infant massage touch

coveted, protected, and savored by all who live there. Not only must parents honor a baby's need for *a lot* of sleep, they quickly will realize that their own sleep habits are directly linked to those of their offspring. Thus it is with a librarian-like zeal bordering on paranoiac ardor that they will attempt to preserve peace and quiet.

The late, great rock-and-roll animal Warren Zevon wrote a song back in the seventies called, "I'll Sleep When I'm Dead." Cancer, not a lack of shut-eye, killed Zevon in 2003 at age 56. But the fact is, while he may have gone long stretches without it, nobody can survive for long without good, solid sleep. That's especially true of babies, for whom sleep is the fuel that powers rapid physical and mental development. A typical newborn needs somewhere between 15–18 hours of slumber each day. Most new parents are thrilled to get about half that amount on a daily basis. The challenge for parents and babies alike is finding and sticking to a routine that accommodates everybody's need for Zs.

From birth, some babies seem to be naturally gifted sleepers. Others seem to emerge from the womb with a perpetual caffeinated wakefulness. What many new parents might not realize is that *all* babies need some degree of coaching to become consistently good sleepers. Little ones don't enter the world with an innate ability to conform to a routine in which they are wakeful during the daytime, unfailingly sleep solidly at night, and nap at other times throughout the day to meet their recommended daily sleep requirement. Neither are most babies born with the ability to soothe themselves into sleep, nor to find a rhythm that allows them to stay asleep, even amid noise or other distractions. These are all qualities that a baby must learn. And as a parent, you have the power to instill sleeping skills in your baby, just as you do basic moral values, motor, communication and interpersonal skills, good manners and personal hygiene, common sense, fashion sense and, of course, proper fly-fishing techniques.

Among all the need-fulfillment activities you undertake on behalf of your baby, sleep is among the most critical. How your lives and your lifestyles unfold here in baby's first year will depend largely on whether there's an abundance or a shortage of sleep in your household. What's more, the good sleeping habits you help your baby develop early in life will lay the groundwork for future sack artistry later in life. Indeed, as vital as sleep is to an infant, it's just as important for us older folk. One recent study out of Great

Britain found that people who do not get enough sleep are more than twice as likely to die of heart disease as those who do. It linked a lack of sleep to increased blood pressure, which in turn has been shown to heighten the risk of heart attack and stroke.

With so much at stake, the goal of this chapter is to help new parents find the philosophies and tactics that work best with their little ones. When it comes to slumber strategies, there is no single formula for success. What works well with some babies might get nowhere with others. Sometimes finding a successful sleep formula comes down to simple trial and error, where after considerable groping you eventually find a routine that works. When you do, by all means stick to it, but do so with the knowledge that as your baby evolves mentally and physically, so, too, will his or her sleep habits. A routine that once worked without a hitch may suddenly, inexplicably and in some instances, permanently, turn ineffective.

All this is enough to keep many a caveman awake at night. But rather than spending restless hours in bed fretting over what the future might hold for the sleeping habits of the people in your household now that there's a baby in your life, you're better served to embrace the unknown. Before you is an opportunity to foster in your little one a valuable skill he or she will call upon frequently throughout life: the ability to answer the body's need for sleep anyplace, anytime. When later in life your kid shows an ability to nod off on a train in rural India that's teeming with people and livestock, in a three-person tent jammed with four other campers and a dog, or during high-stress times that turn average sleepers into insomniacs, he or she will have you to thank.

It's also an opportunity to stare down your own parental fears and feelings of helplessness, to assert the power you wield as a papa to control your own destiny and that of your child, to survive your baby's first 12 months without adding to the baggage under your eyes. The bravado of Zevon's "I'll sleep when I'm dead" slogan might hold some appeal from afar, but you and everyone else in your home are better off adhering to a less macho but eminently more reasonable policy: "I'll sleep when I'm tired."

## WHATEVER GETS YOU THROUGH THE NIGHT...

From the outside looking in, the lengths parents will go to in order to steal some shut-eye for their child and themselves seem downright ridiculous. Remember how you shook your head at the absurd notion of one of your buddies taking his baby out for 3 a.m. car rides just to get the tykster to sleep? Once you're on the inside, however, the absurd suddenly seems sensible. Don't look now, but you and your woman soon could find yourselves seriously considering taking the following measures to stay in the Sandman's good graces:

| | |
|---|---|
| **Household Habits** | Learning exactly which stairs are the creaky ones, and taking stairs three at a time to avoid the offending planks. |
| | Practicing lip-reading or using the closed-captioning feature when watching television. |
| | Leaving doors and windows gaping wide for fear the noise of closing them might awaken the little one. |
| | Postponing chores such as dishwashing, vacuuming, and laundry in order to preserve absolute silence. |
| | Always removing the dog's collar indoors for fear the jingle will roust the sleeping angel. |
| **Relationships** | Tightening and lubricating hardware on the bedframe to limit coital squeaking. |
| | Cursing the neighbor who unwittingly mows the lawn during your kid's naptime. |
| | Second-guessing the decision to invite your buddy with the banshee laugh and his wife the loud-talker over for dinner. |
| | Swearing vengeance against any dog that dares bark while the caveling is sleeping. |
| **Personal Habits & Hygiene** | Holding one's breath when a car horn, siren, train whistle, motorcycle, thunderstorm or other potentially disruptive sound erupts. |
| | Stuffing just about anything into one's nose or mouth in order to stifle a sneeze or cough that could wake a baby. |

| | |
|---|---|
| **Personal Habits & Hygiene (continued)** | Muting normal chewing noises, avoiding belches and throat-clearing, when in a sleeping baby's presence. |
| | Stripping heels from all shoes in the household. |
| | Taking Navy showers or bidet baths, or abstaining from washing altogether, if there's a chance the sound of running water might wake the caveling. |
| | Flogging all rules of john decorum by not flushing the toilet, even after you've turned the bowl into a Superfund site. |
| **Communications** | Answering phone calls in a whisper. |
| | Conversing with your woman only in gestures and hushed tones. |
| | Replacing the "No Soliciting" sign on your front door with a much larger one reading, "Knock softly. Do not ring doorbell. Remove shoes upon entry." |
| **Consumer Habits** | Replacing existing phones with those that offer a silent ring feature, and equipping your woman's hairdryer with a silencer. |
| | Replacing window(s) in baby's room with soundproof, tinted glass. |
| | Trading in the gasoline-powered car for a hybrid model whose quieter drivetrain better accommodates in-vehicle napping. |
| | Covering all exposed floor surfaces in the home with thick, sound-muffling wall-to-wall carpeting, decorating scheme be damned. |

For babies, life presents a constant barrage of new stimuli, sensations, and experiences. Soaking it all up probably gets pretty exhausting, especially when all the while little ones must also devote significant energies to physical and mental development. With all the goings-on internally and externally, babies are creatures who crave their own brand of R&R: **rest** (as in good, solid sleep) and **ritual**. Amid so much newness, they need a few sure things in life. One is a sleep routine. Babies tend to thrive with a structured sleep schedule in which they can count on naptime and bedtime happening about the same time each day, just like the caveman appreciates certain elements of his daily ritual, some too personal to detail here.

In hunting, fishing, dating, and other pursuits involving conquest, a contemporary Cro-Magnon might prefer his quarry to be stationary. To these sporting types, who would rather club a fish than catch it with a perfectly placed cast using an artfully tied and carefully selected fly, a baby's sleep habits might seem particularly confounding, for while a wee one may flourish with a structured sleep regimen, his or her sleep requirements will change frequently over the course of the first year.

Experienced fly-fishermen come to the stream equipped for variable conditions. The good ones know to stock their tackle boxes differently for a caddis fly hatch than for a mayfly hatch. They would never use a woolly bugger when a midge is obviously more to the cutthroat's liking. They're always ready to swap a wet fly for a dry fly when conditions dictate. They most certainly aren't going to use a gold-ribbed hare's ear nymph when the situation calls for a sparkle dun emerger.

Similarly, parents must be flexible and prepared to adjust sleep schedules and strategies on the fly, as the need arises. While every child is different, for the sake of preparedness it surely doesn't hurt to have a rough idea of how your kid's sleep patterns might evolve in the months ahead. Consider this a primer, which we suggest you supplement with additional information from the best-qualified among the myriad sources on baby sleep. This info is everywhere: online, in print, and from primary sources—your friends, family, neighbors, co-workers, bystanders, etc.

Early on in life, a baby's **birth weight** likely will be a key factor in sleep patterns. Heavier babies tend to go longer stretches without needing food, while lighter ones may need to be fed more frequently. Other factors that may weigh heavily in the first-year slumber equation include **teething, digestive issues,** major **leaps in development** (characterized by heightened mental awareness and physical prowess), **illness,** and **imperviousness** to noise and other disturbances (or lack thereof).

There are two alternating types or states of sleep. **Non-rapid eye movement** (quiet) sleep is the deeper of the two, during which the body is hard at work restoring energy, growing, and repairing tissue while releasing hormones to stimulate development. In the REM, or **rapid eye movement** (active) state, the brain is active and dreaming and the body is less active than in NREM mode. For about the first six months of life, babies spend an equal amount of time in each of the two sleep cycles, with each cycle lasting about 45 minutes. After that babies begin to spend more time in NREM sleep.

**Month 1:** *15 to 18 hours of sleep daily*, with frequent naps and wakeful stretches seldom lasting more than two hours, interspersed with feedings, diaper changes, and time to interact. It is during this phase that parents are most apt to marvel at baby's ability to sleep through anything. Indeed, newborns are apt to shut down and sleep when their surroundings become too noisy or overstimulating. Now's the time to grab your woman and, with baby in tow, hit some of your favorite dinner spots, before the little one becomes more alert and thus, at least in some circumstances, less accommodating to such outings. If you're not up for going out, keep the TV off and turn to your slumbering baby for some guaranteed-to-please entertainment, where you can watch the small one flail his or

# DR. BRIAN

*Sleep, There is No Substitute*

From the meltdown at the Three Mile Island nuclear power plant and the *Exxon Valdez's* ill-fated collision to ongoing sleepwalking episodes in the Oval Office, history is full of cautionary tales that underscore the potentially disastrous consequences of sleep deprivation—and the value of a good night's sleep—for infants and adults alike.

The benefits of sleep can be as obvious as a baby waking up happy after a solid night of slumber. Yet many of the benefits sleep showers upon an infant are not so immediately obvious and instead manifest themselves over the longer term. We know that sleep not only allows babies to recharge their batteries, it also provides time for their bodies to repair themselves, ward off illness, and really focus on mental and physical development. The amount of shuteye babies need indicates just how demanding the work of brain and body development must be. By the age of one, most babies will have spent significantly more time asleep than awake. Hopefully you'll be able to count your baby among this group.

But babies aren't the only ones who benefit from solid sleep. Adults need an average of seven to nine hours of the stuff each night. However, recent studies show that a majority of American adults typically get less than the recommended eight hours a night. Those who do get it should benefit from a stronger immune system, less stress, a healthier heart, a sharper mind, and better physical reactions.

On the other hand, chronically poor sleep habits, according to research, can have all sorts of unsavory effects. They can make a person overweight or obese and may cause the body to mimic the effects of aging, while also hampering concentration, memory, judgment, and problem-solving ability. A chronic lack of sleep also may increase the chances of diabetes, cardiovascular disease, and infections.

her limbs, pantomime breastfeeding, and contort the facial features into absurd grimaces, smiles, puckers, and old-feller expressions.

**Months 2 to 4:** *14 to 16 hours of sleep daily.* Regular sleep patterns (circadian rhythms) may begin to emerge as the time between feedings hopefully begins to stretch out, with longer sleep periods of four to six hours occurring more regularly in the evening. Two-thirds of baby's shut-eye may now occur at nighttime, supplemented by several daytime naps. Baby's heightened sociability may mean greater resistance to sleep, while greater sensitivity to noise, light, etc., means it's time to put more emphasis on sleeping environment. At three or four months, it's also time for the baby to start using self-soothing techniques—rhythmically rocking or rooting in bed, or sucking a thumb or a pacifier—that allow him or her to find the slumber zone without outside assistance.

**Months 5 to 8:** *14 to 15 hours of sleep daily,* including stretches as long as nine to 12 hours at night. At six months, about two-thirds of babies have the ability to regularly string together several sleep cycles consecutively in order to plow on through the night without waking. At this point, nighttime feedings may be eliminated and the baby also might be ready to drop from three naps to two. One less nap might mean a shift to earlier naptimes and bedtime. Don't be surprised if sleep is at times disrupted by your baby's burning desire to work on some of the new skills he or she has been developing. Beware separation anxiety, which at about six months can begin disrupting the nice, comfortable sleep-through-the-night routine you've managed to settle into. Separation anxiety is a common phenomenon in which a baby does not understand that separation from someone like a parent is temporary. It can cause a baby to resist going to bed, to cry when a caretaker leaves the room, and to awaken during the night. Sadly this is a phenomenon that some mama's-boys-cum-cavemen never can shake.

**Months 9 to 12:** *14 to 15 hours of sleep daily.* By now, 70–80 percent of babies are regularly sleeping through the night. With a more developed personality comes a stronger will and thus, perhaps, greater resistance to your efforts to stick to a sleep routine. While the little one's overall sleep requirement hasn't changed much, now is the time when it likely will shift from daytime to nighttime, with less time for naps and a longer overnight sleep session. Potential sleep disruptions may arise as baby begins wrapping his or mind around a move to crawling, standing, and/or walking.

Sleep is a fairly straightforward exercise, something a typical caveman can do with his eyes closed. There is little mystery to his nightly bedtime routine, which, if he's not busy with baby duty, goes something like this:

1. **Acknowledge signs of weariness**—thousand-mile stare, 60-second-long blinks, slumping, twitching, drooling, snoring.

2. **Freshen up**—shed day's clothing for sleepwear; visit bathroom to wash, take care of dental hygiene and elimination responsibilities; 100 strokes through the mane with a hairbrush.

3. **Bedroom rites**—banish dog or cat from pillow; peel back covers; brush loose particles from sheets; fluff pillow; assume horizontal position; make half-hearted advances toward woman and if rebuffed, reach for reading material; return to horizontal position; several minutes of non-retentive reading; remove book from face; renew advances toward woman; if re-rebuffed, extinguish light; commence buzz-saw snoring.

Men who perceive sleep—the build-up to it and the actual act itself—as a routine, automatic process will be amazed at the encyclopedic body of information dedicated to the sleep dynamics of people in the youngest segment of the populace: what gets them tired, what gets them to sleep, what keeps them asleep, and what keeps them awake. As parents, we are assaulted with hundreds upon hundreds of secrets, short-cuts, and sure-fire solutions, all of which promise to help our babies, and therefore us, sleep better.

The sheer breadth and volume of all this information leads to two conclusions: (1) that there are many legitimate experts on the subject of baby sleep habits, but also some quacks who are about as qualified to write a book on baby sleep as we are to write one on the first year of fatherhood; and (2) that mankind can (allegedly) clone a sheep but still hasn't been able to identify a single, surefire, one-size-fits-all sleep strategy for babies. Finding one might be a worthy goal, but it just ain't happening.

Though in many ways at Square One of their development, babies still are distinct little people, with unique (though still very formative) personalities and their own relationships with sleep. Somewhere out there is a sleep regimen that likely will work for you and your baby. But odds are you are going to have to custom-design it yourself, based on your own observations of your baby's disposition and your ability to identify, interpret, and act upon the "I'm ready to sleep" signals your baby is sending.

In many cases, however, given the fickle and tenuous nature of infant sleeping habits, there will be times when it's constructive to solicit some outside perspective from true sleep experts, whose insights you can find in libraries, bookstores and on the Internet. The brain trust behind this book elected not to wade too deeply into infant sleep theory, nor to venture to critique the various theories in any depth, because frankly, those are matters better left to you, your woman, and other members of the caveling's caregiving squad. Given that, we *strongly* recommend reading at least a book or two on the subject, for there will be nuggets in there that may prove truly practical and effective, saving you countless wakeful hours of grief and frustration. We also strongly suggest that you approach these information sources with your parental filter on, for they will confront you with a ton of suggestions and positions, some confusing, some conflicting, some not applicable to your situation, and some certainly viable enough to merit your consideration. Below are a few books we found to be particularly insightful and thus worthy of you and your woman's time. Given the huge quantity of information on the subject, you might also want to poll your parenting peers about their personal preferences.

> *The Happiest Baby on the Block*
> by Harvey Karp, M.D.

> *Healthy Sleep Habits, Happy Child*
> by Marc Weissbluth, M.D.

> *Secrets of the Baby Whisperer* and *The Baby Whisperer Solves All Your Problems* by Tracy Hogg & Melinda Blau (not to be confused with the work of our friend, Pat, the *Breast* Whisperer).

> *Touchpoints, Birth to 3* by T. Berry Brazelton, M.D.

With the pieces of wisdom you cull from published sources, plus your own firsthand observations, you and your woman should be able to cobble together a homespun game plan for winning the Sleep Wars, one that turns the Sandman into your ally, not your adversary. What you want are effective techniques rooted in solid, repeatable sleep fundamentals, not gimmicks and short-term fixes.

Finding them entails actually field-testing methods on the infant, a trial-and-error process to see what really works and what doesn't with your little one. Expect progress to come with occasional setbacks and missteps.

With a plan of attack in place, a clan of barbarian cavedwellers that invaded a rival tribe stood a much better chance of successful pillage. Likewise, it will behoove you and your woman to devise a plan of attack for the Sleep Wars—to talk about which strategies you agree with, which you don't, how to divide sleep responsibilities, and as time goes by, what seems to work for your little one and what doesn't. Strictly adhering to a figure-it-out-as-we-go, fly-by-the-seats-of-our-pelts approach will turn the Sandman from friend to foe, one who mocks you before plundering your much-needed sleep reserves. Here are some elements to consider including in such a game plan. If having things in writing gives you peace of mind, consider treating it like a birthing plan (a written labor and delivery strategy/script used by expectant parents), where you have crib notes to which to refer when you're too tired to think clearly.

**Sleeping venue(s):** Will the infant sleep next to you in a cradle/bassinette to start? What are the merits of co-sleeping, where you actually share your bed with the baby? When will baby move from the cradle or co-sleeping set-up to a crib in his or her own room?

**Sleep signals:** What body language is the baby using to signal that sleep is needed and/or imminent? Refer to the sleep tips section that follows for some common cues.

**Schedule:** Over time, sleep patterns should begin to emerge to indicate the times of day for naps, their typical duration, etc. Recognizing these times gives you the makings of a sleep schedule.

**Routine:** What wind-down rituals will you incorporate into baby's naptime and bedtime routines: bath, cuddling, taking a bottle, soft singing, reading, rocking (but never in conjunction with rolling), maybe massage (highly recommended—and detailed later in this chapter)?

**Commitment:** Prick the tips of your index fingers with a sterilized needle and make a blood pact that the two of you (and relevant caretakers) will do your level best to stick to the naptime/bedtime routine and schedule. Even departures of 15 to 30 minutes can throw a baby's schedule out of whack.

**Division of labor:** Who's going to put baby to bed for which naps? Who will wake up to administer which overnight feedings? Will

## Co-sleeping: Catching Winks Walton Style

If for reasons baby-related or otherwise you find yourself channel-surfing on the couch late at night rather than in bed sleeping, you might be lucky enough to stumble upon reruns of a television show called *The Waltons* that had a solid run back in the 1970s. It chronicled the lives of a family living south of the Mason-Dixon line around the time of the Great Depression and World War II. Not only did 11 Waltons—John and Olivia, their seven children, and John's parents Zeb and Esther—live together under one roof, many of them slept in the same bed. While 11 isn't an optimal number to cram into any one bed unless it's at a cuddle party, some new parents believe that when it comes to sleeping arrangements involving an infant, three's a perfect number.

Some families today prefer to keep their babies in bed with them—such as in a three-sided sleep structure, specially designed for a baby, that attaches to an adult bed—rather than in a separate cradle or bassinette. It's called co-sleeping or bed-sharing, a practice begun in prehistoric times that endures today in various cultures around the world. As a sleep strategy, it has strong supporters and detractors.

Advocates of the "family bed" point out that co-sleeping makes nighttime breastfeeding more convenient, fosters a more solid sleep for a baby, and strengthens the bond between parents and offspring. Detractors argue that co-sleeping subjects babies to unnecessary risk (such as being pancaked by a fellow sleeper), makes them overly dependent

you alternate nights? What about late-night diaper changes? If one parent is ill or overtired, will the other one be prepared to pick up the slack?

**Tactics:** What techniques will you employ to soothe a restless baby and send him or her off (or back) to the Land of Nod? Will you use the old-school cry-it-out approach if baby won't go down easily, for example?

**Crisis management:** How will you handle unexpected wakings and other potentially disruptive X factors such as illness? What will you and your woman do to cope with any frustration, anger, and exasperation you might feel when things don't go smoothly?

**Ongoing observation:** A keen ability to notice subtle changes in your baby, and to share what you've observed with your partner, will serve you well in the Sleep Wars, where tactics are always subject to adjustment, as dictated by the baby's evolving sleep needs and patterns.

## LIKE A ROCK: 25 CAN'T-MISS, ABSOLUTELY FOOLPROOF SLEEP TIPS FOR TYKSTERS

What kind of unrest was Dylan Thomas trying to foment among our infants when he wrote, "Do not go gentle into that good night"? A baby who routinely goes gently into that good night is every parent's dream.

But we're not going to sugarcoat things. The path to fulfilling that dream can be elusive. One-third of children ages six to 11 months regularly wake up twice per night or more needing help or attention, according to findings from a recent survey conducted by the National Sleep Foundation. What's more, it found that with 64 percent of babies and toddlers, some sort of behavior—waking during the night, resisting going to bed, waking too early, etc.—interfered with them getting their recommended sleep dosage at least a few nights a week.

This is not a fate to which your family must resign itself, however. *Vee halff vays* of helping babies sleep. Here's a list of tried-and-true techniques to try on a fitful, slumber-resistant youngster, some endorsed by the world's foremost sleep connoisseurs and others derived from our own experience in the Sleep Wars.

**TIP 1:** Provide baby plenty of mental and physical activity and stimulation during awake time. A more active baby tends to sleep better.

**TIP 2:** Learn and heed baby's sleep signals. Common cues include rubbing eyes and face, pulling or grabbing at ears, flailing arms, getting circles under the eyes. Once you see them, launch into the sleeptime routine as quickly as possible.

**TIP 3:** Create and stick to a schedule. You control when your baby sleeps. Consistently missing naps or starting them late can easily scuttle any schedule you try to establish, making for a miserable, sleep-deprived household.

**TIP 4:** Prioritize the baby's schedule above your own. Eventually your commitment to adhere to baby's sleep schedule is likely to be rewarded with more sleep and more adult time for you.

**TIP 5:** Create a sleep-conducive environment. More on this later in the chapter.

**TIP 6:** Create and stick to a ritual. Consistently doing the same things leading up to bedtime is most likely to keep baby in the comfort zone.

**TIP 7:** Don't rush the ritual. You might be in a hurry to catch the last few innings of the ballgame, but the bedtime wind-down routine is one to be savored, not hurried.

**TIP 8:** Try keeping the venue consistent. Babies who are allowed to frequently nap outside their normal sleeping quarters, such as in the car, stroller, etc., may have more trouble sleeping at home.

**TIP 9:** Avoid overstimulating the young lad or lass right before bedtime. You need to wind baby down, not up, before sleep.

**TIP 10:** Don't assume a later bedtime means a longer/later sleep. Keeping the little one up late is a recipe for shorter, more disrupted sleep. Conversely, an early bedtime gives baby a better chance to sleep long and sound.

**TIP 11:** Whenever possible, put baby to bed on the brink of sleep, not while asleep. This gives the youngster a chance to learn how to find his or her own way into la-la land (self-soothing).

**TIP 12:** Don't bolt into baby's room at the first peep of distress. Infants can be noisy and fitful at times, even during slumber. Oftentimes the disturbance is minor enough that the little one, with a little self-soothing, will quickly find his or her own way back to sleep.

on being near parents to sleep, and disrupts much-needed parental sleep. If you're a private type who prefers conducting bedroom business without another entity—human, feline, canine, bovine, whatever—in the room with you, co-sleeping might not be for you.

If you are considering co-sleeping with your infant, keep in mind that the U.S. Consumer Product Safety Commission and the American Academy of Pediatrics warn against allowing infants to sleep in beds designed for adults, where they're at greater risk of suffocation and strangulation. Also keep in mind that eventually you will have to transition your little one into his or her own sleep quarters. The longer babies and parents share a bed, the more difficult the transition may be. Just ask John-Boy Walton.

**TIP 13:** Equip the crib with a few comfort items, like a soft blanket and a stuffed animal, that baby will learn to covet and to use as sleep aids for the comfort they provide.

**TIP 14:** For unexpected wake-ups, first wait to see if the baby goes back to sleep. If you must go see the little one, offer comfort and reassurance while he or she remains in the crib. Picking up can lead the baby to expect more interaction, a bad idea at this time of night—and a potentially habit-forming precedent.

**TIP 15:** With a crying baby, try waiting a few minutes, then, if crying persists, going into the room, offering in-crib comfort (patting, stroking, soft singing), tell baby it's time to go to sleep, say goodnight again, and leave. Repeat if necessary, waiting slightly longer periods between re-entry each time.

**TIP 16:** Share overnight feeding duties to give one another solid blocks of sleep and to give baby some variety in who delivers the goods, so he or she doesn't grow dependent on a sleep ritual involving just one parent.

**TIP 17:** During overnight feedings, keep activity quiet and stimulation to a minimum. The message to baby: This is sleeptime. Enjoy the meal, but you're headed right back to bed.

**TIP 18:** Try to gradually lengthen time between overnight feedings so your baby will sleep for longer stretches. The obvious goal: uninterrupted, through-the-night shut-eye for one and all.

**TIP 19:** Don't be afraid to wake baby for a "dream feed" before you and your woman go to bed at night. The dream feed, in which you gently lift baby out of bed and provide a bottle or a breast as he or she dozes, can be a crucial tool in bridging a little one to through-the-night sleep sessions.

**TIP 20:** Beware tactics that can turn into bad habits. Don't try something once that you're not willing to perform over and over again.

**TIP 21:** Do what it takes to nip habits you don't like in the bud. It may take a few angst-filled nights, but you'll be happy you made the effort to put a halt to behaviors such as bedtime tantrums and unnecessary middle-of-the-night feedings (most babies can be weaned from them at six months, sometimes even sooner).

**TIP 22:** Be willing to try new tactics if the ones you've been using simply aren't working. Persistent problems might warrant a new approach.

**TIP 23:** Expect fits and starts. This is a learning process for everyone. Bad nights will happen. The best way to see they aren't repeated is to stick to your routine and make adjustments as needed.

**TIP 24:** Be patient. Sack artists aren't made overnight. But you may find that just a few days is all it takes to get a baby into a healthy sleep regimen.

**TIP 25:** Seek support and advice. Your pediatrician or family doctor is a good person to approach when you're at wit's end or out of answers. In more serious cases, you may be referred to an infant sleep specialist. More on this later in the chapter.

## SETTING UP A SLUMBER ZONE

Before you is the ultimate challenge: shaping your young 'un into a quality cavedozer, one who not only craves sleep but who, with your occasional steering, easily finds his or her own way to the Land of Nod. Champion sleepers aren't born, they're made. And one way to promote quality sleep on a night-in, night-out basis is to create an environment that's conducive to shut-eye.

The goal is not so much to hermetically seal your baby from all possible disruptions as it is to nurture skills that allow the caveling to sleep in varying conditions, from quiet to noisy. You want disruptions kept to a minimum, of course, but you also want to condition the little one to sleep through some level of noise and other potential intrusions, so that absolute silence is not a prerequisite for solid slumber. You want to avoid creating a sleep environment so unique and prop-laden that baby grows dependent on conditions that can't be replicated anyplace outside his or her own sleeping quarters. If you intend on traveling with your little one, you want to have some confidence that your baby will be able to sleep in unfamiliar surroundings without requiring you to go to extraordinary lengths to recreate the home sleep environment to which he or she is accustomed.

A few of the fundamentals for decorating and equipping a baby's sleeping quarters were touched upon in the nursery discussion in Chapter 4. Here we'll focus more on items specifically geared toward fostering a soporific atmosphere:

- The **sleep surface** (cradle/bassinette/co-sleeping mattress/ crib) should be firm but comfortable, covered in a soft sheet, free of loose bedding, pillows, and other items that could impede

# DR. BRIAN

*The Scoop on SIDS*

This book is a celebration of life with a baby. But occasionally, to celebrate life, we must talk about death. So while Sudden Infant Death Syndrome (SIDS) is still extremely rare, the risk it poses to a baby is substantial enough to warrant a mention here.

SIDS is the unexpected, sudden death of a baby under one year of age for no clear medical reason. About 3,000 infant deaths are attributed to SIDS each year in the U.S. In most cases it afflicts kids who appeared to be in good health prior to death. It is the most common cause of death in children between one month and one year of age, with kids two to four months of age at the greatest risk. It strikes males more often than females, and babies of African and Native American descent more often than Caucasian ones. It strikes more in the winter than in any other season, for reasons that have yet to be pinpointed.

While our understanding of SIDS is increasing, it is far from complete. Research suggests that it may arise from underlying developmental issues that impede a baby's ability to regulate breathing, body temperature and cardiovascular function. Scientists suggest that those development issues, combined with other factors related to the sleeping environment, could trigger SIDS. The National Institute of Child Health & Human Development (NICHD) has proposed a "triple-risk hypothesis,"

suggesting the cause of SIDS is threefold, where the baby is (1) in a critical stage of immune, cardiovascular, and respiratory system development, (2) especially vulnerable due to an undetected developmental weakness or defect, and (3) affected by an environmental factor such as having breathing impeded by bedding.

Identifying links such as those have helped health organizations develop steps to cut the risk of SIDS, which have translated into a sharp drop in the death rate from SIDS. Here's what you can do to keep your baby safe:

- **Always** put baby to bed on his or her back to sleep. Stomach-sleeping vastly increases the risk of SIDS. Inform all caregivers of this back-sleeping policy.

- Provide a firm mattress for the little one and don't allow baby to sleep surrounded by loose, soft bedding and pillows, which can cover breathing passages.

- Avoid overheating the baby with too much clothing and covers and too high a room temperature.

- Encourage smokers in the household (especially moms and moms-to-be) to quit the habit. Expectant mothers who smoke put their babies at a greater SIDS risk, as does exposure to secondhand smoke once the baby is born.

- Periodically check on a sleeping baby.

For more info, visit the National Institute of Child Health & Human Development's website at www.nichd.nih.gov or check the site for the American Academy of Pediatrics at www.aap.org.

breathing. Many sleep experts recommend no pillows or covers in baby's bed until he or she is at least one year of age.

- **Comfort items**. Lifetime bonds sometimes are forged in the infant bed, between a baby and his or her favorite snuggle items, such as a blankie or a stuffed animal. Eventually the baby may use these items to self-soothe, so don't discount their importance. You can also take them with you when traveling to give baby comfort in the familiar.

- Special **sleep aids** might be needed for babies whose slumber habits and/or sleeping location make them especially vulnerable to noise, light and other potential disruptions. A small appliance that produces white noise, such as a humidifier or dehumidifier, can be especially helpful in providing a low-level, non-intrusive wall of sound. You might also consider equipping baby's room with a portable sound system that allows you to play quiet, soothing music to help unwind the little one prior to bedtime. In rooms where sunlight is pervasive, consider heavier light-filtering shades and/or curtains for more of a cave-like feel.

- Many babies are suckers for the **pacifier,** a nipple stand-in that may satisfy an infant's urge to suckle something. Not only can a pacifier in the mouth settle down a restless baby, research shows that using one can also reduce the risk of SIDS. But there are other factors to consider in introducing your baby to a binky. Oral types can grow dependent on a pacifier at sleep time and during waking hours. Those who do may cry out at night if they can't find the little sucker. The longer they use one, the tougher it tends to be to wean them off it. As your kid gets older, prolonged, extensive use of a pacifier can lead to dental issues.

## LET'S WRAP ABOUT SWADDLING

Men who roll their own have always stood a cut above the rest. That held true in old Clint Eastwood spaghetti westerns and it holds true today in the very important practice of swaddling a baby, where a special folding technique is used to bundle the little one snugly but comfortably in a blanket to provide a warm, womb-like sleeping experience.

Not only does swaddling provide snug sleeping quarters to recreate conditions in the womb, it restrains and contains arms and legs, an important feature for babies who may not only wake themselves but also scratch and gouge themselves with flailing limbs. Eventually your baby will grow out of the swaddling routine, but early on it's an invaluable sleep tool.

Like diapering, swaddling is a maneuver even a digitally challenged caveman can learn to perform quickly and effectively. The goal is to perfect a style that suits your baby. Some may prefer the arms-at-the-side position, for example, while others may prefer being swaddled with arms on their chests. The former might work better for more aggressive arm-flailers.

Let's break down the basic swaddle technique into steps:

**Step 1.** Relax, this ain't complicated origami. Take your time and after doing it once, you'll have it down pat. Choose a properly sized and square (preferably), soft cotton or cotton-blend blanket and spread it out in a diamond shape in front of you on a safe flat surface. Fold over the top corner of the diamond shape and place the baby on her back with her little neck just about even with the squared off top of the blanket.

**Step 2.** Fold the top left portion of the blanket over baby's right shoulder and arm. Be sure the arm is snug and comfy but not too tight.

**Step 3.** Using your right hand, hold down the folded portion over baby's right shoulder and arm next to her body and pick up the far left corner of the blanket with your left hand.

**Step 4.** Now draw the far left corner of the blanket across her body to the other side. Make sure that baby's shoulders are squared and that the right shoulder is not pulled too tightly to her body.

**Step 5.** Slightly lift and turn the baby and tuck the folded corner of the blanket beneath her body. Her little weight will keep the blanket in place. Be sure no part of the blanket is covering her face.

**Step 6.** Take the bottom corner of the blanket and fold it upward over the feet, toward the baby's head and over top of the fold you made in the previous step. If the blanket is so big that this part of the fabric would stretch over her face, just fold that extra fabric over itself at about neck level.

**Step 7.** Just like you did on the opposite side in Step 2, fold the blanket over baby's left shoulder and arm this time, and pick up and extend the right corner of the blanket.

The result should be a neatly wrapped bundle of baby, portable and ready for placement on the sleeping surface. Done correctly and used consistently, you will have a valuable technique to add to the arsenal you need to win the Sleep Wars, one proven to reduce colic and fussiness while helping infants sleep better.

## SLEEP CONSULTANTS: 9-1-1 FOR THE ALWAYS EXTREMELY EXHAUSTED

A baby's persistent sleep problems are enough to drive even the sunniest, most even-keeled parents to despair. When you're at wit's end, when none of the methods you and your woman are using to foster and preserve sound sleeping habits seem to work, it is time to call in the heavy artillery: a sleep consultant who specializes in babies. These are people whose background, training and experience make them uniquely qualified to troubleshoot and treat problems like yours. Some PhDs and physicians are even certified in sleep medicine, meaning they completed a special program administered by the American Board of Sleep Medicine. A directory of doctors who are ABSM-certified can be found at www.absm.org. You can also ask for a reference from your family doctor or pediatrician. The National Sleep Foundation's website at www.sleepfoundation.org is another good starting point, with an extensive and searchable national directory of sleep centers. Friends and peers who endured especially bloody skirmishes during the Sleep Wars and lived to tell the tale might also be able to provide suggestions.

**Step 8.** Fold the right corner of the blanket across baby's body and tuck it in beneath her on her right side. Ta-da!

There are lots of sleep consultants out there. The good ones really *can* resolve even the most stubborn and acute cases. Review credentials, references, cost, methods, etc., then throw yourselves at the mercy of whomever you select. That's certainly better than being at the mercy of a screaming baby each night.

One suggestion a sleep consultant might offer is to try infant massage. But you won't need to pay for that advice. Just keep reading.

## INFANT MASSAGE: HELPING HANDS FOR A KNEADY INFANT

Eons ago, somewhere on the African savannah, an ape-like quadruped rears up on its hind legs to pluck a piece of fruit from a low-hanging tree branch. It pauses in the upright position for a tantalizing moment, teeters, then finds, much to its amazement, that it not only can balance there but also can put one hind leg in front of the other to propel itself forward—without using its forelimbs!

Now, having noticed that the appendages attached to its shoulders are dangling free, the mental machinery behind the hulking primate's massive brow ridge kicks into high gear. The first primal reaction by this half-man, half-ape hominid is to wedge the piece of fruit between its Mr. Ed-like teeth, raise its forelimbs to chest level and commence rhythmically pounding its hairy fists against its pectorals in celebratory fashion.

While creationists and Darwinians alike surely will take issue with this half-baked, barely researched account of the dawn of bipedalism, there is no disputing the importance and enduring ramifications of this breakthrough, which probably occurred several million years ago. One by-product of the move to verticality was that it transformed primate forelimbs and the digits attached to them from instruments mainly used for propulsion into something altogether different: true *arms* and *hands* that were available to their owners on a full-time basis for manipulating, grasping, hurling, scratching, gesturing, and all sorts of other pursuits.

Here today, many centuries hence, the hands remain one of mankind's most indispensable instruments. Among the skills passed down from one generation of *Homo sapiens* to the next is the ability to use them as conduits for healing, soothing, and bringing pleasure. In prehistoric times, shamans conducted healing rituals in which they employed massage techniques to draw evil spirits

## Benefits of massage to cavelings

Massage has been shown to enhance neurological development.

Massage has been shown to strengthen and regulate baby's respiratory, circulatory, and gastrointestinal functions.

Evidence suggests massage strengthens a baby's immune system.

Massage relieves a baby's stress and tension.

Infants massaged by a parent before bedtime tend to fall asleep more readily and have better sleep patterns.

Infants who are massaged show better digestive function, meaning fewer gassy episodes and less incidence of constipation to cause angst in baby and parental units.

Infants who receive massage therapy instead of being rocked show greater daily weight gain, less fussiness, and heightened interactivity, sociability, and soothability.

Massage has been shown to relieve the pain of teething.

Babies who receive massage show improved muscle tone, enhanced sensory awareness and self-awareness.

Girls who were massaged as babies exhibit greater self-esteem than those who weren't massaged.

Boys who were massaged as babies show less of a tendency to touch inappropriately later in life.

In preterm infants, massage may diminish pain and lead to more rapid weight gain, decreased autoimmune problems, and enhanced immune function. "Preemies" who were massaged gained 47 percent more weight than those who weren't, became more socially responsive, and were discharged six days earlier, according to TRI.

Preterm infants who are massaged at bedtime tend to fall asleep faster and sleep more soundly. They also tend to gain weight faster than infants who aren't massaged before sleep. Preemies who got massaged as newborns showed greater weight gain and better cognitive and motor development eight months later, according to TRI.

## Benefits of massage to cavemasseurs

Fathers who gave their infants daily massages 15 minutes prior to bedtime for one month showed more healthy interactive behaviors with their infants.

Dads who delivered massage to their babies for three months showed increased parental self-esteem.

Dads who massage babies may enjoy enhanced greeting interactions with their young ones—more eye contact, smiling, vocalizing, etc.

Baby massage better equips dads to read infant body language.

Massage helps Dad reconnect with a baby he hasn't seen much during the day.

Touch establishes an early foundation for father-offspring intimacy and bonding.

Practicing massage teaches Dad to touch safely and appropriately.

Giving good hand is a source of stress relief and endorphin release for the masseur.

Massaging a baby conditions caveman's mitts for heavier hands-on rubbing duty with his woman.

A mom who witnesses Dad's handiwork with the baby may want some of the same for herself.

Moms have breastfeeding to maintain intimacy with baby; massage gives dads a similar means of connecting.

Exotic oils and lotions with flowery aromas might be nice to use on mature hides like yours, but for babies, the simpler the massage oil, the better. No need to visit a high-end boutique to find a substance suitable for baby skin. In fact, the ingredients to make a top-notch elixir may already reside right in your kitchen cabinet. Certified infant massage therapist Desirae recommends the following:

**Use** an all-natural, high-grade vegetable- or fruit-based oil, unscented—olive oil, almond oil, coconut oil, jojoba oil, and mustard seed oil (which has warming effect, good in cold weather) are viable options. Desirae prefers oils to lotions because they have better gliding qualities.

**Avoid** anything containing mineral oil, a petroleum-based substance, contact with which can be harmful to a baby.

out of an ailing subject's body. Massage was similarly embraced in a diverse range of ancient cultures from China to Greece, where in the fifth century B.C., Hippocrates, the man widely recognized as the father of Western medicine, touted rubbing as a necessary skill for physicians. Among natives of the remote Sandwich Islands, massage is known as lomi-lomi. The indigenous Maori people of New Zealand call it romi-romi. To Charo, it is known as cuchi-cuchi.

Regardless of cultural heritage, throughout human history people who are particularly adept at massage have been celebrated for "giving good hand." That designation still applies today to the most skilled practitioners of the art and science of massage, and one needn't be a spiritual healer to earn it. A person who "gives good hand" is one who:

- keeps his hands in massage-ready condition, with calluses filed, nails clipped, and palms dirt- and hair-free;

- pays attention to detail in creating a soothing, distraction-free massage environment;

- never lays his hands on the subject without first asking permission, even when the subject is an infant;

- is gentle, at times firm, but never rough or overzealous with his touch;

- uses a variety of touching techniques—kneading, rubbing, circular motions, and pressing with fingers, palms, and full hands, applying varying pressures;

- focuses on muscles, not bones; and,

- engages the subject with a soft, soothing voice.

A new dad who excels at massage may well discover that through simple touch he has the power to relax and encourage sleep in his offspring, to strengthen the bond between himself and the little one, and to accelerate the caveling's mental and physical development. Indeed, there's plenty of proof that infant massage, when practiced regularly using proper technique, delivers a *huge* array of perks to Dad and baby alike. The Touch Research Institute (an organization that unfortunately does not grant fellowships to troglodytes based solely on their extensive and highly private field explorations) has conducted more than 100 studies on the positive effects of massage therapy—and who are we to question an organization dedicated to skin-to-skin contact? Some of those benefits are detailed on page 191.

One might assume that realizing those benefits would require marathon massage sessions and thus a major time commitment by already busy parents. But no—all it takes, says our resident infant massage specialist and charter CAHFAC member Desirae, are sessions of about five or 10 minutes per day. And the younger your baby is when you start the routine, she notes, the better the chances he or she will embrace it and the sooner those benefits will be reaped.

## GENTLE STROKES FOR LITTLE FOLKS: A GUIDE TO GIVING GOOD HAND

A baby is not a magic genie-in-a-bottle. Simply rubbing a little one's body won't entitle a new dad to all the benefits detailed on page 191, or to automatic membership in the Good Hands Club. It takes dedication, concentration, patience, and of course, dexterity, for an aspiring amateur cavemasseur to become a skilled massage practitioner. But with the right mood, materials, and technique, even a clumsy, ham-fisted knuckledragger can, with practice and the proper guidance, evolve into a massage master, one whose list of satisfied clients includes not only his offspring but also the woman in his life. (See Chapter 9 for on-the-money massage maneuvers more suitable for creating a grown-up kind of intimacy.)

**Materials.** It doesn't take much to launch your own in-home infant massage operation. You will need: a peaceful, quiet location in your home that will become the designated massage spot; massage oil (see tips at left); a smooth, flat surface; a blanket, preferably brightly colored, made of extra-soft cotton or fleece, and used *exclusively* for massage, that your baby will come to recognize as *the* massage blankie, so that when it comes out, baby knows it's massage time.

**Mood.** Once you've settled upon a warm, quiet part of the home as your designated massage spot, and identified a flat, comfortable, and safe surface to work your magic (such as on the floor or a bed), lay down the designated super-soft massage blanket on that surface. Keep the room lit, but not too brightly. Avoid playing potentially distracting recorded music; you want the baby to focus on the sound of your voice and the experience of being massaged. No need for incense, a lava lamp or other perceived mood-enhancers; save those for the woman in your life.

**Maneuvers.** Now you're ready to break out the oil and begin the massage program with a few simple techniques. But before you do, some additional guidelines to keep in mind:

- If your baby has a medical issue or a skin condition, ask a doctor before embarking on an infant massage program.

- Always ask baby's permission before starting your routine, something respectful like, "May I have the honor of massaging you?"

- Babies are creatures who crave routine. Try to start massage sessions at about the same time each day, conduct them in the same spot in your home, if possible, and use the same routine each time.

- Seriously—talk or sing to the little one periodically throughout each session, explaining what you're doing each step of the way. The sound of your voice may not win you a place on *American Idol*, but it engenders a sense of familiarity and comfort in your offspring. Eventually, when the baby gets a little older, he or she may start to identify specific verbal cues and associate them with individual aspects of the routine.

- Don't force the issue. If the infant clearly dislikes the massage experience, discontinue the session and don't take it personally.

- Be patient. A baby who's unaccustomed to massage may initially show signs of sensory overload. But after a little while, if you're properly executing the maneuvers detailed below, your baby should come to crave the massage experience.

- Adjust on the fly. If baby seems to get squirmy or uncomfortable with certain motions or techniques, try backing off on the pressure you apply or move on to another maneuver. If baby seems distracted, try changing the venue. If massage before bedtime seems to overstimulate the little one, try a different time of day.

- Don't give up. Even if you have to end a session prematurely because baby isn't digging the experience, try again the next day. An infant who one day resists your every move may acquiesce the next.

Now it's time to get busy. Pour a small amount of massage oil into your palm, rub your hands together to get them warm and lubricated, ask the small subject for permission to begin, then get the routine underway with...

## LEGS & BUTTOCKS

*Note: The techniques described here are legitimate and massage-therapist-approved for babies. Their names are not.*

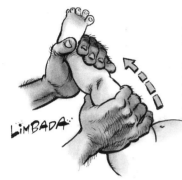

**Maneuver 1:** *Limbada*—Support baby's foot with one hand and stroke the leg with the other hand, starting at the buttocks and working down the outside of the leg toward the ankle, using long strokes. Repeat with the other leg.

**Maneuver 2:** *The Wringer*—Make C shapes with both hands, use both to grasp baby's leg at the hip and, holding hands close together, alternate gently squeezing and twisting as you work toward the ankle. Repeat with the other leg.

**Maneuver 3:** *Solemate, Part 1*—Use your thumbs to stroke the bottom of one foot from heel to toes, then repeat on the other foot.

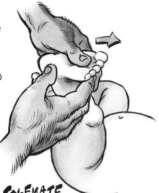

**Maneuver 4:** *Piggies*—Gently squeeze all 10 toes, rolling them lightly between thumb and index finger.

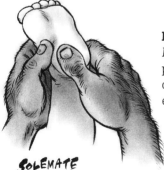

**Maneuver 5:** *Solemate, Part 2*—Use your thumbs to press gently on the bottom of each foot, covering the entire surface.

**Maneuver 6:** *Reverse Limbada*—Same as Maneuver 1, but in reverse, working from ankle to buttocks.

**Touch relaxation:** You've completed the lower body sequence. Now transition to the next sequence with a tension-release maneuver. Support baby's legs by holding behind his or her knees, then gently rock the legs back and forth.

## ABDOMEN

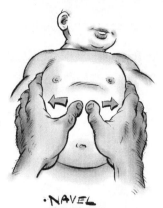

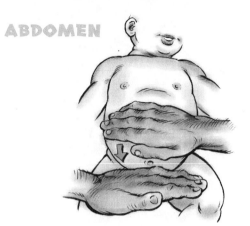

GUT CHECK

**Maneuver 2:** *Navel Patrol—* Place thumbs at either side of baby's belly button and move them gently outward to the sides of the abdomen.

NAVEL PATROL

**Maneuver 1:** *Gut Check*—Using the sides of your hands, make gentle but firm paddling strokes on baby's stomach, starting just below the ribs and moving down to the lower abs.

**Maneuver 3:** *Hands of the Clock*—Use the fingers of your left hand to lightly make a full circle on baby's belly in clockwise fashion, then the right hand to make a half circle from 10 to 4 o'clock. Repeat several times.

HANDS OF the CLOCK.

PHYSICAL GRAFFITI

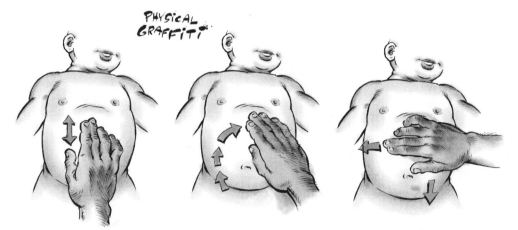

**Maneuver 4:** *Physical Graffiti*—This stroke unfolds in three steps. Start by using your fingers to draw a vertical line on the left side of baby's belly (your right), from lower ribs to navel height. Next use your fingers to make a right angle, upside-down-and-backwards L shape just under the rib cage, moving from your left to your right. Finish by using fingers to draw a closed-end-down horseshoe shape from your left to your right, starting at navel height, up toward the rib cage, then back down to navel height.

**Touch relaxation** again to transition to the next sequence.

## CHEST

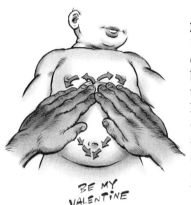

BE MY VALENTINE

**Maneuver 1:** *Be My Valentine*—Use the flats of both hands to stroke baby from the center to the sides of his or her chest along the rib cage, then bring hands around in a heart-shaped motion to meet again at the center of the chest.

"X" MARKS THE SPOT

**Maneuver 2:** *X Marks the Spot*—Place hands on either side of the baby at the rib cage. Move your right hand across the chest diagonally to the right shoulder, then gently massage before retracing the motion back to the original position. By repeating with your left hand, you'll be crisscrossing baby's chest.

**Touch relaxation** again to transition to the next sequence.

## ARMS & HANDS

LIMBADA Upper Version

**Maneuver 1:** *Limbada, Upper Version*—Similar to the technique you used on baby's legs, hold the wrist with one hand and make a C shape with the other. Starting at the shoulder, make long, smooth strokes down to the hand. Repeat on the other arm.

THE WRINGER

**Maneuver 2:** *The Wringer*—Again, similar to the technique used on the legs. With your hands in a C shape, gently and slowly squeeze and twist, working from upper arm to wrists.

THE PALM READER

**Maneuver 3:** *The Palm Reader*—Stroke baby's palms gently with your thumbs.

**Maneuver 4:** *Piggies*—As with the toes, gently squeeze, stroke, and roll each digit.

**Maneuver 5:** *Reverse Limbada, Upper Version*—Use the technique specified in Maneuver 1, only work from hand to shoulder.

**Touch relaxation** again to transition to the next sequence.

### BACK

**Maneuver 1:** *The Sausage Roll*—Gently and very carefully roll the little one onto his or her belly.

**Maneuver 2:** *The Backslide*—Start with both your hands together at the top of baby's back and gently glide them back and forth in opposite directions as you work down the back.

BACKSLIDE

**Maneuver 3:** *Fistful of Butt Cheek*—Use one hand to cup the baby's bottom and the other to glide down the back, starting at the neck and working down the center of the back to the butt cheeks. Repeat several times.

FISTFUL OF BUTTCHEEK

FULL MONTY

**Maneuver 4:** *The Full Monty*—Support baby's feet with one hand and with the other, repeat the same gliding motion from the neck, this time all the way down the legs to the feet.

**Maneuver 5:** *The Rake*—Spread your fingers and gently comb down the baby's back from neck to buttocks, repeating several times.

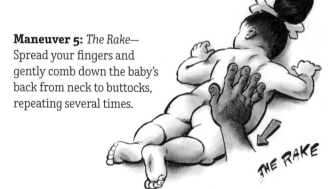

THE RAKE

**Touch relaxation** again to transition to the next sequence.

## FACE

(Desirae's advice to the amateur masseur: no oil or lotion for this sequence, wipe off massage substance if necessary; take extra care to be soft and gentle and don't be surprised if it takes longer for baby to grow accustomed to facial massage.)

FORE!

**Maneuver 1:** *Fore!*—Make small, soft circles on the sides of baby's head, then still using your fingertips, stroke from the center of the forehead outward to the sides of the forehead.

HIGHBROW!

**Maneuver 2:** *Highbrow*—Use thumbs to lightly stroke from inner to outer corners of baby's eyebrows.

OVER THE BRIDGE!

**Maneuver 3:** *Over the Bridge*—Run your thumbs and/or index fingers down the sides of baby's nose, starting from the eyebrows and ending with a gentle finger press.

**Maneuver 4:** *Lip Service*— Run your thumb across the upper lip to the cheek, then likewise across the lower lip.

JAWS TOO

**Maneuver 5:** *Jaws Too*—Use fingertips to lightly draw circles around baby's jaw in clockwise fashion.

GRAND FINALE

**Maneuver 6:** *Grand Finale*— Conclude matters by using your fingertips to stroke around baby's ears and under the chin.

Let the little one know the session is over. By now you should have a relaxed, pliable, and content infant on your hands, one who is primed for a long, strong slumber.

Your first-year journey of self-discovery and need-fulfillment, however, is far from done.

# CHAPTER 8

# COMMUNICATION, SOCIALIZATION & STIMULATION

HELP YOUR BABY MAKE SENSE OF THE WORLD—
AND BECOME A WISER MAN IN THE PROCESS

I T IS CLEAR FROM YOUR EMBRACE OF FATHERHOOD THAT
you are not one who shrinks from a challenge. Back in the first
chapter, you courageously broke out your No. 2 pencil and took
the Fatherhood Aptitude Test (F.A.T.) to assess your knowledge
of baby-related facts and other barely relevant postpartum
information. It turns out that was only the written segment of a
two-part exam, however. Now, ready or not, comes the second phase
of the test, this one more physical in nature. It will challenge your
motor skills and coordination. For this part of the test, you will
need an arm, a hand, a head, and a brain. No special preparation is
necessary, so let's begin.

First, extend your left arm straight in front of you. Now, bend it
at the elbow and bring your left hand to the left side of your head.
Slide your fingers along your unibrow until they reach the place
where your forehead ends and your hairline begins. If your head
is anatomically similar to that of most other *Homo sapiens*, your
fingers should now be resting on a region known as the temple.
Apply light pressure to the temple, moving your fingers in a circular motion. Congratulations—you have located a general area of the
skull beneath which resides a part of the brain called **Broca's area**.

The test isn't done quite yet. Before returning your left arm to
the resting position, slide your fingers two or three inches farther
back on your cranium, so they now rest on an area an inch or two
above the left ear. Explore the area with your fingertips. Very nice

What the caveman stands to gain from
reading Chapter 8:

- The ability to pinpoint parts of the
  brain responsible for communication

- A keen understanding of how babies
  develop communication skills

- The acuity to interpret a baby's body
  language and cries

- The know-how to glean meaning
  from unintelligible infant noises

- The tools to turn up a baby's brain
  development dial

- Insight into the secrets of sign
  language and how to converse with a
  baby without uttering a sound

- A grasp of how music can benefit a
  baby's brain

- An arsenal of songs guaranteed to
  get the whole household rocking

- A clear understanding of the risks TV
  poses to babies

- Familiarity with the phenomenon
  known as infant amnesia

- The know-how to build a baby's toy
  collection wisely

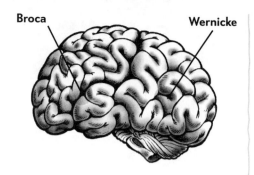

Broca

Wernicke

job—you have just located a part of the brain called **Wernicke's area**, and traced a neural pathway called the *arcuate fasciculus* that connects Wernicke's area with Broca's area. Located in the brain's left hemisphere, these two areas are crucial to mankind's ability to communicate with one another. Their functions help separate humans from other members of the primate family. The chief function of the part of the brain's frontal lobe known as Broca's area, we now know, is to help with speech production (output), while the main function of Wernicke's area within the temporal lobe is to help us understand spoken language (input).

For being the first to identify the distinct locations and functions of these critical areas of the brain, Messieurs Wernicke and Broca have earned a place in the Cultivated Caveman Crevasse of Fame, alongside the likes of Abraham Maslow, male Aka pygmies, Carolus Linnaeus, Captain James T. Kirk, Otzi the Iceman, Warren Zevon, Gronk (of course), and the various other illustrious men who warrant mention in these pages. The Frenchman Paul Broca, whose own brain was encased in a skull partially covered by massive mutton chops, was a 19th-century physician and a pioneer in neurosurgery. In the early 1860s, he was the first to link human speech function to a specific area of the brain. Polish-born Karl Wernicke was a man of equally impressive facial hair and achievement in the fledgling field of neuroscience. In 1874, slightly more than a decade after Broca went public with his findings on the brain, the neurologist and psychiatrist Wernicke published his own findings on the area of the brain that now bears his name.

Before each passed away more than a century ago, Broca and Wernicke performed much of the early investigatory legwork on the brain functions that produce human communication. Now they have passed the communications torch to you, a parent who has a chance to fulfill one of our human destinies: to convey the secrets of speech, conversation, and self-expression to the younger generation. Broca and Wernicke are gone, leaving the moms and dads of the world to do much of the heavy lifting related to fulfilling a baby's need for communication, socialization, and stimulation. This is as it should be, since parents are often in a better position than anyone to help a child learn to express himself or herself and to interpret the world through language and perception.

Teaching communication skills is a pretty cool responsibility for the knuckledragging keeper of the communications flame, one that should be taken neither too lightly, nor too seriously. Communication is a gift we have inherited from our earliest ancestors and one you can start sharing with a little one almost immediately after he or she enters the world. During the newborn stage, it may seem like a one-way street, with adults doing their best to read and interpret the baby's body language without much input from the baby. But things aren't always as one-sided as that. Babies tend to develop quickly as communicators, learning ways to express themselves through sounds and gestures long before they can form an intelligible word, never mind a coherent sentence. By the end of the first year, your baby may be producing babble and various other forms of noise with purpose, inflection, and intonation.

You, your woman, and other mature communicators are a little one's role models in this amazing transformation. It may seem a stretch to call some of the more reserved, monosyllabic unibrows who walk among us "strong communicators." But even a strong, silent type of troglodyte can be a stellar role model of communication and interaction, for the throaty grunts, chattering sounds, brow-knitting, and other primitive mannerisms a baby learns from Dad will serve a valuable purpose until the little one develops more evolved, intelligible forms of speech common to most members of the species here in the 21st century.

As closely as you'll be watching your baby, your baby will be observing you, and others as well, eyeing how you use the muscles of your face to make certain expressions and form words, and listening to the different ways you use your voice. They do this to model their behavior on yours. They're also looking to see how you react to their signals, storing that knowledge to begin making associations that certain actions elicit specific reactions from Mom and Dad. "Hmmm. I sure like the response I get from the big folks when I do that thing with my tongue. Let's try it again."

What takes most youngsters just a fraction of a lifetime to master evidently took our hominid forebears a few million years. Drawing from fossil evidence, evolutionary scholars suggest that the power of speech first emerged with *Homo habilis* (*handy man* in Latin), who walked the earth between 2.4 and 1.5 million years ago. With brains almost as big as those of modern humans, *Homo erectus* further climbed the communications curve when he reigned between 1.8 million and 300,000 years ago, somehow managing speech despite his massive jaws, huge molars, and lack of a chin.

We humans have come a long way since then, having developed oral and written language, gestures, chanting, singing, and story-telling, plus a vast range of methods to promote and accommodate interpersonal communication, from the carrier pigeon and the bullhorn to text messaging, a practice that contemporary cavemen really seem to have taken to because it is the modern equivalent of grunting.

The ability to understand and send a text message doesn't automatically qualify you as an expert in infant communications. But that expertise is within your grasp. In this chapter you'll gain insight into how babies develop communication skills, plus you'll learn fundamentals in interpreting what a baby's body language and babble might be telling you, in conversing with a little one without intelligible words, and in giving a baby a means of self-expression through sign language, music, and other methods.

This is unfamiliar and groundbreaking territory for baby and parents alike. Finding a common ground for communication between adult and infant relies heavily on the powers of observation and interpretation. For only through watching a baby on a regular basis can you begin to glean meaning from those seemingly random facial expressions, cries, gurgles, and movements. The success of your needs-fulfillment efforts during baby's first 12 months will depend largely on your ability to read your baby and react accordingly. For example, you may be able to distinguish between the cry the little one uses to say, "I'm famished" and the one he or she uses to say, "Give me some attention, Pops." An ability to respond to the infant in kind often means the difference between a cooing, satisfied little human and a hysterical, inconsolable one.

With you, your woman, and the baby working together to find a common wavelength, you'll be amazed at the steady progress you make in unlocking the mysteries of human communication. The channels you open with your offspring here in the first year will serve you well going forward, at least until the caveling hits adolescence or the teenage years, at which point the paradigm shifts and you may find yourself back at square one, in search of a clue for how to get through to a kid who *knows* he's smarter than you. Strategies for tackling that mammoth challenge will be offered in the sixth book in this series, working title: *Old and in the Way: A Stone-Ager's Guide to Surviving a Teenager.*

The brain is a mighty complex organ. So much effort has gone into studying it, yet even with the contributions of Broca, Wernicke, and many others, we have only scratched the surface of neurological understanding.

As a proud and curious papa, you likely will spend long hours studying your little one, wondering what's going on inside that adorable melon. For answers, let's again wade into the world of vintage science fiction, as we did in Chapter 5's homage to Captain James T. Kirk of the Starship Enterprise. This time our point of reference is another vessel with a different esteemed troglodyte helmsman: Captain Bill Owens of the submarine *Proteus*, from the 1966 movie *Fantastic Voyage*. Aided by technology that shrinks people and objects to microscopic dimensions, Owens, his crew, and the *Proteus* are reduced to a size that allows them to be injected into the body of a man who lies in a coma. Their mission: to bring the patient back by venturing into his brain, resolving a blood clot there, and exiting before white blood cells attack.

You're scratching your head, wondering what a B-movie that came out before you were born has to do with you and your baby. Well, about as much as Captain Kirk has to with baby clothing: absolutely nothing. Even so, wouldn't it be cool to make yourself miniature and take a fantastic voyage of your own into the head of your baby? Let's get small and find out what makes a baby tick upstairs.

A sleeping infant may look placid, angelically peaceful. But inside a little one's brain, wheels are furiously turning. All the stimulation, sleep, and nutrients a baby should be getting are stoking a great deal of activity inside the caveling's cranium. Broca's and Wernicke's areas are both bustling as the newborn's brain begins processing impressions from the *ex utero* environment.

Neonates typically are born with the ability to see things only at close range, though not in full color. Their hearing is fully developed, and they come with a keen sense of smell. Still, it will take time for them to learn how to process all the input their senses provide, and to develop the ability to respond to that input with some form of communication. That doesn't mean babies are born silent, however. Crying is another skill babies feature from the get-go. In fact, it is perhaps their first and most effective communication tool—and one they will frequently fall back upon, not only during the fourth stage of labor but throughout their lives. Some will raise crying to an art form later in life, developing highly nuanced weeps, wails, sobs, chokes, and gasps, plus an ability to summon those sounds instantaneously when the need arises.

Given how frequently babies tend to cry, the sooner you and your woman grow accustomed to hearing it, the better off you both will be. Babies spend an average of one to two hours crying each day. Keep your fingers crossed that time doesn't occur all at once but rather in small, digestible bites. When the cries come, your work as an interpreter begins. Babies have distinct cries for different situations—a cry for attention, a cry of pain, a cry from fatigue, and another from discomfort, a cry in hunger, and a cry to say, "Enough, I'm on sensory overload." Odds are you'll be hearing those cries enough that in a matter of days you and your woman will learn to identify your baby's signature sounds, even in a roomful of other infants.

When was your last good cry? During a recent viewing of *Brian's Song*, perhaps, or in the gourmet shop, when you finally found the perfect cheese to complement your favorite bottle of Bordeaux. How about your woman? Watching her shed tears probably makes you uneasy, particularly if your actions happen to be the cause of the waterworks. Crying is different when it comes from your own offspring. Every parent reacts differently to it. Some are calm, others are driven to extreme distraction.

By embracing the notion that a baby's cries have a purpose and a message to convey, you might begin to take a calmer, more clinical approach to your little one's howls. Sure, the sound makes the hairs on your neck (and there are many) stand on end, but exactly which cry is that? What is he or she *really* trying to tell you? This detached, interpretive approach might provide a caveman with some much-needed clarity and diversion during moments of acute confusion and frustration resulting from an infant's crying.

Thankfully, there's much more to baby communications than just crying. Within the first few weeks of life, your baby should start to recognize your voice. Meanwhile, your own tremendous powers of observation will help you to recognize the cues (verbal and body language) your little one uses to indicate hunger, tiredness, etc.

Touch—holding, cuddling, rocking, massage, and the like—is another way to become fast friends with a baby. It helps establish a bond and trust, as does close-up, face-to-face interaction between the two of you. You'll know baby's been watching your facial mannerisms when he or she cracks her first smile, usually at an age of two months or less. By three months, many babies are making vowel sounds by themselves and in response to interactions with another.

By about the fifth month, the mental machinery is really working, for this is when many babies discover causality, a realization that if they perform a specific action, they will get a specific result. Now the pace at which communication skills develop can be staggering. Sometime around the eighth or ninth month, many babies start using and practicing babble containing solid syllables, with more mature inflection and rhythm. At this point your hearts are likely to be warmed with a lot of "mamamama" and "dadadada." No matter that baby hasn't yet attached your specific identities to those sounds. It feels good for the baby just to say them and good for you both to hear them.

You could have a fully operative gibberish machine on your hands by the end of baby's first year. By then, the sounds he or she emits may have the rhythms and inflections of regular speech. And those sounds may come in longer (but no less unintelligible) streams, where you're able to pick out a word or two here and there. At this juncture the caveling's babble likely will be accompanied by expressions of emphasis and gestures such as pointing. He or she should begin showing an ability to respond to very basic commands and requests.

"Quiet, please" might not be one they respond to, however. Babies tend to develop communication skills in leaps and bounds. Many learn to love the sound of their own voices. And how can you fault them, since every day makes for new discoveries and breakthroughs? As you and your woman surely will conclude, these newly discovered methods of communication sure beat crying.

# BABY TALK:
# A TRANSLATION GUIDE
# FOR TROGLODYTES

When babies flap their gums, you best be paying attention to what comes out, because these are the cues and clues to use to gain insight into what's going in a caveling's head. Generations of confounded parents who came before you have dedicated a mountain of brain cells to identify and assign meaning to some of the most common sounds babies make. Below, for your benefit, are the fruits of their labor—a rudimentary vocabulary to make sense of the guttural grunts, playful squeaks, boisterous bleats, and other cryptic sounds a little one emits. We've also included points of Cro-Magnon linguistic reference especially for cavemen seeking to trace these sounds back to their most archaic origins.

| Sound | From the Cro-Magnon expression for... | What he/she might be trying to tell you in baby lingo |
|---|---|---|
| Ahhh[1] | **Relief**: That saber-toothed tiger could have taken a lot more than just my leg. | My latest diaper masterpiece is now ready for viewing. |
| Ahhh[2] | **Satisfaction**: I can't remember ever tasting sloth entrails so delicious. | That was the tastiest breast nectar I've had since, well, two hours ago. Must sleep now. |
| Ahrrgh | **Pain/discomfort**: Something sharp has lodged itself in my neck. Kindly extract it or summon the shaman. | I just swallowed a huge quantity of air. Some help releasing it, please. |
| Daaaa (sometimes pronounced "duuhh") | (1) Father, fatherhood or father figure; (2) Slack-jawed, dimwitted. | That big fella with the unibrow—he's goofy looking. Are we related? |
| Eeeee | A shrill warning sound used to ward off threat. | Hey, don't change the station. I'm digging this Snoop Dogg song. |
| Eheheheh | Sarcastic expression of supremacy: We may not look as smart as you Neanderthals, but we did figure out how not to become extinct. | The joke's on you, Pops. Those breasts are mine, on demand (sound often accompanied by wink that appears involuntary). |
| I-e-i-e-i-e | An expression of revelry, celebration or self-indulgence: The feeling of felling a wildebeest with one club swing; there's nothing like it. | Just wanted to remind everyone that I love the sound of my own voice. |
| Maaa | (1) Mother, motherhood, mothering; (2) The cave of one's birth. | I love what you do for me, girl. Don't ever leave my sight (or stop breastfeeding). |

| Sound | From the Cro-Magnon expression for... | What he/she might be trying to tell you in baby lingo |
|-------|---------------------------------------|------------------------------------------------------|
| Ooowaa | To ogle, admire or look longingly at another: Me likee that minx in the puma pelt. If only we weren't so closely related... | So that's what I look like. Blue really is a good color for me. |
| Pffflaahh | **Frustration:** I've been striking these rocks together for the past six hours, but still no spark. | How many times must I make this sucking motion with my lips before someone offers me liquid refreshment. |
| Yayayayaya | **Gratitude:** I never thought I'd live to the ripe old age of 25; spirits willing, I might even make 30 and become clan elder. | For all you do, Mom and Dad, this one's for you. Thanks for taking such good care of me. I wouldn't make it in the world without you. |

# TURBOCHARGE YOUR TYKE'S DEVELOPMENT IN 20 STEPS

We often talk about the golden opportunities that parenthood presents to proactive primitives. The chance to be a catalyst to your baby's development is certainly one of them. Little ones crave interaction with their environment and the people around them. In that regard, they are putty in your palms, ready to be sculpted by the oversized, hairy hands of a master. Now, by becoming your baby's mirror, sounding board, and sensory mentor, you have an opportunity to help the caveling fulfill an innate desire to experience and interpret life while at the same time speeding his or her development.

Before you and your woman is one of those chances to make a genuine, lasting, and positive impact on another member of the species. All the better that this person is your own flesh and blood, the fruit of your loins, a member of your own clan. The impact the two of you can have on the development of your little one is far-ranging. Babies are like sponges, desperate to soak up as much as they can as their brains and bodies develop. The goal isn't to raise a child who's all bod and no brains or vice versa, as an infant's mental and physical development tend to feed off one another. Your developmental efforts thus should strive for balance, focusing as much on the physical as the mental.

The power to affect your offspring so profoundly is a mighty cudgel to have in your arsenal, so you might as well wield it. Here are some suggestions for how.

## To bolster mental/cognitive/communication development

Chat up the caveling. Little ones comprehend a lot more than they let on. Use downtime during car rides, baths, diaper changes, and the like to practice words, point out body parts, recite the ABCs, etc.

Be your baby's bard. Babies tend to find the voices of their parents soothing (even when few others do), so reading or telling stories is a good way to relax the little one. Babies also model their own attempts at speech after the sounds they hear coming from your mouth. Reading a book with someone allows a baby to learn speech and to associate words with images. It also conditions them to listen attentively, and to crave reading and books.

Tune in. So what if dogs in the neighborhood howl when you sing "I'm a Little Teacup?" Music and song stimulate a baby's cognitive development, as detailed later in this chapter.

Broaden baby's horizons by exposing your offspring to different people and environments. Variety is the spice of life. The greater a baby's exposure to new things, the more adaptable and less resistant to change he or she may be.

Travel with your young troglodyte in tow. By train, airplane, automobile or bus, it's helpful to get your offspring accustomed to going places.

Square peg, square hole. Provide toys that help babies understand shapes, spatial relationships, etc.

## To bolster physical/motor skills development

Get aquatic. For babies, the water's where it's at. They spend months immersed in it while in the womb, so being back in water is like a homecoming. Swimming encourages muscle development and coordination while strengthening the bond between parent and infant. It also has been shown to stimulate cognitive development.

Give your tiny trog regular supervised tummy time. While legitimate concerns about SIDS means babies should sleep on their backs, they still need to spend time on their stomachs to strengthen the muscles that allow them to hold their heads up, roll over, etc.

Furnish your little primate with a bouncy chair, exercise saucer and/or swing to help develop the lower body and coordination. Here's a good way for baby to get exercise while Mom or Dad takes care of household chores. It's good sport just watching how one of these can bring out a baby's monkey tendencies.

Provide colorful, dangling objects. Babies spend big blocks of time prone on their backs, so better provide them with stuff to engage them, such as items you suspend over a play mat, crib, carseat or from the roof of a stroller. They let your baby practice reaching out, touching, and grasping things.

Conduct frequent, supervised household decathlons. Provide outlets for a little one to pursue challenging (age- and motor-skill-dependent) activities, such as rolling over, climbing stairs, pulling oneself up to the standing position, rolling, tossing and catching a ball, etc.

Support motor skills development by providing toys with moving parts that let baby practice hand-eye coordination and different motions, such as dropping the ball in the hole, opening and closing, etc.

## To bolster mental/cognitive/ communication development

Play games. Engage the baby in simple games like peek-a-boo, hide-and-find-the-object, build-a-tower-of-blocks-then-topple-it, and fill-the-container-and-dump-it. A game like peek-a-boo teaches object permanence—that the object is still there even it can't be seen.

Face-off. Spending time face-to-face with the baby not only allows you to get to know one another better, it lets baby study the movements of your mug for modeling. Eye contact also can strengthen the connection between the two of you.

Walkabout. Take regular walks or hikes with baby in a chest pack, sling, backpack or other carrying device. With baby's head close to yours, you can point things out, whisper sweet nothings, work on conjugating verbs in Latin, and generally nurture a healthy intimacy between the two of you.

Encourage serious silliness. Make time to make funny sounds and faces, laugh, dance, and goof around together.

Teach your baby sign language. The benefits are potentially huge, as detailed later in this chapter.

## To bolster physical/motor skills development

Help baby make a racket. Provide devices and musical instruments like drums, rattles or cymbals to scratch the primal itch to make rhythmic noise. It also teaches cause and effect—that a rattle makes noise when shaken.

Expose your baby to the great outdoors. Fresh air, sunshine, colorful flora and fauna—the sights and sounds of nature heighten a baby's senses and allow them to connect with their natural surroundings.

Encourage self-propulsion, from rolling over and rising up on all fours to pulling up to the standing position, crawling, and finally walking.

## LET BABY'S FINGERS DO THE TALKING

Back in Chapter 7, we suggested infant massage techniques as a way for a troglodyte dad to put his hands to good use and keep them out of trouble. Digitally intensive manual labor also is integral to performing your parental responsibilities, from laundry to diapering to dressing a little one. Still, there will be times when the caveman finds his hands idle and his mind wandering to potential ways to keep them occupied. Here's a chance to curb your self-centered, blasphemous urges and channel your energies (and the baby's) toward a mutually mind-expanding pursuit with all sorts of

DAD

MOM

HELP

HURT

benefits for parents and infant alike. It's called sign language and as useful as it is to communicate with people who have a hearing impairment, it's also an amazingly valuable tool for stimulating a baby's cognitive development and providing the little one with an outlet for relaying his or her thoughts, desires, and needs. As a mode of communication, signing sure beats screaming, crying, and other potentially grating forms of vocalization little ones are likely to resort to, particularly when they're frustrated because the message they're trying to relay isn't getting across.

While screaming and crying likely will always be part of your baby's vocal arsenal, a little one who has the ability to self-express through signs is apt to do less of each. Months before babies develop the ability to express themselves verbally, they can learn to understand and use signs to communicate. That takes a lot of the guesswork out of needs fulfillment. It also provides major benefits by:

- giving babies the means to convert thoughts into expressions;

- giving parents new insight into how a baby's mind works;

- giving everyone in the household more common ground to communicate;

- opening the lines for two-way communication, which strengthens the baby-to-parent/caregiver bond;

- accelerating development of a baby's brain; studies have shown that babies who sign learn to speak sooner, with a broader vocabulary;

- positively impacting kids long-term; in studies, children who used signing as babies scored higher on IQ tests at age 8;

- serving as a bridge to verbal speech;

- giving baby and parents something they can succeed at, thus building their sense of achievement and self-esteem.

If chimpanzees can learn to sign, so can a caveman and his offspring. So when to start the process? While you can begin using signs as soon as baby emerges from the womb to accustom everyone to signing as a medium for communication, experts suggest the best time to introduce the concept in earnest is sometime around the sixth month or later. By the time a baby reaches the nine-to-12 month range, he or she should be primed for signing, with the cognitive aptitude to understand the relationship between a sign and the object or need it represents, the memory to remember that connection and build a vocabulary, plus the motor skills to actually perform the movements.

That's the when. What about the how? Here are a few fundamentals to guide your efforts in teaching a baby sign language:

- As you make a sign, always say the corresponding word.

- Always use the proper corresponding word, lest you cause your baby and others profound confusion.

- Start with a few words and build the sign vocabulary from there.

- Don't expect immediate results. It takes time for a baby and a caveman to wrap their minds around the unspoken language.

- Repeat and practice using signs with the right words.

- Make the process fun, like finger puppets.

- Expect your kid to personalize the signs he or she uses. The sign your little one uses for a certain word may not be executed in textbook fashion, but if everyone in the household understands it, go with it.

By now your palms are probably getting itchy to begin. The following signs, most of which are part of standard American Sign Language, can serve as a good starting point in your efforts to converse with the caveling.

**Daddy:** With the palm of one hand open and facing forward, fingers spread, bring hand up to touch the forehead with the tip of the thumb.

**Mommy:** With the palm of one hand open and facing forward, fingers spread, bring hand up to touch a cheek with the tip of the thumb.

**Help:** With the closed fist of one hand resting in the open palm of the other hand, move palm upward; *alternative: touch open palm to chest.*

**Hurt:** With both index fingers in a pointing position, touch the tips of those two fingers together.

**Eat:** Bring the tips of the fingers and thumb of one hand together into the shape of a bird's beak and touch the beak to the mouth.

EAT

DRINK

MILK

MORE

FINISHED

BOOK

SLEEP

**Drink:** Make like the Fonz by forming a thumb's up sign, then tip arm up, bringing the tip of the thumb to the mouth.

**Milk:** With palm open, clench the fingers of one hand into a fist, as if squeezing a cow's udder.

**More:** Use fingers to form a bird's beak with each hand, then touch the fingertips of each hand together like two birds touching beak-tips.

**Finished:** With hands at chest level, palms toward body, move hands down and out in a swooping motion.

**Book:** With palms together at abdomen/waist level, open hands as you would open the middle of a book, so palms are joined on the pinky edge, open, and facing up.

**Sleep:** With palms pressed together in prayer position, raise them to cheek level and rest the head on them, as if they're a pillow.

## YOUNG MINDS ARE MADE FOR MUSIC

Illuminated by a full moon, a group of Cro-Magnon men, women, and children sits around the remains of a fire, weary but satisfied by a day of highly successful hunting and gathering. Now, everyone having finished devouring the catch of the day, boar, ginger root, and pine nuts, one of the clan elders retrieves an intact bone from the embers of the fire and begins rhythmically thumping it against the hollow log on which he sits. One by one, other clan members follow suit. As the percussion escalates in intensity, a female in the group rises, aims her chin toward the sky and releases a throaty, undulating bay from the depths of her diaphragm. Others join in the chorus. Heads bob, hips sway, and knuckles pound in unison. Suddenly the clan is a band.

Music could very well be the oldest art form known to man. And as it turns out, the primitives who first began making it happened upon a means of expression that, according to modern research, provides huge benefits to those who make it and those who are exposed to it, babies included. While the preceding recreation of an evening of Paleolithic entertainment is pure conjecture, recent studies have drawn a link between music and intelligence, suggesting that listening to music at an early age strengthens brain development, thus bolstering intelligence later in life. Some findings suggest that music helps infants remember things better. Other studies conclude that young kids who make music are stronger in language and math skills, better-adjusted socially, and more skilled at solving problems.

Scientists aren't exactly sure how, but many now agree that music provides far-ranging benefits. Making music, some have posited, exercises the entire brain, positively impacts neurological systems, and bolsters brain capacity. Music may also provide a developmental boost to babies born prematurely. In one recent study, premature babies who heard lullabies while in neonatal intensive care gained more weight while registering lower blood pressures and stronger heartbeats than premature babies in the same intensive care unit who weren't exposed to music.

As a society, the power of music has begun to dawn on us. These days, music classes for kids as young as a few months can be found in many communities. But the beat can begin immediately at home. Not only can parents start playing music for a baby right from birth, as soon as a little one is able to grasp items, he or she can begin making primitive music with a rattle, a drum, a bell, a tambourine, even pots, pans, and kitchen utensils. So put down the TV remote, caveman, and grab your lute. Here's your chance to make some constructive noise in the name of your baby's brain.

## INFANTS AND THE IDIOT BOX

For better or for worse, television is here to stay. And that's lucky for us, because without it we would never have been introduced to the likes of Bart Simpson, Johnny Drama or Ryan Seacrest. Given that, how bad can TV watching be for a baby, especially if he or she exclusively watches educational programs, videos, and DVDs developed specifically to help little people learn?

So, how much TV should your baby be watching? The answer: **None**. The American Academy of Pediatrics explicitly recommends zero TV viewing for children under age 2. Ignore that advice at your child's risk; recent research shows that a consistent diet of heavy TV viewing (more than two hours a day) throughout early childhood can cause behavior, sleep and attention problems later in childhood.

Americans don't appear to be heeding the AAP's advice, however. A 2007 study from the University of Washington found that 40 percent of three-month-olds (and 90 percent of two-year-olds) reg-

## Postpartum Playlist: Now Is the Time When We Dance

The Partridges, the Van Halens, and the Von Trapps—these folks know how good it feels to rock as a family. You want music everyone in the clan can enjoy and move their bodies to, stuff whose appeal endures through multiple listenings. You gotta help a little person tap the primal urge to groove. Rock, soul, R&B, reggae, ska, bluegrass, country, hip-hop, house, be-bop, trance, gypsy, salsa—cue it up, turn it up (but never to decibel levels that pose a risk to a baby), and turn your little one on. For balance, augment with quieter sessions involving classical music, jazz, etc. Here, then, is a list of tunes to load in a playlist, burn, and play anyplace—at home, in the car or at a campsite. Even better if you bring your own instruments and play along.

*Yellow Submarine*
The Beatles

*Puff the Magic Dragon*
Peter, Paul & Mary

*I Want Candy*
Bow Wow Wow

*Rubber Biscuit*
The Blue Brothers

*Honky Cat*
Elton John

*Magic Bus*
The Who

*The Name Game*
Shirley Ellis

*Bad, Bad Leroy Brown*
Jim Croce

*Shout!*
The Temptations

*The Sidewinder Sleeps Tonight*
R.E.M.

*These Boots are Made for Walking*
Nancy Sinatra

*Blitzkrieg Bop*
The Ramones

*Magic Carpet Ride*
Steppenwolf

*Raindrops Keep Falling on My Head*
B.J. Thomas

*Chicken Payback*
Band of Bees

*I'm From the Sun*
Gustafer Yellowgold

*Joy to the World*
Three Dog Night

*Gimme Back My Dog*
Slobberbone

*Dancing Queen*
Abba

*Get Off My Cloud*
The Rolling Stones

ularly watch TV. "While appropriate television viewing at the right age can be helpful for both children and parents, excessive viewing before age 3 has been shown to be associated with problems of attention control, aggressive behavior, and poor cognitive development," explains Frederick Zimmerman, lead author of the UW study.

According to Zimmerman, "Exposure to TV takes time away from more developmentally appropriate activities such as a parent or adult caregiver and an infant engaging in free play with dolls, blocks or cars."

Other research suggests it ain't called the idiot box for nuthin'. Some studies have concluded, for example, that television watching during infancy, when parts of a baby's brain are rapidly developing, can have long-term ramifications on the wiring of the brain—how the synapses develop and fire. So while research on the impact of television viewing on a baby's brain is ongoing, those kind of findings are compelling enough for many parents to keep their infants and toddlers away from the boob tube altogether.

That's not an easy thing to do in many households, however. So if you are going to allow your baby to watch TV—and we're not advocating doing so, despite all the high-quality programming filling the airwaves these days—experts recommend that it be for short periods (maybe 15 minutes or less), with content that is slow-paced, without lots of rapidly changing images.

Rather than sticking a baby in front of the tube (even if it's one of those newfangled plasma or liquid crystal display models that emit no radiation) while you cook a meal, put the little one on the kitchen floor near you, provide a few pots, pans, and wooden utensils, and let him or her make some noise. It may not be music to your ears, but at least it won't turn your baby's brain to detritus.

A quick glance at the scorecard for this chapter yields the following: Parental interaction with baby: good. Sign language: good. Music: good. TV: bad. Before we move on to the final level of the needs-fulfillment pyramid, there's one more facet of baby communication/stimulation/socialization that demands exploration: Toys!

As a parent you likely will develop a love-hate relationship with them. The ones that seem to have little purpose other than producing a lot of repetitive, cloying noise—you can usually identify them by their brightly colored plastic parts and their voracious appetite for batteries—tend to be the first to land in the trash, then a landfill, leaving scores of disinterested babies and agitated adults in their wake. Toys that babies return to again and again, that hold their attention longest, and actually challenge their motor skills or their minds, without annoying everyone within earshot, tend to have much greater staying power.

The best toys from the infant and parental perspectives are those that engage and exercise a baby either mentally or physically. In most cases, simpler is better. Fancy features don't make much of a difference to kids this young. What you want are items that stretch, not shorten, a baby's attention span. All the better if they are made from a natural material like wood or cloth that biodegrades relatively quickly, not chemically engineered stuff like non-biodegradable plastic that's going to clog landfills for centuries to come.

Like clothes, cribs, and other baby gear, toys don't have to be purchased brand-new for a kid to make good use of them. The resourceful, budget-conscious troglodyte can find secondhand toys that are still in good condition by scavenging garage sales, second-

# DR. BRIAN

## *Infant Amnesia: Why Babies Draw a Blank*

Stop and smell the roses, people urge you. Cherish the memories of this first year of life with a baby. There will be lots of them, and it's a good thing you and your woman will be present for most of them, since your baby isn't capable of remembering these experiences, at least in any vivid, recallable detail.

Human neonates are like luxury automobiles; they come equipped with many high-end features, such as suckling know-how, the ability to coo and to cry right out of the womb, and the ability to suck their own toes, to name just a few from a lengthy list.

Long-term memory is not something they are blessed with at birth, however. During this first year, you and the folks close to you will rejoice in celebrating things such as holidays, birthdays, and other milestones with the baby—first tooth, first time uttering "mama" and "dada," first solid food, the progression from rolling over to crawling, standing, and eventually walking. Your little one will remember none of them. Therein lies an interesting conundrum: The offspring to whom you and your woman are dedicating so much time and effort parenting, while surely benefiting from the attention, care, and love you're providing, isn't in a position to retain memories of those experiences. Neuroscientists have labeled this phenomenon "infantile amnesia" and linked it to development of the brain's frontal cortex, a vital vault for event-memory storage and one that doesn't really hit stride development-wise until after the baby hits one year of age. For a recent study, researchers at Harvard University (Conor Liston and Jerome Kagan, "Brain Development: Memory Enhancement in Early Childhood," *Nature*, Volume 419, Issue 6910, October 2002) attempted to teach babies ages nine, 17 and 24 months toy-building techniques, then revisited them several months later to see if they could repeat the feat. It turned out only the older two groups of children could recall how to put together the toy.

While research is ongoing to solidify the link between long-term memory and cortex development, we know it takes time for babies to develop the ability to retain memories of events. Sure, they're seemingly fully aware of what's happening to them in the moment. But your little one will be depending on you and your woman to record those special times during the first year for later viewing. Without the still and/or moving footage you capture and store for posterity, there will be a void in baby's *Year One* book of memories.

hand stores, and the like, and via hand-me-downs and swaps from friends and family. Here are a few simple staples to consider adding to your little one's collection—toys that have entertained generations of little ones:

- Musical instruments (rattle, recorder, triangle, drum, etc.)
- Soft blocks
- Pull toys
- Duplo (big Legos for small children)
- Lincoln logs
- Squeeze-to-squeak toys
- Crayons, fingerpaints, and paper (supervision required)
- Balls
- Dolls
- Trains and train tracks
- Containers that open and close
- Mobiles
- Push toys (for babies who can stand and are ready to take steps)

The great thing about many of these toys is that they can provide you with hours of enjoyment, too. After all, your offspring isn't the only one in the household who needs stimulation, along with communication and socialization. To maintain a physical and mental edge during baby's first year of life, the cavecouple needs their own playthings, plus their own dedicated playtime. All work, no joy can make moms and dads feel like surly, subservient, out-of-shape, and antisocial girls and boys, and that's the last thing a baby needs.

Even during this labor-intensive phase of childrearing, it's crucial that you and your partner maintain touch with one another and with your individual identities, interests, and needs. So after eight chapters of material mostly addressing what you can do for your little one, it's finally time to focus on what you can do for *yourselves*.

# CHAPTER 9

# COUPLE & CAVEMAN MAINTENANCE

DEDICATED TO PRESERVATION OF THE ADULT SELF, COUPLEHOOD, AND SANITY DURING BABY'S FIRST YEAR

**Cro:** *dialectical form of the French word "creux," meaning* cavity *or* hollow.

**Magnon:** *augmentative form of the Old French word "magne," from the Latin word meaning* large *or* great.

THE WISDOM YOU HAVE ACCUMULATED OVER THE COURSE of this journey through baby's first year has turned you into an etymological anomaly. For although "Cro-Magnon" from the French translates roughly to "great, hollow cavity," the cavity that sits on your shoulders is anything but empty.

Physically you remain true to the troglodyte bloodline. Hair continues to account for one-third of your body weight. Your ability to touch your toes from the standing position without bending at the waist or knees still impresses at cocktail parties. But in your case, appearance is deceiving. Having absorbed all the baby-related stuff jammed into the preceding eight chapters, your hatful of hollow (at least as it applies to your lack of fatherhood experience) is now a vast reservoir, full of childrearing wisdom, knowledge, and common sense, to be applied and shared liberally from this point forward.

Not only have you demonstrated a great capacity for learning, you deserve special commendation for rising to meet one of the most formidable challenges any man will face: fatherhood. As you clamber to the pinnacle of the needs-fulfillment pyramid and speed toward one year with a baby under your belt (where does the time go?), your daddy résumé now sparkles with amazing evolutionary accomplishments and milestones that put you head and shoulders (but not neck—you don't have one) above many of your Cro-Magnon peers.

Your skill set is now so broad it is coveted by men and women alike. It is a repertoire that now includes conversiveness in sign language, proficiency in infant massage, a newfound aptitude for

## Grow with Gronk

What the caveman stands to gain from reading Chapter 9:

- An appreciation for all he and his lady have achieved in baby's first year
- The perceptiveness to read his woman's mind
- An intimate grasp of sexual issues facing the postpartum couple
- Keen insight into postpartum issues that may affect his woman
- A mastery of massage techniques to use for relief, release, and foreplay
- Entrée into the magical, mystical world of yoga
- Tips on staying healthy amid all the stress
- Strategies for handling the critics
- The know-how to fashion a viable postpartum social life
- Creative suggestions for staying true to his troglodyte self
- A clear idea of the odds of conceiving again, so soon after birth
- The impetus to make his baby's first birthday an extra-special celebration

household responsibilities and other forms of manual labor, the know-how to keep a baby healthy and out of harm's way, a keen eye for baby clothes that are both fashionable and functional, the finesse and persistence to coach a baby to be a solid sleeper, newly discovered wizardry in the kitchen, and an ability to keep your household afloat when your woman leaves town or is otherwise unable to perform baby-related duties.

All this has been building toward a revelatory first-year denouement, one that the two of you might even get to experience at once. Say you're both standing in front of the bathroom mirror one morning as you've done so many times before. Only this time, when you wipe the fog away, the people whose reflections you're gazing at have somehow acquired a different aspect, something you can't quite pinpoint. Has someone secretly replaced your normal reflective glass with one of those shape-shifting funhouse mirrors that make people look like dwarves and giants? Nope.

What's changed is the two of you. When you look at one another, you now see a man and woman who, besides being friends, lovers, partners, and playmates, are *parents*—and pretty good ones at that! Suddenly you've gained the perspective to see beyond your moment-to-moment daily existence, as relentlessly paced as it has become since the baby came along. In this sublime flash of clarity it dawns on you just how much each of you has grown and evolved as individuals, and how much has transpired in your little nuclear family since your baby was born. Feelings of gratitude, pride, love, and humility wash over you. Then the air of reverie is abruptly broken by the sound of your infant crying in the room down the hall.

What lingers long after the moment passes is the wisdom that as much as life has changed since that little chip cleaved off the old block, and as much as the two of you have grown since becoming parents, you're still basically the same people. The needs, desires, passions, and qualities that give you your identities as individuals and as a couple are still very much intact, it's just that at times they become enmeshed with, or take a back seat to, the baby's. Bury, overlook or neglect these aspects of yourselves at your own risk. Your individuality needn't wither on the vine just because you now have a kid.

While much of what you have read to this point is about fulfilling another's needs, only by staying true to your inner troglodyte, your respective adult identities, and your strengths as a couple will the two of you reach the pinnacle of the first-year needs-fulfillment pyramid. Men and women who feel fulfilled as individuals generally make better parents. This chapter is dedicated to helping the cave-couple strike a balance where meeting the needs of a baby doesn't preclude them from fulfilling their own needs.

We'd like to say this chapter will focus mostly on sex, but that's not the case. There are means other than copulation to keep you thriving as individuals and as a couple, and in the pages that follow we'll explore some of the most indispensable, including things you undertake together, such as massage, cultivating a social life, staying healthy and fit, and fielding criticism of your parenting techniques, and things you may pursue separate of one another, such as hobbies, guys-only and ladies-only time, and activities one parent does while the other hangs out with the little one.

First let's talk communication. Good things come to cavemen who listen closely and say and do the right thing, with their partner's best interests in mind. It's the kind of behavior that, dare we say, might even lead to sex.

## CAVEMAN MINDREADER, THE SEQUEL

By mastering baby signs and baby-speak, you've acquired a couple of indispensable darts to use in your communications blowgun. But by keeping your highly sensitive rabbit-ear antennae pointed exclusively at the little apple of your eye, you run the risk of tuning out other, equally important signals: those emitted by the sunshine of your life, your woman.

Never in your relationship has it been so vital for the two of you to remain on the same wavelength. Your woman, like your offspring, will frequently send you signals so nuanced and pregnant with meaning that deciphering their intent requires an extra degree of perceptiveness and interpretive skill. Taking statements by your partner only at face value may have you wearing a mystified look and a daddy dunce cap more often than you care to. The following is a quick-reference translation guide to help keep the lines of communication (and your eyes) from getting crossed. Keep it accessible for those especially mind-bending moments.

| Mom Says | Mom Means |
| --- | --- |
| *How was your day, honey?* | A quick capsule of what's going on in the outside world would be much appreciated. I'm too fried/busy to focus long enough on the newspaper or the TV news. |
| *If I were a drinker, I'd be pouring myself a double.* | It's been one of those days. Anything you can do to help relieve my stress, get busy. |
| *I don't know how much more crying I can take.* | If the baby didn't cry so loudly and persistently, the sound you'd hear would be my own cries for some caretaking help. |
| *My breasts feel tender.* | That little sucker is turning my nipples to hamburger. |
| *All these baby meet-and-greet visits are becoming a little tiresome.* | I don't mind close friends and family stopping by occasionally, but no more surprise visits from those guys from the bowling team who stare at me when I breastfeed. |
| *I can see how some new moms might go a little stir crazy.* | Cut me loose for a couple hours so I can think of something, anything, other than the baby. |
| *Weird—falling asleep standing up is much easier than I imagined.* | Exhaustion has set in. How about taking the baby for the afternoon so I can take a nap? |
| *I miss my friends.* | All this time with the baby makes me feel like I'm neglecting my friendships. |
| *I'm drained.* | This kid is sucking me dry with his/her huge appetite. How about fetching me a milkshake/frappe/malt/smoothie. |
| *I need to put my feet up for a minute.* | You'd be my hero if you let me kick back for a while. |
| *My body just doesn't feel the same.* | The birth, breastfeeding, and a lack of sleep and exercise aren't doing much for my self-image and self-esteem. |
| *I'm so out of shape!* | Being able to exercise for even just a half-hour a few times a week would be a big bonus. |
| *I haven't even thought about dinner.* | Cooking is the last thing I want to do at this moment. How about you step up to the plate tonight? |
| *I can't remember the last time I had a block of solid, uninterrupted sleep.* | All this waking up at night to feed the baby is catching up with me. |
| *I just don't think I have it in me tonight.* | I'm reading your signals loud and clear, big guy, but it ain't happening for us tonight. |
| *I'm feeling romantic.* | Wipe that sad puppy look off your face, caveman. Tonight is your lucky night. Light some candles, turn on the smooth jazz, and let's make slow, sweet love before the urge to sleep overcomes me. |

| The Uncultivated Dad's Response | The Cultivated Dad's Response |
| --- | --- |
| If it's fantasy football stats you're after, I'm your man. Otherwise I'm as clueless as you. | Commits to providing woman with a nightly five-minute recap of news headlines, including two minutes dedicated exclusively to celebrity gossip. |
| Don't you have a Valium you could take? | Administers a 10-minute neck-and-shoulders massage, then draws his lady a hot, sudsy bath. |
| Aren't your mom and dad going to be in town next week? If you can just hold out until then… | Suggests they begin searching for a babysitter to watch the baby for at least five to 10 hours a week. |
| They may be painful, but baby, believe me when I tell you they're a pleasure to look at. | Fetches cool cabbage leaves from the fridge, suggests she apply them to breasts—a legitimate homeopathic remedy he read about in a book. |
| My bowling buddies may come off as a bit abrasive, but all that good booze they've brought us as baby gifts has the liquor cabinet pretty well stocked. | Vows to immediately stem the tide of visitors/breast-gawkers and to honor her desire for privacy. |
| I hear you, babe, but we all make sacrifices. I haven't been to the driving range in weeks. | Volunteers to take the caveling two mornings a week to free her up for yoga, coffee with girlfriends, etc. |
| Rest up, hunbun. I'd be there with you but gotta go—you know I like to be on time for those pregame tailgate parties. | Asserts to woman that her being that tired is unacceptable; promises to let her sleep late three times a week and clears schedule to permit her to nap both days of the weekend. |
| Not to worry—if they're true friends, they'll stick with you through this. | Purchases spa gift certificate for his woman and a friend of her choice, suggests that she take one night a week out with the ladies. |
| How about I bring you one of those sugar-free popsicles from the freezer? They taste great and they're less filling. | Recognizing breastfeeding woman's need to replenish nutrients and her occasional desire for comfort food, bee-lines to closest ice cream shop. |
| Sure, sweetheart, take a load off for a couple minutes. By the way, when's dinner going to be on the table? | Insists that woman remain on the couch while he cooks, cleans, and handles all baby-related duties. |
| You're right—the demands a baby puts on the female body are huge. Reason No. 1,235 why I'm glad I'm not a woman. | Tells her she's everything he could ever want in a woman. Retrieves copy of poem he wrote for her in college and recites it with Romeo-like earnestness. |
| The elliptical machine in the basement is collecting dust. Why don't you jump on it after you put the baby down for the night. | Says it's time she focused more on her health and well-being; the same week furnishes her with a package that includes multiple personal training sessions and babysitting. |
| That's funny, because dinner was all I could think about on the ride home. What's on the menu? | Seizes opportunity to prepare one of the recipes he recently found in that book about what's-his-face the caveman. |
| Just a couple more months and we'll have that caveling sleeping through the night. | Insists on assuming more middle-of-the-night feeding duties until the little one begins sleeping through the night without needing nourishment. |
| Give me a chance and I guarantee I can get you in the mood. | Calls off full-court press, suggests she make herself available for a massage instead. |
| Hold that thought, honey. It's the ninth inning and the winning run is on third base. | Strikes Heisman pose, hurdles coffee table, and bolts upstairs to transform bedroom into shrine to Aphrodite. |

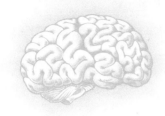

*Inside Mommy's Mind: Installment 3*

## Your Lady's Libido

Extensive research by CAHFAC members Stasia and Gina on the subject of sexuality among new parents yields the following insights about the postpartum female libido.

- Our breasts are for giving, only not to you.

- Various erogenous zones are temporarily closed until further notice. We'll let you know when they are open for business. In the meantime, non-sexual touching (like a massage) may lead to more. It's your best shot.

- If we are not exercising during that first year, you're probably not getting any.

- If you arrange for a babysitter even once in a blue moon, we'll go down on you.

- Most doctors say to wait six weeks or thereabouts after giving birth before having intercourse. C'mon. Emotionally we may be ready after six weeks, especially when we watch you feeding, diapering, and playing with the baby. But physically we aren't ready (nor are we really **brave** enough) until about 10 weeks. So please don't push it.

## SEXY TIME: A DISCOURSE ON INTERCOURSE

Regardless of how upright a cavemen walks, how much Dostoevsky or DeLillo he reads or how much cologne he wears, there is no denying his primate lineage. And however much we *Homo sapiens* might try to bury it, rationalize it, and exercise it away, we are creatures with a rich sexual heritage.

Humans and primates alike have long feasted on forbidden fruit. Some prehistoric scholars suggest, for example, that primitive societies practiced group sex and used sex toys on a widespread basis. A recent study by British archeologists hypothesizes that a 25,000- to 30,000-year-old limestone statue of a naked woman called the Venus of Willendorf and an ancient stone phallus of a similar vintage represent the earliest direct evidence that sex for people of the Paleolithic wasn't just about making babies, nor was it always heterosexual or monogamous. They posit that it was a form of body language—a way to communicate, interact socially, and explore the mysteries of one another's bodies. What better way to keep warm while holed up, weathering one of those interminable Ice Age storms? Our close relative the chimpanzee swings, too, and not just from trees. According to primatologists, groups of adult Bonobo chimps practice indiscriminate sex to relieve tension.

You may have an innately strong drive to celebrate and further this carnal heritage by having sex on a regular basis. And now that you're a fledgling father, your need to relieve tension and stress might be stronger than ever. But one of the realities you must try to wrap your mind around as a new parent is that supply will not always meet demand. The simple fact is that it takes time for a woman to rebound mentally and physically from childbirth, whether baby came via vaginal or Cesarean delivery. The bottom line, caveman, is that it likely will be a month from baby's birth, and often longer, before you and your woman can resume intercourse.

It may have been quite a while since you endured a dry spell of that magnitude, particularly if you and your woman had to work (difficult to fathom, but sex can become "work," especially when it is performed with clinical precision, solely for reproduction) long and feverishly to conceive in the first place. Reading about the sexploits of our Paleolithic forebears—check out *Clan of the Cave Bear*, book or movie, for more graphic fictionalized detail—might get you yearning for the good old days—the really, really old Ice Age ones or the more recent ones when supply kept pace with demand.

Yearn all you want, but keep in mind, too, that when it comes to any postpartum alterations in sexual habits, often the reasons aren't as one-sided as locker room talk might lead you to believe. As it turns out, new moms *and* new dads might find that adding a baby to the mix changes the sexual dynamic, though certainly not always for the worse. Besides the physical limitations that may keep women from intercourse in the first weeks and months after delivery (Dr. Brian expounds on those on the next pages), other internal and external factors are sure to impact your respective sex drives. With so much of your time, energy, and devotion now diverted to the baby, sex at times may slip a few notches on the priority list, and perhaps further still for women engaged in the physically draining (but potentially hugely rewarding) practice of breastfeeding. The too-pooped-to-pop phenomenon is very real for many a cavecouple.

Each of you is channeling so much affection toward the caveling, you may need to drill a little deeper to once again tap the reservoir of intimacy and passion that once lurked so close to the surface. Some couples find it easy to get back on the proverbial horse. For others, it takes time to figure out how to get their heads, their hearts, and/or their parts back in the game. When you're both ready, when the mood is right and the opportunity is there, it will happen.

It may not happen soon enough or frequently enough for some folks, however. Of course there will be times when the mood strikes neither of you, or one of you but not the other. There also will be times when you're both in the mood but the baby's awake, eyes wide open, contently cooing away in the bassinette right next to your bed. Remember the discussion in Chapter 8 about a baby's inability to retain specific, detailed memories from the first year of life? To seize the moment in these instances you must have faith that infant amnesia is indeed very real, that the lights are on but nobody in baby's memory department is home.

Unfamiliar feelings and sensations might accompany your return to sexual activity. An act that seemed to come so naturally for both of you now might be accompanied by new anxiety, uncertainty, even trepidation. To what extent have things changed down there? Will it hurt her? Will the fit still be snug enough to satisfy both parties? The only definitive way to answer these questions is to *go for it*.

Once the doctor has cleared your woman to resume intercourse,

- We may want it emotionally, but we're embarrassed about how our bodies may feel different than they used to. We're afraid you could drive a Mack truck into our vaginas and neither of us would know it.

- **Incontinence!** There's a pretty good chance that after giving birth, we will have no control. We cough, we pee. We laugh, we pee. We hurry across the street to make it before the walking man stops flashing, we pee. So…we orgasm, we pee? We are afraid that during sex we might pee on you (or worse, your face, depending on what's going on down there). This condition is usually temporary, but we take it seriously while it lasts, so you should, too.

- We are exhausted. Please make sex easy for us with lots of foreplay and whispers of sweet nothings.

# DR. BRIAN

## *Insight on Her Insides*

The female body is an alluring and mysterious temple at which many a caveman will spend a lifetime worshipping. From the male perspective, it can take a lifetime merely to make sense of the female mind-body dynamic—what's going on inside a woman physiologically and how that might manifest itself psychologically. That dynamic can be especially difficult for a caveman to fathom during the postpartum period, given the physical and mental issues associated with childbirth and first-time parenting.

The time you spend with your woman makes you ideally situated to monitor these issues as they unfold, and to help her address them if the need arises. Here are a few worth watching for:

- In the aftermath of pregnancy and childbirth, conditions in the holiest parts of the female temple may confound even the most devout worshippers. After birth, for example, the new mom must contend with fairly copious amounts of vaginal discharge, called **lochia**. It's a combination of remnants of the uterine lining and blood. She may also pass blood clots. Discharge should gradually dissipate over a period of several weeks after birth.

  To absolutely no one's surprise, her vagina likely will be exceedingly sore and swollen after **vaginal delivery**. If she had an episiotomy, there will be stitches that should dissolve/disappear after a couple weeks. Her vagina in its postpartum state is like any wounded part of the body. It needs time to heal. As with treating other wounds, your woman will need to use a pad (dressing) and gently cleanse the area. She will likely take "sitz" baths, which is basically where she sitz in a bath. At this point, you may be thinking plenty about intercourse, but from a purely physical standpoint, don't even go there until her genital area (perineum) is comfortable, the

episiotomy has healed (three to five weeks) and any bleeding has stopped.

- While having a baby by **caesarean section** is easier on the vagina, there will still be plenty of discharge. It's abdominal surgery, in which a cut is made through the muscle and connective tissue of the abdomen, so it's going to hurt afterwards and it will take four to six weeks for the incision to heal (absolutely no intercourse before then). A note about managing her pain after a C-section: It's best to "stay ahead" of the pain. If she waits until it gets intense before taking the next dose of pain meds, she may need more medicine to dull or rid the pain. If she takes medication *before* the pain gets too severe, she may actually use less of the pain drug overall.

- Adding insult to injury, many women develop **hemorrhoids**—dilated, inflamed rectal veins—from pregnancy and childbirth. You can comfort your woman by telling her hemorrhoids generally should shrink and disappear over time, but what she wants most is immediate relief, which she can get from over-the-counter products as well as prescription hemorrhoid medication.

- **Hormones** are the postpartum elephant in the room. Your woman may look placid on the outside, but after childbirth her hormones are churning in order to facilitate breastfeeding and to otherwise normalize to pre-pregnancy levels. Lactating women produce high levels of **prolactin**, the principle hormone stimulating milk production, or lactogenesis. Infant suckling stimulates production of the hormone, whose effects may include difficulty concentrating, according to CAHFAC member Pat, aka the Breast Whisperer.

  **Oxytocin**, another hormone, not only triggers milk letdown, it has been found to stimulate bonding and maternal behavior in women. Lactation, which is partly stimulated by oxytocin, has been shown to have a calming effect, so women who breastfeed may have a less intense reaction to stress. It's also worth noting that oxytocin is the hormone involved in uterine contractions during childbirth, so some women may experience "after pains" (pelvic pain) after breastfeeding. The benefit here may be that breastfeeding shortly after giving birth makes the uterus contract quicker, decreasing maternal bleeding.

And let's not forget the **thyroid gland**, which regulates many of our metabolic processes, acting as a sort of a gas pedal for the body. A woman's thyroid may either be over- or under-active after childbirth.

The **baby blues** affects some 50 to 80 percent of new moms. Symptoms, including feelings of loss, confusion, anxiety, fear, and being overwhelmed, tend not to disrupt the daily routine. They usually peak five days after birth and resolve within a few weeks.

If those symptoms persist and intensify instead of subsiding, they may be signs of postpartum depression, which is less common but more acute than the baby blues. Depression may first appear during pregnancy and continue after the birth, manifested by sleep problems, fatigue, guilt, feelings of worthlessness, a lack of energy for, and interest in, activities, problems concentrating, appetite changes, and even thoughts of harming herself or the child.

**Postpartum depression** affects eight to 20 percent of women. It usually starts during the first month after birth but can occur anytime in baby's first year. If you suspect your woman might have it, act decisively but tactfully to help her get treatment, as it is a condition that not only can impact a mother's ability to interact with her baby, it can have both short- and long-term effects on the child's development and behavior as well as family dynamics

Your first instinct might be to try to lift her spirits yourself. But if depression is the issue, it's best to seek professional help. As a starting point, gently suggest to your lady that she talk to her OB-GYN or family doc about how she's feeling. The sooner the problem is diagnosed and addressed, the better. Treatment might include therapy and/or medication. Whatever the course of action, support from you and other family members is crucial. The following websites offer solid information and guidance on postpartum depression: www.4woman.gov; www.postpartum. net; www.depressionafterdelivery.com; and www. postpartumstress.com.

All these possibilities might be unnerving to the caveman. By now you may be eyeing the liquor cabinet for something—anything—to calm your racing mind. But before you pour yourself a tall glass of cooking sherry, there's more. **Fatigue** may also be an issue for your woman, as may **swelling** and fluid **retention**, **night sweats**, **mood swings**, persistent **hunger**, and even **hair loss**.

You best be worshipping your lady, given all the stuff she must endure.

the sooner you attempt to rediscover your sexual intimacy, the more opportunity you'll have to figure things out mentally and physically, and to accordingly recast your sex life in the brave new postpartum era. You may be tempted in your first postpartum sexual forays to release the caged beast inside you. But it's in both your best interests to be a gentle giant and take it slow.

As is the case with many equipment-intensive pursuits, you don't want any vital parts to grow rusty or fall into disrepair from neglect. Balls do occasionally need re-inflating; skis do require periodic waxing. There is, of course, more than one way to keep one's equipment in good working order. There will be times when the person you rely upon to grind, wax, buff, and tune your gear isn't open for business. Hopefully over the years you've learned how to perform those functions yourself, so that when the need arises, self-service is an option.

## THE CAVEMASSEUR STRIKES AGAIN

In indigeneous cultures, shamans were (and in some cases, still are) tribal troubleshooters whose healing powers and wisdom about the workings of the body and spirit earned them immense respect within their clans. The shaman of prehistoric times was versatile, serving the public as a healer, sorcerer, priest, and tribal leader. He or she was a ritual leader who gained special powers through an ability to straddle the material and supernatural worlds.

The hands and digits were among a shaman's most indispensable tools, for they provided the means to transfer some of that healing power to his or her cavedwelling subjects. It was the shaman who raised the practice of "giving good hand" to an art and a science.

To earn your stripes as the shaman of your household, you, too, must give good hand, and not just to your little one using the infant massage techniques outlined in Chapter 7. When they're not dragging in the dirt, those things attached to your wrists can be honed into powerful tension-release tools, skilled conduits of pleasure that through simple touch help you and your woman re-establish intimacy after the baby is born. When sex isn't an option, the cave-couple can use massage as a stand-in. And when it is an option, they can use it as foreplay.

All you need to know are a few simple techniques. Executed properly, at the right time and in the right environment, these maneuvers can bring the masseur and his subject much-needed relief from the rigors and stress of the day.

First some basics. Among the many "schools" of massage, the Swedish technique is by far the most commonly practiced in the U.S. It uses five basic strokes: (1) **effleurage**, in which the whole hand or the thumb is used to make long, gliding strokes; (2) **petrissage**, a gentle grabbing and lifting of muscles away from the bone, followed by light rolling, pressing, and squeezing to encourage deeper circulation; (3) **friction**, where circular movements of the thumbs and fingertips are used for deep muscle penetration; (4) **tapotement**, where the edge of the hand, fingertips or a closed hand are used to make tapping motions; and (5) **vibration**, where fingers are pressed and flattened on a muscle, then used to shake the area for a few seconds.

When performed with proper shaman-like technique (applying the same principles of good hand-giving outlined in Chapter 7), even a few minutes of massage can provide your woman much-needed relief. And once you're done, she can reciprocate. It's a skill the two of you can use for a lifetime, not just to stoke the passion but to maintain a level of intimacy that only touch can provide.

To get started, choose a quiet, private, softly lit venue and get your supplies in order—massage oil, proper surface, candles, perhaps some gentle, non-intrusive mood music. As a warm-up you may want to draw your woman a bath and allow her to soak while you make preparations. Here are a few techniques our resident massage therapist and Caveman's Ad Hoc Advisory Council member Desirae suggests incorporating into the routine.

**Shoulders, neck & head:** A breastfeeding woman's neck and shoulders are apt to get tight from peering down at the baby during feeding sessions and from lifting and toting the little one around. With your woman sitting backwards in a comfy chair or laying on her belly, start with a few sweeping motions through the neck, shoulders, and mid-back. Then warm the tissue with gentle squeezing and kneading. Next use your thumb to apply pressure from her spine across to the tops of her shoulders, then from the spine to her shoulder blades (you should always work from the spine outward).

- Now use the fleshy part of your thumbs to make small circles in specific spots that require extra attention because they are particularly tight or tense, adjusting pressure according to your woman's direction. Areas along the tops of the shoulders and tucked down near the collarbone often need extra work. Use small, circular motions with the fleshy part of your fingers to get in there deeply.

- In the neck area, use fingertips to gently massage the sides of the neck and the lower head, behind the ears, and on the sides of the head. Use your thumbs on the back of the neck and along the outside of the upper spine. With feedback from your woman, identify tender points and massage them slowly with circular motions. Now begin working her head lightly with your fingertips, moving around the ears, the sides and top of her dome. Using your thumbs as pressure points, have her tilt her head back slightly onto your thumbs, creating counter-pressure on an area called the low occipital, where the neck and head meet.

**Foot, ankle and calf:** Position your woman so that she is lying in the bath, feet and ankles poking out of the water, or lying on the bed, feet just off the edge, or seated in a comfortable chair. You can also perform a foot/ankle massage while she's breastfeeding, if it's not too distracting to her or the baby.

- Start stroking the top of her foot, using both hands to make long, slow rubbing motions. Be firm with your thumbs. Gradually slide your hands along the entire length of the foot, from toes to ankle. Now shift to the bottom of the foot. Make circular motions with firm fingers and knuckles, then slide them up and down her arch. Next, slowly and gently, but firmly, pull each of her toes.

- Now for the ankle. Grasp one of her feet in your hands and move it in a circular motion, then use your fingers to gently work the area. Finish by moving up to the calf, where you'll use your fingers to pull and spread the muscles there.

**Lower back and glutes:** With your woman lying on her belly, use your thumbs to massage the area where her hips meet her spine. Find the area of soft tissue around her lower back, then press and release on the tissue using your knuckle or thumb. Hold the position for three seconds for tension-release.

- Now onto the butt cheeks. Staying close to the sacrum area, make little circles with thumbs and fingers, gradually expanding the coverage area of your strokes until they encompass the entire butt cheek. Work the ball and socket area; also wander a bit to the front of the thigh. If she identifies specific spots as being particularly tender, sustain firm pressure there for several seconds, then release and move on to another pressure point.

## YOGA PARTY:
## ALL IT TAKES IS TWO

Remember the rubber-band-boy you grew up with who could bring his toes behind his back and up to touch his shoulders, the freak-of-nature who would leave everyone in gym class gawking by pulling off a double flip from a standing position then dropping right into a split?

Here in the cultivated caveman universe, Dr. Brian is our resident rubber-band-man. And he has yoga to thank, not just for his Gumby-like flexibility but also for his superior balance, calm demeanor, and strong sense of well-being. These benefits are well within reach for you and your woman as well. By exploring the ancient practice of yoga together, you not only stand to gain flexibility, strength, and a new means of stress-relief, you may also discover erotic avenues that lead to eye-popping sexual vistas. If you've ever been intrigued by tantric sex and the *Kama Sutra*, yoga can provide entrée into these mystical worlds, where tapestries flow, incense burns, sitars play, and body parts intertwine like a pit full of oily, writhing snakes.

But let's not allow your imagination to get too far ahead of your body. If you and your woman are new to yoga, it's in your physical best interests to start practicing slowly, perhaps with a few introductory classes to provide a solid foundation for your future private explorations.

Yoga, which originated in India as many as 5,000 years ago, is practiced to benefit both mind and body. It involves poses designed to stretch and strengthen while promoting balance and concentration. Many practitioners find that it not only provides a workout but instills a sense of inner peace and fosters a connection between spirit, mind, and body. There are many different styles of yoga, among them Anusara, Ashtanga, Bikram, Iyengar, Integral, Jivamukti, Kripalu, Kundalini, Raja, Sivananda, Tantra, Yinhatha, and Hatha, which is the one most commonly practiced in the U.S. Each comes with its own distinct approaches, some more meditative and some more physically demanding. What unites most of the styles practiced here in the West today are the common "asanas," or poses, they incorporate. All the poses in a series are designed to be coordinated with breathing.

You might be tempted to dismiss yoga as a fad, just another excuse to put on tight, formfitting outfits. But today an estimated 20 *million* Americans are doing it. Rather than trying to forget the stress of the day with a visit to a maddeningly crowded health club or with a post-work cocktail, why not use yoga to transcend those tensions? It's been working for people since well before anyone could dream up aerobics, Pilates, and workouts built to turn buns into steel and abs into six-packs, it works for legions of busy guys like Dr. Brian and it can work for you, too.

One of the beauties of yoga is that it doesn't demand that you invest in any special equipment or a membership, nor that your practice be limited by a class schedule. While it's probably worthwhile to invest a few bucks in a good non-stick yoga mat and a couple of introductory classes, you can practice at home, anytime your schedule allows. Once bitten by the yoga bug, it might not be long before you find yourself practicing several times a week and shopping for a contour-hugging, super-comfy yoga outfit along with other widely used props, such as a block and a strap. These props can be used in a variety of imaginative ways, but we'll let Dr. Brian explain those in another book.

In the meantime, once your woman has been cleared to resume physical activities after the birth, here are a few poses for the two of you try in the privacy of your own home. Where they might lead…well, the possibilities are as boundless as your respective imaginations.

## 1. Notice Your Breath

Paying attention to your breathing is an essential part of yoga practice. Begin your session with a breathing exercise/meditation to establish the "connection" to your breath.

Sit in a comfortable cross-legged position on a mat or the floor. If you are uncomfortable in the cross-legged position, try sitting on a yoga block or folded towel to elevate your bottom. Relax your hands on your knees and sit tall.

Relax your face and mouth, close your eyes, and breathe naturally, without effort, through your nose. First try just noticing how your breath feels—the sensation as it passes in and out of the nostrils, how the chest and abdomen move with each inhalation and exhalation. Then try to make the inhalation and exhalation equal length, counting as you breathe in (1 . . 2 . . 3 . .) and counting the same number as you exhale. Gradually increase the count, but don't struggle too hard. A big part of yoga is learning where to expend effort and what tension you can let go. After a few minutes of this you can return to natural breathing and open your eyes.

To practice this pose in connection with your partner, sit facing one another, knees lightly touching, and hold each other's hands. You may find that touching your partner during the breathing exercise adds an emotional and energetic quality.

Initially, breathing and meditative exercises may be uncomfortable, and you might find that you want to move, or that your mind is racing. With time, however, you will probably find that breathing exercises are both energizing and calming at the same time. Sharing this quiet time with your partner may be strongly bonding. In the frenetic life of new parents, it isn't often that you can truly relax together.

As a general rule in practicing yoga, try to stay mindful of your breath, and if you ever find yourself struggling or uncomfortable, remember to refocus on the breath.

## 2. Mountain Pose & Forward Fold

Stand up, facing one another, your eyes open, about five feet apart. Use your most upright posture, with your feet about hip width apart and your shoulders tending to move backward (shoulder blades toward each other) and down (shoulders away from the ears). Notice your breath again, and continue taking even inha-

# DR. BRIAN

## Germ Warfare

New dads and moms have to be at the top of their games to handle the responsibilities that come with parenting. The baby isn't going to sleep any longer or spare you from diaper duty simply because you're feeling under the weather, so you must take steps to stay healthy. Here are some tips to keep the caveman and woman strong like bull and off the "physically unable to perform" list:

- **Stay fit.** Even 20 minutes of exercise per day a few times a week can better equip your body to battle—and bounce back from—illness and exhaustion.

- **Find outlets to relieve stress.** Yoga, massage, paintball, poetry readings—whatever methods you find most effective at releasing pent-up tension and anxiety.

- **Eat right.** A healthy, well-balanced diet keeps your body working more efficiently.

- **Get enough sleep.** Easier said than done with a new baby in your home. But every facet of life suffers for people who don't meet their quota for Zs. Sleep as much as you can at night and if necessary, make up any deficit with quick daytime catnaps under your desk at work.

- **Take vitamins.** Ask your doctor to recommend supplements to help keep you strong amid the rigors of raising a baby.

- **Curb vices.** Harmful habits like smoking and excessive alcohol consumption can ruin your health. You're no good to your caveling, your woman or anyone else when you're ill or dead.

- **Laugh a lot.** Frequent laughter isn't just good for the soul, it's good for your health, studies have shown.

- **Dress appropriately for conditions.** Don't head out on an ice-fishing expedition wearing only your lightweight summer pelt.

- **See a doctor.** Get a physical before or right after baby is born so you know where you stand health-wise.

lations and exhalations. On an inhalation, raise your arms up sideways toward the ceiling. Reach high, fighting the natural troglodyte inclination to hunch the shoulders. On the exhalation, fold forward at the hips, as if you are making a slow swan dive, taking care not to butt heads with your woman, who is likewise folding forward. Try to keep your back flat by leading the fold with your chest. Let your arms come down and place your hands wherever they fall naturally, which may be at your shins if you have tight hamstrings or squarely on the ground if you're a knuckledragger with Dr. B-like flexibility. If there is discomfort in the hamstrings or low back, feel free to bend the knees slightly. Relax the neck so the head hangs without effort. Breathe. After a few carefully paced breaths, on an inhale rise up as if you are reversing the dive motion, lifting your arms back toward the ceiling. On the exhalation, lower your arms back to the side. Repeat these moves a few times.

These movements are the beginning of a series of moves, synchronized with the breath, called "sun salutations." Sun salutations are a commonly performed series of yoga poses.

## 3. Turtle Pose

Face each other on the floor, sitting tall with a straight back, legs spread wide. You're about to start taking turns stretching one another. Place your feet on the inner side of your woman's lower legs. Have your woman lean forward and gently hold each other's upper arms. Gently stretch your woman toward you, being careful to move slowly. Let the stretch occur gradually to foster a sense of trust in each other. Switch roles. This posture can also be coordinated with the breath: on the inhalation, the person being stretched lengthens and straightens their spine and on the exhalation lets go into the stretch. Another variation of this pose is to gently rotate each other in a circle, first one direction, then the other, being mindful not to pull too hard. This pose allows you to physically connect, develops sensitivity to each other's bodies and trust.

## COPING WITH THE CRITICS

All this talk of tension release and stress relief, but little mention of where the stress and tension actually originate. What, besides the everyday rigors of life with a baby, causes new parents to turn to outlets such as yoga and massage?

Oftentimes, it's the critics. People will be Ebert-and-Ropering your parental performance and many will be generous with their advice, praise, and criticism, whether you invite it or not. Some comments surely will be constructive and worth taking to heart; others are best allowed to escape into the ether unheeded.

Here it's worthwhile to hearken back to two of the Ten Commandments for New Fathers detailed in Chapter 1. One says, *Thou shalt exercise healthy skepticism and heed useful information.* Another says, *Thou shalt use levelheaded common sense.* When confronted with a comment or criticism you find particularly offensive, the best policy for preserving peace and your reasonably clean criminal record is to curb the immediate urge to fire back at the source and instead take a few moments to craft a more diplomatic response. At right are some examples on which to model your behavior.

## TWO ON THE TOWN

There is an inherent tension to becoming a parent. For while humans are naturally social creatures who crave the company of other *Homo sapiens*, for new parents the drive to interact with others often takes a backseat to a phenomenon known as the nesting instinct, where the overriding urge is to hunker down in your baby bunker to revel in the trappings of your newly created nuclear family. During the nesting phase, the extent of your contact with the outside world could be limited to the time you spend at work, plus periodic errands to restock household supplies and the occasional housecall from friends and family. Phone messages, personal hygiene, and poker games may be ignored.

Wanting to revel in the powerful, primal, and very new feelings associated with parenthood is perfectly normal and fully understandable. But eventually you and your woman must re-emerge from the cave to connect with the outside world—your friendships, social lives, leisure pursuits, community activities, and the like. For outside of family, these are what help define you as a person. The

| Offending Remark | First Thought Through Your Mind | The Tactful Response |
|---|---|---|
| We used to dress ours in secondhand clothes, too, but we got tired of people staring at him/her as if he/she was a hobo/tramp. | *I'd rather my baby dress like a ragamuffin than a mallrat.* | A lot of the hand-me-downs he/she wears have sentimental value. Those booties were mine when I was a baby, for example. |
| You'd never see our little one wearing something like that outdoors on a day like today. | *That's because you never let your poor kid outdoors.* | He/she is the kind of kid who lets us know if he/she is uncomfortable. |
| Isn't that stuff too fattening to feed a baby who's already so chubby? | *Shouldn't you be more concerned with your own muffintop?* | In our home, we believe you can't ever have enough chins. And the doctor says he/she is right on track height- and weight-wise. |
| That food might be good for a baby, but there's no way he/she can possibly like the taste of it! | *How would you know? The only vegetable you eat is ketchup.* | We keep feeding it to him/her and he/she keeps eating it. |
| Our little Olympian walked at nine months and he/she will be up on skis by 18 months. | *…and I'll wager he/she will be the first among his/her peer group to have ACL surgery.* | No hurry—our little dugong will take a step when he/she is ready. |
| I feel so bad for you guys, having to cram your baby's carseat into that little old sedan. It's why we traded up for a supersize SUV. | *… and I feel so bad for you guys, having to cram $75 worth of fuel into that beast each time you fill the tank.* | There's one SUV we like, but we're waiting for a hybrid-electric version to hit the market. |
| With all the newfangled baby equipment and gear out there, parents have it easy these days. | *It's called progress. And I choose to embrace it.* | You're right. I can't imagine what we'd do without things like diapers, cribs, carseats, and kiddie leashes. |
| We would never tolerate that behavior from our kid. | *Just because I don't share your belief in "tough love" doesn't mean we tolerate that behavior.* | We just subscribe to different parenting philosophies, I guess. |
| Leave that little one with me for a week and I'll have him/her doing things you never would have imagined. | *One week with you and my kid is likely to come home a chainsmoker.* | A very generous offer, but I don't think our little one is quite ready for the kind of wisdom you can impart. |
| I know you're used to it, but all the clutter has got to drive you nuts. It's why we absolutely *had* to buy a bigger house. | *I've seen your new place. It's not square footage you lack but interior design taste.* | A little more space would be nice. But with the real estate market like it is, we're staying put for now. |
| Any sentence starting with, "I know you mean well, but…" | *My mother-in-law said that to me… once.* | Any sentence starting with, "I know you have nothing but good intentions in pointing that out, but…" |

sooner you and your woman resume efforts to circulate following the birth of your baby, the easier it likely will be to re-establish your lives outside the cave.

Hearken back to your childless days and you may recall that certain friends and acquaintances suddenly turned into J.D. Salinger types with the arrival of a child, seemingly dropping out of circulation and off the face of the earth. It's true that the baby factor changes the dynamics of some couple friendships, particularly when one couple becomes parents while the other remains childless. Suddenly one couple isn't nearly as socially accessible as they were pre-caveling. And when they do go out socially, much of their discussion centers around their little one. An exhaustive Pampers vs. Huggies debate isn't exactly riveting conversation material for a childless couple. Having a baby may indeed infringe on some of the common ground on which certain friendships with couples are built. But if you value the friendship you and your woman have with a couple, it's worth finding ways to keep it strong.

One way to do so is to carve time out of your schedules for a social life separate from the caveling. Periodically going out just the two of you or with friends can keep your social connections strong, your batteries charged, your perspective fresh, and your sense of freedom intact. Whether it's once a week or once a month, just a few hours at a time, the short stretches you spend away from your baby can give you an even deeper appreciation for the little one.

Common sense and the law dictate that someone be home to care for your largely helpless infant when the two of you are out, so cultivating a postpartum social life entails that you establish relationships with parental pinch-hitters—reliable folks to serve as babysitters. Capable and affordable babysitters are often tough to come by, so your best route is to find at least two or three whom you trust and whom your baby seems to like. Since babysitters can get expensive, your most affordable option might be to groom a family member or generous friend for the job, keeping in mind that while they might not demand financial compensation, it's probably in the best interests of you and the baby to reciprocate their generosity in other ways—meals, rides, gifts, etc. If free sitting help isn't an option, get ready to reach in your wallet. Either way, you want someone who knows how to handle anything a baby is apt to throw at them: soiled diapers, bouts of crying, and the like. If you don't know the person well, check references and administer the F.A.T. in Chapter 1 to weed out the weaker candidates.

In some cases you and your woman might be divided on whom to use as a regular babysitter. You may favor the nubile 19-year-old cheerleader recommended by one of your buddies ("eye candy," he calls her) while your woman would prefer the blue-haired spinster she met at the yarn store. For obvious reasons, this is a battle the caveman is better off not fighting, particularly if winning means souring the mood of his date, whose only cryptic comment is, "Remember what happened to the Kennedy guy who was hot for his kid's teenage babysitter…"

With a reliable stable of caregivers from which to draw, you not only can maintain existing friendships but also seek out new ones. Some of the best candidates for expanding your social horizons, you may find, are new parents just like you, folks you might meet in birthing class, through daycare, at the pediatrician's office, the coffee shop or the playground. The fact that you both have babies provides instant common ground. You will have plenty of notes to compare, tips to share, anecdotes to chuckle over, and things to bitch about, so conversation won't be lacking. And since you're all likely to be fairly exhausted, your evenings together figure to end relatively early, so you'll owe the babysitter less money.

## EMANCIPATE YOURSELVES

Inevitably the invitations will come, and with them, the urge to say, "I'll be there." One of the caveman's mates will call to implore him to join a golf foursome, a backcountry camping expedition or a weekend junket to Las Vegas. His woman likewise will begin fielding similar invitations from her female friends. The will to accept those invitations will be there. And so, too, will the way, for in one another, the two of you have a built-in babysitter, one who won't charge you a penny for services rendered (but who may require other forms of compensation).

One of the hallmarks of a strong parenting partnership is the reciprocity moms and dads show one another in various areas, including a willingness to provide single-coverage childcare to periodically free up the other for some well-earned and much-needed time all to himself or herself. *Thou shalt remain true to thy inner troglodyte,* reads one of the 10 Commandments for New Fathers (see Chapter 1). You need small tracts of time apart from your woman and baby to follow your own cavemuse, just as your woman needs time to cultivate her own interests.

There will be times when all you want to do is be together with

your nuclear family. But at other times each of you will feel the call of the wild, an urge to find the kind of fulfillment neither your partner nor your offspring can provide. Rather than fight the urge, you're better off yielding to it, lest you start feeling confined, neutered, and separated from your inner troglodyte. In fact the baby and both parents stand to benefit from occasional short-term stretches of single-parenting. Spending time alone with the little one not only provides free time to one parent, it gives the baby and the other parent (the one doing the babysitting) an opportunity to focus on their one-on-one relationship. When the caveman is doing the babysitting, this dedicated "daddy time" may also bolster the confidence a guy has in his own skills as a father and a parent. That confidence might not come easily early in the postpartum period, particularly for dads who aren't accustomed to much solo parenting because of work.

Some guidelines to follow to make the dynamic a healthy one:

- Discuss the babysitting reciprocity policy to make sure you're both clear on why you're doing it and how you'll approach it.

- Clear plans with your partner, the would-be babysitter, before formalizing them. Never assume your woman will be inclined or able to babysit on the day and time you have in mind.

- Present the potential engagement as a request, not a demand or an order. And try to submit your request with plenty of advance notice.

- Offer something in return. Be clear about what's in it for her: back rub, foot massage, a reciprocal babysitting session by you, a surprise gift, whatever it takes.

- If she's not up to the task, don't push it. Babysitters have the right to cancel if they're under the weather, etc. So does your woman.

- Don't let self-time turn one-sided. If you seem to consistently be getting the longer end of the stick, you stand to alienate your woman and perhaps lose privileges unless you make an effort to even things out, perhaps by forgoing the next guy-time opportunity that comes your way and instead insisting you stay home with the baby while your woman heads out.

- Be sure self-time doesn't replace the time the two of you have set aside to spend together as a couple, without the baby.

- Don't treat a babysitting request from your woman as an imposition or inconvenience. Treat those requests as you'd want your own to be handled—receptively, with a positive outlook.

## PARTY IN TODDLERTOWN

As the Chairman, Frank Sinatra, used to sing, "It was a very good year"—the caveling's first 12 months of life and the caveman's first 12 months of fatherhood. While the baby has been busy exploring, absorbing, developing, and generally exhausting his or her parents, the caveman and his woman have been similarly immersed, overcoming periodic bouts with exhaustion to fulfill the responsibilities of parenthood and develop as moms and dads.

Reaching this point of the book means you are close to attaining the pinnacle of the postpartum needs-fulfillment pyramid. Not only does this earn you the right to call yourself a cultivated caveman, a *Homo sapiens* in the true Linnaean sense of the word, it gives you plenty of reason to *party* to honor the day and what it represents. Your baby hasn't just survived 12 months with you as a dad, he or she has truly thrived, thanks in large part to a stellar overall parenting performance by you and your lady. Now, as your baby's first birthday approaches, you have a miniature prodigy in the making. This calls for a celebration.

Your baby's first birthday is reason enough for a blow-out. And any party you throw will of course honor your little one first and foremost. However, once the candles have been blown out, the cake smeared, and the presents opened, the celebration needn't end. Before you is an opportunity to make this more than a birthday party. We're talking a gala to mark the caveling's first birthday as a rite of passage, a graduation, and a matriculation for the little one's parents. You have achieved much individually and as a partnership. Here's a great chance to celebrate your past, present, and future together. You have graduated from your first year as a dad with flying colors and now you, your woman, and your baby are ready for your respective matriculations into the next phase: life with, and life as, a toddler.

What kind of party will you throw? Beyond cake, presents and other typical birthday party trappings, there are a few ways to make the event extra special. You can:

- surround your little one with his/her favorite people. She smiles at the mailman whenever she sees him, so let's invite him...

- avoid inviting clowns and mimes; they freak out little kids (and adults).

- assemble a photo album or scrapbook of images and keepsakes from the first year, then cozy up with the baby to page through it as a family, you or your woman providing a sort of "This Is Your Life" narrative, with occasional interjection from the little one.

- if you've documented the first year with video footage, sit down with the little one and your woman, hook the camera to the TV, and view what you've captured (this will, of course, be the only television the baby will watch in his/her first year).

- once you've put the offspring to bed for the night, let the romance begin. Make a nice dinner, pop a bottle of good wine, stoke the fire, enhance the mood with candles and some vintage Miles Davis, talk and laugh about all you've been through together through the first year, then get down to some serious lovemaking, just as you did some 92 weeks ago when your sperm met her egg and made this whole thing possible. If you're not looking for them to repeat that performance (see the Dr. Brian box on the next page), use contraception.

Your baby won't have any recollection of his or her first birthday bash, however it unfolds, but you and your woman will recall it fondly as the culmination of one amazing year. From the moment you first held the caveling until now, the memories and the wisdom you carry with you from these first 12 months will serve you well during your kid's time as a toddler and for the remainder of labor's fourth stage, however long it might last for you.

Ready or not, on the immediate horizon loom milestones:

# DR. BRIAN

## A Close Second

You and your woman are still basking in the postpartum afterglow. The idea of conceiving again so soon after your child's birth is, well, inconceivable. But one look at your odds of doing so might have you ready to rescue the goalie—your chosen form of contraception—from prenatal exile.

New moms, whether they are regularly breastfeeding or not, can and do conceive within weeks or months of giving birth. If that's not exactly what the two of you have in mind, if you prefer to shoot but not score, to produce your next offspring on your own terms, it's time to consider contraception. You may take comfort in knowing that breastfeeding full-time tends to postpone postpartum ovulation (a phenomenon called lactational amenorrhea or LAM), and that your woman can't conceive without ovulating. Even so, there are no guarantees. There is a chance, albeit a relatively remote one, of you impregnating her.

During the first six months after giving birth, a woman who breastfeeds full time (nursing at least every four hours during the day and at least every six hours at night) and hasn't experienced a period has only about a 2 percent chance of ovulating. That's because a breastfeeding woman's body produces mammotropic hormone, which besides stimulating lactation also suppresses ovulation. New moms who don't breastfeed their babies tend to resume their menstrual cycles sooner than do those who breastfeed full-time—as soon as four to 10 weeks after giving birth (45 days on average), compared to two months and perhaps much longer. Some moms don't get their periods again until they quit breastfeeding altogether.

Once a new mom begins breastfeeding less frequently and supplementing with formula and solid food, however, the odds of her ovulating increase and so too do the chances of conceiving. So, sports fans, unless you're prepared to pitch both ends of a very grueling doubleheader, you'd better have a reliable catcher.

- in **personality development**, where the offspring's temperament, sense of humor, and tantrum-throwing ability gain further definition.

- in **communications**, such as the little one's initial and repeated usage of the word *no*.

- in **boundary-testing**, where your kid explores the ramifications of doing exactly the opposite of what you asked.

- in **self-propulsion**, where the toddler progresses from walking to a spastically frenetic style of running borrowed from contestants in Monty Python's "Twit Olympics."

- in **sleep habits**, where the caveling drops from two naps a day to one.

- in **artistic expression**, where the tyke uses any available media—permanent marker, smeared food, fingerpaint, even doo-doo directly from the diaper—to make a mark on the world, without regard to the surface he or she is working on, be it furniture, walls, floor, clothing or his or her own skin.

- in **dining habits**, where the little one not only wants to eat what mommy and daddy are eating, he or she also demands utensils with which to bludgeon it.

- in **dress habits**, where your kid no longer will be content to wear outfits you have selected and instead begins asserting his or her own fashion preferences.

- in **hygiene**, where getting the caveling to participate in everyday practices such as bathing, tooth brushing, and hair combing becomes a major undertaking.

But let's not get too far ahead of ourselves. Better now to savor this event and reflect upon all the stuff, good and bad, that led up to it. Having emerged from the first year relatively unscathed, you have earned the right to party hearty. But be sure to save your strength, caveman, because the next test, parenting a toddler, is no cakewalk. As a wise man, a genuine, upstanding *Homo sapiens* who has proven he can evolve, you're unquestionably ready to rise to the challenge.

# INDEX

## Acknowledgments

They say childbirth is easier the second time around. However, that rule does not necessarily apply to the process of birthing a book, especially one whose subjects are babies and childrearing. Producing this, the second volume in the Cultivated Caveman series, was just as taxing and just as fulfilling as the first time around. We couldn't have done it without a strong supporting cast.

Immeasurably valuable guidance and insight came from new and holdover members of the Caveman's Ad Hoc Female Advisory Council: Kelli Jennings, a registered dietician and prenatal nutritional expert in Crested Butte; Desirae Manering, a registered doula and certified massage therapist in Denver; Pat Shelly, founder and director of the Breastfeeding Center of Greater Washington, D.C.; and Gina Raith and Stasia Droze Jost, California residents who have been researching a book on human sexuality and relationship dynamics.

We owe a huge debt of gratitude to Charlie Nix and George Scott of Scott & Nix for patiently coaxing us through the process and to Gideon Kendall for his consistently hilarious illustrations. Hearty thanks also to the folks at Barnes & Noble/Sterling— particularly Nathaniel Marunas—for their support and for meeting our outlandish contract demands.

We've reserved extra-special caveman hugs and kisses for Emily, Jane & Lila, and Diana, Juliette & Zane. The irony of us occasionally disappearing from their lives in order to write books about being a "present" parent and partner is not lost on them. Without their love, encouragement and patience, we never could have ventured out from the cave to write this book.